The Invention of Native American Literature

The Invention of Native American Literature

ROBERT DALE PARKER

Cornell University Press

ITHACA AND LONDON

First published 2003 by Cornell University Press
First printing, Cornell Paperbacks, 2003

Printed in the United States of America

Library of Congress Cataloging-in-Publication Data

Parker, Robert Dale, 1953–
    The invention of Native American literature / Robert Dale Parker.
       p. cm.
Includes bibliographical references and index.
    ISBN 0–8014–4067–X (cloth : acid-free paper) — ISBN 0–8014–8804–4 (pbk. :
acid-free paper)
    1. American literature—Indian authors—History and criticism.   2.
American literature—20th century—History and criticism.   3. Indians of
North America—Intellectual life.   4. Indians in literature.   I. Title.
    PS153.I52 P37 2003
    810.9'897—dc21

                                        2002010492

Cornell University Press strives to use environmentally responsible suppliers
and materials to the fullest extent possible in the publishing of its books. Such
materials include vegetable-based, low-VOC inks and acid-free papers that are
recycled, totally chlorine-free, or partly composed of nonwood fibers. For further information, visit our website at www.cornellpress.cornell.edu.

Cloth printing   10 9 8 7 6 5 4 3 2 1
Paperback printing   10 9 8 7 6 5 4 3 2 1

Contents

Preface

Native American literature has arrived. It has best-sellers. It has anthologies. It gets widely taught. Widely read journals publish articles about it, and scholars writing primarily about other topics increasingly take Indian writing into their frame of reference. College and university English departments occasionally set out to hire specialists in Native American literature—or in "multicultural literature," by whatever name, with Indian lit as one of the permitted flavors. And scholarship in the field now appears at a rapid pace.

Native American literature has arrived—or has it? All too predictably, the visibility of best-sellers has the accidental side effect of letting a few writers take over the landscape of Indian writing and blot out the many other Indian writers both past and present, just as for years courses in American literature included no women writers and no African American writers or, if any, then only one, chosen from a tiny repertoire that rarely reached beyond Richard Wright, Ralph Ellison, and Emily Dickinson. Some might even argue, fairly or not, that the work of the few most marketed and widely taught Indian writers confirms rather than challenges the usual clichés about Indian culture or even (more subtly) the expected patterns of Indian resistance to those clichés. The anthologies often provide little information about the cultural setting of the writers and works they represent, making Indian-written works into yet more texts in the still resilient new critical museum of verbal icons propped up to be read in an echo chamber of self-sufficient reference. Most colleges and universities still do not offer courses in Indian literature; fewer offer such courses regularly; and we might wonder how well integrated Indian literature is into courses not specifically dedicated to it. Some scholars even challenge the idea that the study of American Indian literature should be integrated into the study of American literature.[1] At the least, we need to think seriously about what we gain and lose when we teach Indian literature in Indian literature courses or in American literature or more general courses, and when we write about it in articles, journals, or books that concentrate on Indian lit or in forums that see Indian lit as part of a wider literary canvas. Scholarship in the field may come out now at a rapid pace (at least by comparison to a decade or two ago), but much of it appears as the new hot thing, with little sense of the history of Indian literature or the scholarship about it, let alone the cultures it comes from.

But if the scholarship on Indian literature is a new hot thing, it is also in serious ways older than the scholarship on other American literatures, even on that phantom we still call, oversimply, the "canon." Since time immemorial, Indian people have studied their own verbal expression, including specialists, so to speak, who sometimes work in long apprenticeships and with enormous elaboration. Decades before the new critics established the principles that founded modern literary criticism in the nineteen thirties, forties, and fifties—a blend of scholarship and interpretation that focused intensely on individual literary "texts" (those verbal icons), careers, circles, movements, and genres—a vast written scholarship had grown up around American Indian verbal expression, produced by professional and amateur anthropologists, often with federal support. Their language study, textual recording, and textual and cultural interpretation, while often suspect or worse by later standards, nevertheless provide an enormous legacy of intellectual and cultural traditions and problems for the contemporary study of American Indian literature.

In short, Native American literature wasn't born with the recent writings that have made it newly and uneasily popular, and the scholarship around it wasn't born with the surge of study that focuses on recent Indian writing. Most writing about Indian literature concentrates on materials published since the late 1960s, but Indian writing, including fiction and poetry, has a longer history. This book reads the state of contemporary Indian writing and the scholarship about it in relation to that history. In recent years, more scholars of American Indian literature have enlarged the discussion and changed the field by joining the various debates in literary studies at large, and an increasing number of American Indian scholars have contributed their perspectives and taken leading roles in defining the direction of American Indian literary studies. In this book I seek to join and continue that enlarging discussion. I approach the project as part of a pervasive dialogue in contemporary international critical theory and often through comparison to African American literary and cultural studies, and I seek to accelerate the critical interest in gender in

Indian writing. At the same time, I also engage a broad range of cultural and material research, drawing on tribal histories and ethnographies, obscure contemporary book reviews, transcripts of tribal council meetings, recordings, local newspapers, letters, manuscript archives, and other sources.

As criticism is changing, literature is changing as well. The rapid increase in numbers and prominence of Indian women writers over recent years is altering the shape of Indian literature and can help critics see patterns in the history of Indian literature that may not have stood out so sharply before, including preoccupations with the uneasy position of restless young Indian men. This preoccupation is a legacy that some Indian women writers, most notably Leslie Marmon Silko, hold onto even as they reshape Indian literary history. Before writers such as Joy Harjo, Paula Gunn Allen, Louise Erdrich, Wendy Rose, Linda Hogan, Beth Brant, Lucy Tapahonso, Betty Louise Bell, and many others, and before the reinvention of reading set off by feminist critics, it was possible for readers to see the preoccupation with uneasy masculinity in such novels as John Joseph Mathews's *Sundown* (1934), D'Arcy McNickle's *The Surrounded* (1936), or N. Scott Momaday's *House Made of Dawn* (1968) as simply natural, the way things are. That is, it was possible *not* to see the preoccupation with uneasy masculinity at all. Now, for better and worse, Indian literature has arrived on the landscape of American literature, and is being reinvented by women writers and the male writers they influence. To understand that reinvention we need to understand the earlier invention of Native American literature that the new writing sometimes builds on and sometimes replaces. The earlier invention assigned Indian peoples to the sometimes overlapping and sometimes contradictory categories of young men's threatened masculinity, the oral, and the poetic. In the process, the dominant culture asked Indians, not least Indian writers, to represent an authoritative Indianness, and many obliged by challenging stereotypes and proposing alternatives to those stereotypes. More recently, other writers—and here I take Ray A. Young Bear and Thomas King as prime examples—have been rewriting their relation to gender, orality, and the poetic outside the scripts of authoritative representation, not so much claiming a superior authority (though not forswearing it either) as thinking outside the concept of authority altogether.

Other critics might cast this net in a variety of different patterns, and I hope that they will. The rapid increase in writing by Indian women, in particular, is leading to a refreshing openness to literature that centers on women and on female characters, which can help us recognize how underdeveloped women's concerns are in earlier Indian writing by men. We can all recognize more categories of things Indian besides restless young men, orality, the poetic, and independence from authority. We can also pick out the usual lugubrious stereotypes—the wise elder, the earth mother, the natural environmentalist, and so on—and those stereotypes and others sometimes enter my argument. The point is not to survey the range of representations or stereotypes, however. Others have already done that work well (e.g., Berkhofer; Utter; Mihesuah, *American Indians*). Nor do I suggest that interest in a few key preoccupations through a diversity of traditions has been a bad or stereotypical thing for Indian literature, or that Indian writers, wrapped in internalized racism, are pitiful victims of the stereotypes that others project onto them. Quite the contrary. Indian writers typically defy those stereotypes, and to see a series of repeated patterns is not to equate them with stereotypes. Any tradition chooses certain features potential within it to develop with special intensity. That's a good thing: it builds continuity, ongoing dialogue, a sense of shared history and identity. Here I seek to sketch that tradition, trusting that other critics will add to the discussion by sketching it in different ways.

Every age sees itself as a turning point, and our own age is no different. Indian literature seems to us to have reached a threshold. If it has not definitively *arrived*, it at least has reached the point where such a notion of arrival calls for contemplation and skeptical review and sets out Indian literature as a tradition that both new and established Indian writers can revise and reinvent. Indian writers of course are indeed remaking the old and forging the new, which puts a special value on the task of characterizing the tradition that they are building on, reshaping, and sometimes even leaving behind.

With fond memories of challenging dialogues and exchanges, I thank the people who listened to me talk about this book's arguments or who read from the work-in-progress and offered questions or suggestions for revision: Amanda Anderson, Nina Baym, Michael Bérubé, Stephanie Foote, James Hurt, Simon Joyce, Laurence Lieberman, William J. Maxwell, Brian McHale, Bruce Michelson, Cary Nelson, Kenneth Roemer, Siobhan Senier, Michael I. Stark, Zohreh T. Sullivan, Julia A. Walker, and an astute anonymous reader for Cornell University Press. Many other people helped the work on this book in a variety of ways they may not even remember, but I recall their conversation and encouragement with grateful appreciation: Janice N. Harrington, Susan Brill de Ramirez, Ramona Curry, Brenda Farnell, Walter Feinberg, Ann Haugo, Frederick E. Hoxie, John McKinn, Carol Thomas Neely, Christopher Nelson, A. LaVonne Brown Ruoff, Vivian Wagner, Robert Allen Warrior, Marlie P. Wasserman, Richard P. Wheeler, Ray A. Young Bear, Paul Zeleza, and the editors and anonymous readers for the journals that published early versions of several chapters, including Edgar A. Dryden and Gordon Hutner. I am grateful to Bernhard Kendler, my editor at Cornell University Press, who shepherded this book through the acquisitions process; writers need good editors. I am also grateful to my colleagues at the University of Illinois at Urbana-Champaign who took seriously an area of interest that often receives little support.

Having the good fortune to work at one of the world's great libraries, I take pleasure in thanking the librarians and staff at the University of Illinois at Urbana-Champaign Library and the countless librarians at other libraries who did so much to make this book possible.

I have found the scholar-critics and teachers who write about Indian literature a generous, committed, open-minded group of colleagues whom I have learned from enormously, and for that I am deeply grateful. I try, however feebly, to make my writing and teaching do justice to their personal and intellectual kindness.

In earlier versions, chapter 3 appeared in *Modern Fiction Studies* 43 (1997), chapters 4 and 5 in *The Arizona Quarterly* 53 (1997) and 50 (1994), and chapter 7 in *American Literary History* 5 (1993). Excerpts from "The Dream of Purple Birds in Marshall, Washington" and from "Quail and His Role in Agriculture" are from *The Invisible Musician: Poems* by Ray A. Young Bear (Holy Cow! Press, 1990). All rights reserved. Reprinted by permission of the publisher. Excerpts from *Winter of the Salamander: The Keeper of Importance* reprinted by permission of Ray A. Young Bear.

This book is dedicated to Janice N. Harrington, who transforms the daily life of reading and writing into a love supreme, and in the best ways.

R.D.P.

Champaign, Illinois

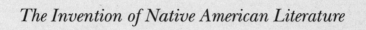

The Invention of Native American Literature

CHAPTER 1

Tradition, Invention, and Aesthetics in Native
American Literature and Literary Criticism

This book proposes an interpretive history of the ways that Indian writers drew on Indian and literary traditions to invent a Native American literature. In the process, I distinguish two thresholds in Native American literary studies. The first is a threshold in the literature, which has now reached sufficient mass for critics to move beyond the worn generalizations about rediscovered identity, eloquent simplicity, nonlinearity, orality, and so on. The second is a threshold in the criticism, which has now succeeded (despite continuing difficulties) in establishing the texts and the field of Native American literary studies and is increasingly contributing to the theoretical debates raging across the international study of literature and the humanities.

Nevertheless, the bulk of the large, growing body of American Indian literature remains unknown to most critics and teachers of American literature. This book cannot give a complete picture; it cannot even accommodate all my own favorite works. Rather than writing a survey, therefore, I have pondered a selection of works as part of a broader effort to understand the growth of Indian literature historically and in formal terms. Like other peoples, American Indians have a long history of telling stories and taking aesthetic pleasure in language. Amid widespread confidence and pleasure in literature as an aesthetic category, and with widespread literacy, it makes sense that we see an ever-growing number of Indian writers, including writers of great skill and power. The same could be said of many other groups. Yet to many people the invention of Native American literature comes as a surprise, because it violates hardened stereotypes of Indians. Those stereotypes deflect attention from Indian intellectuality and literacy and often from Indian articulateness. Even for critics and teachers of Indian literature, or critics and teachers of American literature who have a passing acquaintance with Indian literature, the contemporary often shoulders aside the earlier history of Indian writing, especially the history before N. Scott Momaday's 1968 *House Made of Dawn*, which ushered in what came to be called the Native American literary renaissance.[1]

This book takes the presence of Indian writing for granted, while recognizing that Indian writing has often had to confront the expectation that it doesn't exist or at least that it can't be very impressive artistically. The current tendency among some critics (though not so many as is often claimed) to set aside literary form and aesthetic taste has the accidental effect of allowing conservative readers to think that noncanonical works aren't terribly interesting as art. But the declining interest in literary aesthetics and the rising interest in understudied writing have partly separate histories. For some critics, an interest in literary form is contaminated by the history of the so-called new critics; many scholars came to identify the new critics' attention to literary form with their conservative politics. But an interest in form can come in many flavors; the conservatives don't own it. Even amid an array of competing or varying aesthetic tastes, there can be no brief for the noncontingent aesthetic taste that the new critics took for granted and that to much of the populace has come to seem like the only way to understand judgments of literary value. For such people, to make a claim for an art object is to make an absolute claim, but if art were absolute then we wouldn't need to think about it critically. As Barbara Herrnstein Smith has influentially argued, and as the prolific enthusiasms of popular culture testify, aesthetic taste has a thousand faces.

Meanwhile, the recent explosion of interest in understudied writing receives its impetus from urgent social motives, and for that reason some of its proponents have tried, with deliberation or obliviousness, to pry aesthetic questions away from criticism. But many of us who recognize the social imperatives driving us to read understudied writing also recognize aesthetic imperatives. We *like* this writing. We like the rhythms and resonances of its phrases, sentences, episodes, and ideas. The politics and the aesthetics of Indian writing (or any writing) are not the same, but they are not separable either. The new critics and their followers often masked their politics by posing their political judgments as aesthetic judgments and pretending to write politics out of criticism. They saw politics as the stuff of naive criticism, especially criticism from the left. By contrast, scholars and teachers devoted to noncanonical literature see no conflict in reading politically and reading aesthetically. We read for politics and aesthetics, and we read the rhythms and resonances of one as part of reading the rhythms and resonances of the other.

Much as I take the presence of Indian writing for granted, then, I also insist on the aesthetic value of Indian literature, together with its identity as *Indian*. There's nothing necessarily artistic in cultural identity, but in the act of expressing itself cultural identity takes on aesthetic form. It's not just that audiences will identify the expressions of Indians as Indian painting, writing, music, and so on, whether they are distinctively Indian or not, but also that what Indians do makes (and hence changes) what Indians are (Stuart Hall, "Cultural Identity"), often in defiance of or obliviousness to what audiences expect (even some Indian audiences).

To point these interests through a historical lens, then, takes us to a history of ways that Indian literary writing expressed itself as literary and as Indian. In the process, Indian writers invented a body of literature that we've come to call Native American literature, imagining an internal coherence we produce by our culturally driven need to imagine it. They laid the foundation for later Indian writers to connect to a tradition and to do something else—to break the paradigms that their predecessors labored so hard to establish, a process now well under way.[2]

In this context, *The Invention of Native American Literature* identifies a series of key issues in the emerging, imaginary coherence of Native American literature over roughly the last century. Specifically, I argue that the desire to invent a Native American literature returned Indian writing over and over to a set of topics partly chosen by and partly chosen for Indian writers. I identify four topics that in overlapping ways address gender, sexuality, stereotype, and the appropriation of Indian cultural and intellectual property. Those four topics are: young men's threatened masculinity, the oral, the poetic, and Indian cultures' aloof renegotiations of what the dominant culture understands as authority.

After beginning with a skeptical reconsideration of scholars' and writers' efforts to theorize an Indian aesthetic, I turn to a topic not addressed by earlier critics but made newly accessible by the revolution in feminist criticism and gender studies, namely, the preoccupation with a pattern of restless young men with nothing to do. At least, the restless young men suspect or feel pressured to believe that they have nothing to do. For they live amid the often misogynist cultural mythology that contact with Euro-Americans (even long after such contact is routine) has deprived Indian men of their traditional roles without a similar displacement of Indian women's roles. Moreover, their world has not managed to construct an Indian, unassimilating way to adapt masculine roles to the dominant, business-saturated culture's expectations of 9–5 breadwinning. I ask not whether such a mythology is accurate or inaccurate. Instead, I consider its effects on early Indian literature's efforts to reimagine Indian culture while inventing a specifically Indian literature, especially in a pair of land-mark but understudied novels from the depression that much influenced later Indian writers.

Meanwhile, the accelerations of modernity, with the almost irresistible excitements and enticements of mass culture and the reconfigurations of what Walter Benjamin called "the work of art in the age of mechanical re-production," contributed to an international modernist craving to pre-serve, recover, or memorialize a nostalgically imagined past. Amid the ex-ploding growth of literacy and print culture, that past was often identified with orality—hence the growth and popularity of "folklore" and the vast project to transcribe and translate a supposedly disappearing American Indian oral culture. Many others have already noted the central role of oral storytelling in Indian culture and literature, and I do not wish to un-dermine their insights. Instead I reread those insights through the broader lenses of modernist nostalgia and its drive to construct the oral as a touchstone and core of Indian distinctiveness. That nostalgia helps open the door to the naive identification of orality with Indianness in a world of print literacy that condescends to orality, even as condescension is the tacit accomplice of romanticizing exaltation.

Jacques Derrida, in that vein, decries the western tendency to see oral and written cultures as radically different from each other. He critiques Claude Lévi-Strauss's "The Writing Lesson," a chapter in *Tristes Tropiques* that recounts introducing writing to Nambikwara Indians in Brazil (Lévi-Strauss, 294–300; *Of Grammatology*, 101–40). To be sure, for Lévi-Strauss and many others since, the desire to see the oral and written as separate takes the anticolonialist form of championing orality and sometimes of understanding orality as a special characteristic of Native peoples fading tragically before the colonialist onslaught. But Derrida casts that desire as ethnocentrism in the guise of anti-ethnocentrism; he sees it as ethnocen-tric for Lévi-Strauss (and others) to suppose that oral discourse lacks the intricacy of written discourse, a supposition typical even among those who, like Lévi-Strauss, romanticize oral culture.

Thus while the representation of orality and oral storytelling becomes a means for Indian writers to imagine an Indian literature, and for their characters—including the restless young men—to rethink their relation to the past, it also becomes a means for non-Indians to imagine escape from modernity, conflating Indians and Indian orality with a romantically recoverable past that can merge with the oral, often in the form of poetry. As poetry becomes the preferred form for representing traditional Indian oral narrative in print, the insistence on the poetic mystifies storytelling, orality, and poetry itself, and it displaces the actual poetry written by In-dian writers. I write a new history of the aesthetics of Native American literature, therefore, through the linked preoccupations with restless young men, storytelling, orality, poetry, and Indian notions of authority as they come together in a series of precedent-setting novels, bodies of poetry, and bodies of theory about Indian oral storytelling as poetry.

In the central five chapters of this book, I identify a series of concerns or issues that American Indian writers have faced as they invented what eventually seemed to cohere as Native American literature. I use the word *invention* to suggest an air of the provisional, of ongoing process and construction, as opposed to a natural, inevitable effusion of Indian identity. To see Indian art as such an effusion is to suppose that Indian identity is ahistorical, static, and absolute rather than always being produced by Indians and, however cavalierly, by other people. After all, without non-Indians, no one could imagine Indians as a category. (The notion of invented here has more to do with Gerald Vizenor's view of Indianness and what he calls the "post-Indian" than with James Clifton's idea of "the invented Indian.")[3] I trust that other critics can identify issues beyond those addressed in this book. Still, I argue that these issues weave together to establish a Native American literature.

Chapters 2 and 3 read the preoccupation with restless young men with nothing to do in two Indian novels published during the depression, John Joseph Mathews's *Sundown* (1934) and D'Arcy McNickle's *The Surrounded* (1936), a preoccupation that continues with remarkable consistency through later Indian writing, including writing by women. The restless young men so absorb the wider culture's devaluing and emptying out of their roles that they can find nothing to do, or they so little value their doing that they misread it as nothing. Even sexually, they don't do much. They procrastinate, and what little they do, they do indifferently, hinting at but holding off a potential homosexuality or (more modestly) an interest in queerness. Their uncertain, passive masculinity offers a troubled medium for Indian modernity and gender relations, yet it also offers possibilities for rethinking gender, masculinity, sexuality, and an ethic of Indian work in ways these early novels find hard to imagine or follow through on. The depression proves provocative for such rethinking, because the great difficulty in finding paid work put pressure on the dominant culture's conflation of masculinity with business-oriented labor just when Indian writers were trying to reconcile their own relation to intersecting ideologies of labor, masculinity, business, and changing traditional cultures. While *Sundown* unwinds with little sense of any way out beyond an economic assimilation that it refuses, *The Surrounded* turns to traditional oral storytelling to construct Indian modernity and articulate it to an outside world. Meanwhile, that outside world seeks to temper the new age of mechanical reproduction by turning to a nostalgically recovered orality—often recovered, ironically, through the mechanical reproduction that prints Indian oral stories in written form as parts of novels and as Indian "poetry."

Picking up on that notion of orality, then, chapter 4 looks historically at the transcription of traditional Indian oral stories and the cultural translation of transcribed, translated stories into Indian "poetry," a new "Indian literature" that happens not to be written by Indians yet remains foundational to many non-Indians' imagination of what Indian writing might be. Here I critique a body of translation and transcription theory that has proved enormously influential in Indian studies and the wider study of oral literature and folklore. As McNickle's prose fiction captures the dominant culture's growing identification between orality and Indianness, the production of Indian oral stories as literary poetry merges that identification between the Indian and the oral with an identification of the Indian, the oral, and the poetical, which poses a problem for actual Indian poets.

Chapter 5, therefore, takes up the poetry of Ray A. Young Bear, whose lyrical poems scorn the non-Indian appropriation of Indian cultures and of the purportedly Indian poetical and oral, including the way that such appropriations can displace actual poetry actually written by Indians. But contrary to the dominant expectation of resistance, Young Bear and other Indian poets, such as Wendy Rose and Chrystos, don't counterpoise an authoritatively transcendent real Indianness to bulldoze over the faux-Indianness they find so preposterous. Simply to reverse who holds which position in the relation of dominator to dominated would lock in the structure of authority that Young Bear's poetry defies. By contrast, and in accord with traditional Meskwaki notions of authority, notions not incongruent with those of many other Indian peoples, Young Bear's epistemology is indifferent to the dominant presumption that culture and knowledge admit authoritative, stable readings. Young Bear's assumptions about authority cycle us back to the restless young men with nothing to do portrayed by Mathews, McNickle, and many later Indian writers, including Young Bear. For a lack of interest in authority won't translate into the Babbitt-ridden, business get-up-and-go of Euro-American masculinity that Mathews paints as descending onto the calmer, less hierarchical world of early twentieth-century Osage ways. The focalizing consciousness of Mathews's novel relies on regressive fantasies of a return to supposedly traditional ways imagined through an idealizing nostalgia, without the cultural repertoire to reenvision what the dominant ideology misreads as "nothing" and to translate it into cultural advocacy, into an epistemology of ordinary Indian living—something to do indeed. Young Bear provides an alternative of the sort that Mathews and McNickle sought and helped lay the groundwork for in their writing and their political activities but that, in an earlier, differently pressured age, they could not find the cultural vocabulary to envision.

With the achieved invention of Native American literature, we have that vocabulary now. In a culminating chapter, then, I follow how all these issues come together in two relatively recent novels about restless, passive, young or not-so-young men, Leslie Marmon Silko's now canonical *Ceremony* (1977) and Thomas King's less known but delightful *Medicine River* (1989). (King is better known for *Green Grass, Running Water*, 1993.) Both novels include oral storytelling, with *Ceremony* presenting oral stories in poetic form and *Medicine River* spoofing what non-Indians often don't get about storytelling while crafting its narrative structure on oral models and centrifugal assumptions about authority. Though I set this chapter up partly as a test of the larger argument, I don't approach it as an experiment so much as I set out to read the fate of these preoccupations as they all come together climactically in key novels of the Native American renaissance.

My final chapter continues to address Native American literature but this time as one among many American literatures. It poses more directly a question implicit in the rest of the book: when critics and teachers of literature broaden the range of materials that they study and teach, inciting what I call a "post-canon," how does that broadening change not just what we study and teach, but how we study and teach? Too often, critics and the general public address the movement to study texts from a wide range of social groups as if it were isolated from what we say about those texts, or assume that merely to widen the traditional range of texts is to reinvent what we say about literature and its representations. But the reinvention of literature offers more challenges than the writing about that reinvention usually supposes. This chapter brings together the active but still largely separate projects of retheorizing representation (how does a text represent or not represent a group of people whom the author does or does not belong to?—how does an Indian text represent or not represent Indian people?) and retheorizing canonicity (which texts and what range of texts should we write about and teach?). Each of these projects has gained its recent sophistications partly at the cost of ignoring the dialogues that are retheorizing the other. If a post-canon is to live up to its post-canonicity, it cannot reapply a discredited confidence about representation to a wider range of texts, assuming, for example, that a text by an African American writer bears a one-to-one relation to the representation of African Americans in general. Instead, a post-canon must think through the constraints of representation that impel us to a post-canon in the first place. Then our reading of Native American and other literatures can live up to the promises of post-canonicity by reinventing both the reading of representation and the representation of what we read.

My motives for studying Indian literature are aesthetic and literary. I cannot recall another critic of Indian literature who comes right out and says that, probably in part because it is difficult to say what we mean by aesthetic and literary pleasure. Many people who do not read much Indian writing never expect those of us who read it to seek it out and return to it for aesthetic reasons. But anyone who spends much time among critics of Indian literature will sense their excited pleasure in the writing.

What does it mean to say that I like what I read? It is easier to say what it doesn't mean. It doesn't mean that there is a universal standard of value, epitomized by such writers as Dante, Shakespeare, and Tolstoy and fulfilled again in Indian writing—or in any writing. It could mean that Indian writing offers a radically different set of standards and pleasures from canonical writing, so that if only readers would get a feel for those standards, then they would learn to love Indian writing as they or others love the writing of Dante, Shakespeare, Tolstoy, and their canonized cohorts. I hoped for that before starting to read Indian literature, and sometimes I found it, especially in some of the translated and transcribed oral stories of traditional storytellers, such as the violent tales from the northwest (see Jarold Ramsey, Siobhan Senier) or the trickster stories that Gerald Vizenor tries to embody in his extravagant fiction and theoretical writing. But for the most part, that's not what I found. Instead, I found the cadenced, resonant understatement of D'Arcy McNickle, Ray Young Bear's lyricism (whatever obstacles I also found in Young Bear's thicket of obscure references), Joy Harjo's common touch and lyrical anaphora, Louise Erdrich's lapidary metaphors, and Thomas King's wistful, amiable ironies. In other words, I found many of the same pleasures that I found in canonical writing, and plenty of other pleasures too, for Indian writers often write about different worlds from those of non-Indian writers. With modest exceptions—Mathews's and King's sense of plot, Young Bear's difficulty(or is that difficulty not so different from James Joyce's, Ezra Pound's, T. S. Eliot's, or Melvin Tolson's?)—I didn't need to come up with a noncanonical notion of aesthetics to appreciate Indian writing. Indian writing stands out (at least to me) not only for its differences from other writing, its profound differences of cultural reference and understanding, but also because so much of it is as good as the best other writing and good on pretty much the same terms as the other writing. Indeed, that matches a broader strain in the continuing history of contact between Indian and non-Indian cultures. Non-Indians—and Indians influenced by non-Indians (more precisely, Indians internalizing the dominant culture, which they are already influencing and part of)—often expect something exotic in Indians and Indian writing. But one of my goals in this book is to recover the extraordinary sense of ordinariness in Indian writing, an ordinariness that has profound aesthetic connotations through its pleasure in routine, in the beauty of continuity and daily life, in simply—as Young Bear and many others put it repeatedly—"being."

In that spirit, I am arguing that abstract descriptions of form (e.g., symmetrical, asymmetrical, linear, circular, lyrical, narrative) have no cultural specificity. This has everything to do with the arguments in chapters 4 and 6 about poetic form in oral narrative and in Silko's *Ceremony*, and in chapter 7 about the thickness of cultural description and study we need to see how a text uses form. In particular, I draw on the notion that communications theorists call the fallacy of technological determinism, namely, the fallacy that a given technology (the printing press, railroads, radio) necessarily produces a given cultural consequence. By contrast—the argument goes—the cultural consequence varies with how the technology gets used, despite our tendency to read a consequence back onto the technology itself. In the same way, a literary form, such as the novel, the autobiography, free indirect discourse, parallelism, repetition, and so on, doesn't inevitably carry a predictable cultural meaning or context (such as Indian or non-Indian), though we might read back onto it a cultural context that we have come to associate with it, as we might associate Navajo prayer with parallelism ("My feet restore for me, my legs restore for me, my body restore for me, my mind restore for me, my voice restore for me"—see chapter 7). Navajo prayer has much to do with parallelism, but parallelism doesn't inevitably lead to Navajo prayer. Any form that we might connect to Indian writing (or to the writing of any given Indian people) might also appear in other people's writing. If we deny that pliability of form, then we limit our chance to read what any particular tradition—such as Creek or Navajo, or a more broadly Indian tradition—does with that form.

It is therefore anything but a matter of discovering that Indian literature is worth reading because it abides by European or falsely universalized forms. On the contrary, my approach seeks to get at what Indian writing does with form. Such an approach has the effect of deprivileging and de-Europeanizing forms associated with literature written by whites and often glibly described as "complex," whereas the forms of "minority" literature are often described as "simple" (see chapter 7). But I don't suggest a deracializing or deculturalizing of form. Readers and writers will still culturalize form, and to the extent (debatable and variable) that we live in a race-saturated world, they will racialize form as well, with whatever mélange of cultural insight or oversimplification. The point is to identify the site of racialized and culturalized forms in the ways that we read instances of those forms, rather than in some essentializing way inherently in the forms themselves.

Yet, we might expect Indian writing to have a different aesthetic from non-Indian writing, and many critics claim that it does. For me to incline otherwise is to buck a growing trend. A novel like Silko's *Ceremony*, so the argument goes, is cyclical, rather than linear, fitting an Indian sense of nonlinear time. Paula Gunn Allen puts the argument famously in the title essay of her influential *The Sacred Hoop*, and the poet and critic Kimberly M. Blaeser has returned to it in an elegant article. Still, for readers of modernist and contemporary writers who defy linearity, from Woolf and Faulkner to Borges, Angela Carter, and many others, as well as earlier writers like Cervantes, Swift (e.g., *A Tale of a Tub*), or Sterne, Silko's commitment to nonlinear plot, however defining of *Ceremony* and her other writings, and however fascinating her version of nonlinearity, might not seem distinctive for its nonlinearity per se. As Sandra Adell says about efforts to construct a black aesthetic, "the more the black theorist writes in the interest of blackness, the greater his Eurocentrism." Adell's argument recalls Derrida's idea that Lévi-Strauss's anticolonialist desire to separate orality from literacy ends up as ethnocentrism in the guise of anti-ethnocentrism. In Indian studies, we might remind ourselves that Indian identity is unthinkable without contact and exchange between Indian and non-Indian cultures. Before that, there could be no concept of Indians. Hence the notion of an Indian aesthetic depends on non-Indians, just as the notion of non-Indian or "western" culture gathers its illusory coherence by depending on the worlds it seeks to expel. That does not necessarily mean there is no such thing as an Indian (or European) aesthetic, but it makes it recursively tricky to pin down what an Indian aesthetic might be. Thus, when Adell goes on to quote Lewis Nkosi writing that "the further back the African artist goes in exploring his tradition, the nearer he gets to the European avant-garde,"[4] we need to match Nkosi's insight by remembering that European, modernist avant-garde art depended on African and, broadly, on so-called non-western art.

I fear, then, that Blaeser's eloquent argument mostly comes down to platitude. "The works of Native American writers," she says, "both inadvertently and self-consciously embody literary processes and genres unlike those of the old canon. Many Indian authors have chosen purposefully to ignore standard rules and forms ill suited to Native storytelling. They strive to introduce different codes. Their works teach readers and critics new ways of reading and interacting with voices on the page" ("Like 'Reeds through the Ribs of a Basket,'" 266). All this sounds nice, but the same claims are often made for almost any group of writers. The romantic claim for newness and the structuralist claim for "codes" have their own histories apart from any connection to Indian writing. After some excellent readings of texts, Blaeser concludes with in effect a prose poem characterizing Indian writing and its aesthetic:

Contemporary story told in a nonlinear fashion. The interweaving of the realities of this world and time with that of other worlds and other times. The transgressing of the boundaries of genre. The use of the circle as an aesthetic form instead of a straight line. The refusal to write an end to story because story always continues. The creating of characters whose beliefs and actions violate certain standards of morality or good taste. . . . Not explaining "logically" in cause and effect but believing in the chance of life and the chance of a story. . . . Writing reality. Not writing literature. Writing revolution. Not writing literature. Writing life. (275)

These are common, almost platitudinous claims for many writers, Indian or not. More non-Native than Native writers practice the aesthetic (or collection of aesthetics) that Blaeser describes; nor is her aesthetic necessarily congenial to all Native writers. Native writers hold no privileged link to reality, revolution, or life; and not all Native writers stand ready to forswear genre, endings, characters who abide by morality or good taste, logic, literature, or even linearity.

To understand *Ceremony,* we need to ponder its nonlinear structure, but tying its structure to being Indian will not necessarily describe what other Indian literature is or prescribe what it should be. Duane Niatum, the poet and anthology editor, writes that he has "an arrow to chip" on this topic: "It is my opinion that there is not a Native American aesthetic that we can recognize as having separate principles from the standards of artists from Western European and American cultures. And anyone who claims there is encourages a conventional and prescriptive response from both Native Americans and those from other cultures. The result is that the reader's imagination is actually inhibited. Stereotypic expectations break down the free play between reader and writer" (554). In a similar if more politicized vein, Robert Allen Warrior says that "we do not have to wait to discover some essentially Indian form of writing. . . . However much these writers are performing an activity somehow continuous with that of storytellers and singers, they are also doing what poetry has done in its European forms and in other non-European contexts. . . . These poets have taken a European written form thousands of years old and transformed it . . . to become a form of resistance against other European forms and systems" (117). Niatum goes on to draw connections between the Kiowa writer N. Scott Momaday or the Blackfeet and Gros Ventre writer James Welch and Joyce, Woolf, Faulkner, Hemingway, and Camus (557–61). But it's a tricky argument. He looks at a poem about a storm by Ted Hughes, the British poet (and later poet laureate), and finds features in it that sound Indian. "There is one exception, however," Niatum adds, going on to say—in intriguingly qualified language—that "a Blackfeet or a Navajo or a Swinomish writing about a similar experience—*if* well versed in the traditions of his or her ancestors *and* caring about the values enough to integrate them into his or her art—*might* respond to this storm, but far more humbly and openly (without Hughes's arrogance), having discovered from the people's songs, ancient sparks, that the way is to be with the turning earth, the blowing mist, the cycle of human as well as earthly changes" (557; emphasis added). According to Niatum, then, there is no Native American aesthetic, in the sense of a specifically Native form, but there are tendencies and topics (as Niatum hints wittily when he says that he has "an arrow to chip"), at least among Native writers who have the knowledge and desire to weave their writing into Native traditions Niatum's inelegant exchange ("exception," "if," "might") seems to me exactly right and more trustworthy than any elegant formulation, any well-wrought urn we might craft to contain Indian aesthetics.

To critics of African American literature, the outlines of the debate might sound like a familiar echo after the Black Arts and Black Aesthetic movement of the 1960s, though the particulars and tones differ enormously. Niatum's inelegant exchange bears a likeness to the call of Henry Louis Gates Jr., arguing against the notion of a Black Aesthetic (*Figures in Black*, 38–46), for "a theory of criticism that is inscribed within the black vernacular tradition and that in turn informs the shape of the Afro-American literary tradition" (*Signifying Monkey*, xix). Niatum's playfully ironic "arrow to chip" and humble songs of "the blowing mist," with their nonlinear "cycle of human as well as earthly changes," aspire to such a vernacular for describing Indian writing. Whether that adds up to an Indian aesthetic, a specifically Indian form, might depend on the needs of the beholder, which can cycle and change from one setting to another.

Moreover, the classic statements from theorists of the Black Aesthetic often bear a good deal more nuance than their critics bequeathed to cultural memory. In "Towards a Black Aesthetic" (1968), Hoyt W. Fuller identified an array of black styles, but he began by lamenting the silly idea that black artistic expression is inevitably about blackness or suffering. He defined a black aesthetic as "a system of isolating and evaluating the artistic works of black people which reflect the special character and imperatives of black experience" (9). He never suggested that all artistic works by black people fill that function or that they do nothing else. Nor did he claim that all black writers whose work reflects black experience reflect it in the same way. Thus, Fuller advocated a black aesthetic without taking up the banner that scares off Niatum, the banner proclaiming that art without a black aesthetic isn't black, or that art without an Indian aesthetic isn't Indian. As Gates puts it:

> A descriptive formalism cannot bring a contrived unity to a tradition defined in the first instance by "ethnicity." Further, expectations that authors must be

accountable spokespersons for their ethnic groups can well nigh be unbear-
able for an "ethnic" author. If black authors are primarily entrusted with producing the proverbial "text of blackness," they become vulnerable to the
charge of betrayal if they shirk their "duty." . . . These burdens of representation can too often lead to demands for ideological "correctness" in an author's work, not to mention a prescriptive criticism that demands certain
forms of allegiance and uniformity. ("'Ethnic and Minority' Studies," 294)

Critics such as Allen or Blaeser (and I name only two of the best such critics as examples) end up implying, perhaps without meaning to, that to be
an Indian writer you need to follow certain prescribed forms, such as nonlinearity, and that without the prescribed forms, writing cannot be Indian.

By contrast, many of the most separatist Black Aesthetic theorists argued against defining a Black Aesthetic. Julian Mayfield wrote, "I cannot—will not—define my Black Aesthetic, nor will I allow it to be defined
for me" (29). Even Don L. Lee wrote, "Finally, the Black Aesthetic cannot
be defined in any definite way. To accurately and fully define a Black Aesthetic would automatically limit it" (246). Instead of describing the Black
Aesthetic as typifying black writing, many Black Arts theorists rejected earlier black writing, unlike most Indian critics, who address their traditions
with more deference. Instead of identifying with the past, many Black Arts
and Black Aesthetic critics saw their ideas as a program for the future.
"The Black Aesthetic, if it is anything," wrote Mayfield, "is the search for a
new program, because all the old programs spawned out of the Judaeo-
Christian spirit have failed us" (28). In Fuller's terms, the Black Aesthetic
"is seeking new forms, new limits, new shapes" ("New Black Literature,"
346). To Larry Neal, "the Black Arts Movement proposes a radical re-
ordering of the western cultural aesthetic" (272). The differences between African American and Native American literary histories are at least
as cautionary as the similarities may be instructive. But the outpouring of
writing about a black aesthetic in the late 1960s and early 1970s offers a
sounding board and stimulus for thinking about Native American aesthetics, even as the civil rights and black power movements helped inspire
political change and assertiveness in Native America (and non-Anglo
America in general).

Thomas King laments that "in our discussions of Native literature, we
try to imagine that there is a racial denominator which full-bloods raised
in cities, half-bloods raised on farms, quarter-bloods raised on reservations, Indians adopted and raised by white families, Indians who speak
their tribal language, Indians who speak only English, traditionally educated Indians, university-trained Indians, Indians with little education,
and the like all share. We know, of course, that there is not."[5] Underlining
the inevitable unrepresentativeness and incompleteness of even a long

list, King leaves off expected categories like full-bloods on reservations or quarter-bloods in cities. And we can multiply King's comments by the many groups of Indian people, racially quantified or not, that he doesn't mention.

I return then, circularly, to the representative example of nonlinearity as a potentially defining characteristic for a Native American aesthetic. Especially in narrative writing, which privileges—though it does not confine us to—reading from left to right (or in some languages from right to left), from top to bottom of the page, and from page to page in the same direction, nonlinearity is not an independent function. It never exists apart from linearity. Even when we see the circular or nonlinear as the negative of linearity, we still make linearity and nonlinearity partake of and define each other. The difference between them may apply more usefully to comparing Indian and non-Indian autobiography, as, historically, traditional autobiography depends on a linear, progressive model. But even a traditional autobiography begins where it ends, with the writing that the plot leads up to. In narrative theory, variations in linearity govern the defining formula of narrative, the *fabula* as opposed to the *sjuzet* (as the Russian formalists famously put it, in Russian);[6] the story as opposed to the plot (the Russian formalists, in English translation), to the narrative (Gérard Genette), to the discourse (Emile Benveniste, Seymour Chatman), or to the text (Shlomith Rimmon-Kenan); or, as I prefer to put it, the tale as opposed to the telling. The tale is the sequence of events as they happened, and the telling is the sequence of events as they are told—for example, told by a novel that narrates the tale. We can read the tale or the telling as linear or nonlinear, progressive or repetitive, but either way, the binary between tale and telling equally fits (and equally distorts) all narrative, Indian or not.

Hertha Dawn Wong points out that, while nonlinearity has been claimed as defining Indian autobiography, it has also been claimed as defining feminist autobiography (23). More broadly, nonlinearity plays a signal role in Hélène Cixous's controversial efforts, like those of Luce Irigaray, to define what Cixous has called *l'écriture féminine*, or feminine writing, efforts that have met at least as much scorn as acclaim, for many feminists fear that such terms clothe women's language in a dressed-up version of the same misogynist clichés about women's frivolous chatter that feminists set out to overturn. Even Cixous describes *l'écriture féminine* as a style of writing produced by male as well as female writers.

In the same vein, we might enjoy how Sherman Alexie's poem "One Stick Song" (*One Stick*, 35–40) plays riffs on the rhythms of a stick game song (a popular game in his part of Indian America), but in another context a non-Indian or an Indian writer might choose a similar form that would attract different associations. The form itself does not carry a cultural determinant apart from the context we read it through, even though that context makes his poem's form very Indian indeed (or very northwest Indian). Thus my approach differs from approaches that seek out transcendent formal characteristics, such as nonlinearity, as a means to define Indian writing. I read the Indian in Indian writing historically, rather than formally. I offer formalist readings but read form historically, not as a transhistorical vessel of essentialist identity.

"Scholars who write about an ethnic group to which they do not belong," notes bell hooks, "rarely discuss in the introductions to their work the ethical issues of their race privilege" (*Talking Back*, 44). I am white and lament that, as hooks notes, some people may unwittingly attribute greater authority to the work of white scholars. I would rather that people approached my work with extra skepticism. There is a great deal that some Native critics will understand that I would never anticipate. But just as my failures cannot reduce to my whiteness, so to reduce Native scholars' insights to their Nativeness would demean the work it took to reach those insights.

The community of scholars and critics has grown, in recent years, by increasingly recognizing the need to think through our perspectives and biases and by recognizing that we can never think them through entirely. I have my biases, and they range beyond color. I am—or try to be—a formalist and a politically poststructuralist, feminist, socio-historical critic on the left. I seek to write criticism that reads the social meanings and structures of literary forms and the formal structures and meanings of social representation, including gender. I lament the widespread tendency to read form and social representation as some kind of seesawing binary, as if when attention to one goes up then attention to the other must go down. On the contrary, I assume that form and social representation never separate, despite many readers' investment in imagining them separately, and even though no one kind of form (e.g., "Indian form," "western form," nonlinear form) can predict any particular kind of social representation.

But if we increasingly recognize the need to reflect on our perspectives and biases, we also fortify bias when we reduce it to essentialized racial categories, as we sometimes (and I put weight on the word *sometimes*) do when we say things like, as a white critic, I think such and such, or as an Indian critic, I think such and such, or as an Indian or white critic, someone else thinks such and such. I don't want to rule out those expressions, for their meaning varies with their context, and I think it's more useful to contemplate expressions like that and the need or pressure to use them than it is to rule them out or insist on them.[7]

In the meantime, some critics persist in misreading the project of writing about a people or its literature as writing for that people, in effect, as speaking for them.[8] Speaking for Indians is the furthest thing from my mind. Elizabeth Cook-Lynn denies, as well, that Indian poets can speak for their people, an idea that she calls "one of the great burdens of contemporary American Indian poets today, for it is widely believed that we 'speak for our tribes.' The frank truth is that I don't know very many poets who say, 'I speak for my people.' It is not only unwise; it is probably impossible, and it is very surely arrogant, for *We Are Self-Appointed*" ("You May Consider Speaking," 58). In an interview, Thomas King says that to

> speak for Native people . . . isn't a role I'm even interested in. . . . There are enough people from the various tribes who speak both languages, who have very close ties, which I don't, to their tribe, who can do that for each one of the tribes. Everybody tries to hit upon one particular Indian at any point in time to answer all the questions about Indian affairs in the whole of North America. Most Indians won't take that job, so people go looking for someone who will. Most times it's a non-Indian who thinks he knows all about Indians or a social guru like, say, Lynn Andrews. I get fairly appalled when that begins to happen. I don't really care if the person is Native or non-Native. But to put anybody into a role like that, particularly a non-Native, is maddening. (Interview with Hartmut Lutz, 109)

As Cook-Lynn and King indicate, plenty of Indians speak perfectly well for themselves, with no thanks needed to anyone else.[9] Their work has, among its least notable attributes, inspired this book and many others.

Happily, Indian literature offers much to choose from: this book could well address writings beyond those it concentrates on. Critics write about what moves them most and where they think they see ways to make a useful contribution, and in my case, that comes with fiction and poetry. As it happens, despite a proliferation of autobiography and the growth of Native theater,[10] poetry and fiction still rest at the center of what we see, ideologically, as "literature," thus playing a central role in the emerging imaginary coherence of Native American literature that this book sets out to describe.

My title, *The Invention of Native American Literature*, merges two different meanings of *invention*. One meaning describes the creation *of* Native literature: how it got started, historically. The other meaning describes the creation *by* Native literature: the ideas it invents. The second sense, less familiar in contemporary usage, comes from theories of rhetoric and refers to the act of imagining what to write about. In that context, I tend to concentrate on writers' early, formative work—McNickle's first novel, poems from Young Bear's first two books, Silko's and King's first novels. Warrior has spoken to the tendency of teaching and scholarship to focus on the first novels of Indian writers and neglect their later work. Many readers (including this one) were disappointed in the long-awaited second novels of Momaday (*The Ancient Child* [1989]) and Silko (*Almanac of the Dead* [1991]), but these novels have a following, and Momaday's and Silko's other writings have attracted much interest, especially *The Way to Rainy Mountain* (1969) and *Storyteller* (1981). I expect that Silko's *Gardens in the Dunes* (1999) will also attract much critical interest. The novels that Louise Erdrich published after her spectacular debut novel, *Love Medicine* (1983), have won a large audience, and Thomas King's second novel, *Green Grass, Running Water,* has received far more critical commentary than his first, promising that his continuing work (beginning with *Truth & Bright Water* [1999]) might attract considerable interest as well. But Warrior is right; first novels by most of the best-known Indian novelists (Momaday, Welch, Silko, Vizenor, and even Erdrich) have captured the bulk of critical and pedagogical attention, and I do little to change that. By concentrating on the formative works of writers who later go on in a multitude of additional directions, I bring those works together in their roles as bricks in a larger structure, the invention of Native American literature.

Close concentration on formative texts serves my nonessentialist approach, for essentialist assumptions have a tough time holding up under close study. Warrior notes that "a commitment to essentialized indigenous worldviews and consciousness, over the course of the decade [of the 1980s], became a pervasive and almost requisite feature of American Indian critical writing," but that the "dominating influence of essentialist understandings of Indian culture" has drawn increasing challenges (xvii). He concludes that American Indian studies "continue[s] to be preoccupied with parochial questions of identity and authenticity. Essentialist categories still reign insofar as more of the focus of scholarship has been to reduce, constrain, and contain American Indian literature and thought and to establish why something or someone is 'Indian' than engage the myriad critical issues crucial to an Indian future" (xix). In line with Warrior, my attention goes not to why or whether someone or something is Indian, but to *how* they are Indian. In itself, anti-essentialism has become a critical commonplace (even while some people remain—as Warrior notes—oblivious to it). Still, it retains an edge in Indian studies that it may be losing in many other conversations, because, again as Warrior and Jace Weaver note, in Indian studies there remains so much pressure to essentialize.[11] Moreover, the nonessentialist approach of this book is not the point. If it were, this book would only rediscover a sometimes forgotten truism. Instead, the nonessentialist approach is an instrument, one among many, to readings of these texts' social and aesthetic energies and interests.

For literary criticism to seek the social apart from the aesthetic, as many readers expect, especially for criticism of literature written by people who are not white, is to reduce the critical project to what Gayatri Chakravorty Spivak aptly scorns as mere information retrieval ("Three Women's Texts," 243). Thus I return at the end of this introduction to where it began, with the writings that this book addresses as texts that offer their readers pleasure. The pleasure of these writings comes in the cultural, intellectual, and literary challenges they lay down, in turns of phrase, plot, imagination, and representation that invite us to pause and at the same time urge us to keep on reading, cycling on through Niatum's "human as well as earthly changes."

CHAPTER 2

Nothing to Do: John Joseph Mathews's *Sundown* and Restless Young Indian Men

EDNA: You're a four-star bust! If you think I'm standing for it much longer, you're crazy as a bedbug!
JOE: I'd get another job if I could. There's no work—you know it.
EDNA: I only know we're at the bottom of the ocean.
JOE: What can I do?
EDNA: Who's the man in the family, you or me?
JOE: That's no answer.
—Clifford Odets, *Waiting for Lefty*, 1935

Scattered through the massive archives of Native American studies, a good deal has been implied about the cultural history of the articulation between contact and gender, but it deserves more concentrated study. It is sometimes hinted that contact with European peoples displaced traditional Native American masculine roles and work patterns more than it displaced traditional feminine roles and work patterns, although Paula Gunn Allen suggests that such a belief reflects the colonial privileging of men's experience.[1] Whether accurate history or colonialist and misogynist presumption, that belief contributes to the image of aimless, restless young men with nothing to do who populate the line of Native American novels beginning with John Joseph Mathews's understudied *Sundown* (1934) and D'Arcy McNickle's *The Surrounded* (1936). While many recent novelists—especially women novelists—leave that focus behind, including Betty Louise Bell, Linda Hogan, Susan Power, and Anna Lee Walters, the fascination with restless young men with nothing to do continues through the novels of N. Scott Momaday, James Welch, Leslie Marmon Silko, and on to Sherman Alexie's *Reservation Blues* (1995).

Young Indian men in *Sundown* and *The Surrounded* think they have nothing to do, but their sense of *nothing* and of *doing* gradually emerges as a sediment of non-Indian, colonizing ideologies and—especially in *Sundown*—as an invitation to critique those ideologies. The options for youthful masculinity seem contracted into little more than making trouble and getting drunk, superficially appealing options, perhaps, but still options that clear a path for colonizing through self-hatred and the appropriation of mineral and land rights. "Tell me what you think a fellow can do here," the young Archilde Leon asks in *The Surrounded*, "steal horses like Louis? Drink and run around?" (15). Similarly, amid the prosperity of the Osage oil boom, the young Chal Windzer of *Sundown* thinks he and other Indians should be "doing something" (161, and twice on 162) besides living off their oil income, but "No one would give a job to an Indian" (263). Internalized self-hatred makes Chal read Indian activity as doing nothing, whereas Mathews suggests that the colonizers' busyness is hollow, another version of nothing, desperate to impose its frenzy as the criterion of masculine pride. Although some critics have read onto these novels the more optimistic narratives of recent Native hopes for cultural pride and self-sufficiency, neither novel can imagine the ideological equipment that might merge living Indian culture—including Indian attitudes toward work—with an economic restructuring that resists colonization. Instead, the options seem reduced to assimilation and a gradual fading of tribal and Indian cultures before the all-consuming colonialist economic expansion, even amidst the more hopeful possibilities that both novelists imply through their protagonists' yearning rediscovery of meaning in local Indian cultures. Under the influence of *Sundown* and *The Surrounded,* and even more under that of the ideologies and histories they represent and resist, a good deal of later Native fiction continues to revisit the preoccupation with restless young men who have nothing to do, and to reimagine the epistemology of Indian doing in a wider world that so often sees Indians as done to, and not as doing.

Drawing on W. E. B Du Bois's comparisons between white labor and black labor and E. P. Thompson's ideas about work discipline and the rise of industrial capitalism, Eugene D. Genovese, the historian of slavery, has written a risky but provocative account of what he calls "the black work ethic," which he opposes to the industrial work ethic that took hold in nineteenth-century America.[2] He reads the industrial work ethic not as a white ethic but rather as a time-clocked, regularized, often factory-based development of the Euro-American Protestant work ethic, often anathema to American rural, Catholic, or immigrant laborers of whatever color. Genovese argues that waves of white and often immigrant workers were driven into the new industrialized work ethic in the nineteenth century despite considerable resistance, even as black slaves and workers, adapting to and resisting the conditions of United States slavery, developed not the lazy ethic often invented to describe black labor but instead a specifically African American work ethic, pre-industrial and relatively independent of clock-time and standardized regularity. The risk, of course, comes in reducing African Americans to a potentially degrading or romantic stereotype—a problem that Genovese addresses with considerable subtlety—and in underestimating the many directions that African American work has taken since emancipation. Labor historians such as David R. Roediger have developed the ideas of Du Bois, Genovese, and others to chart the way that white male workers adapted to the industrial economy by identifying with whiteness and projecting their own resistance to the new work ethic onto African Americans, thus in some ways actually creating whiteness—as American popular culture has unconsciously come to understand it—through demagogic race-baiting.

It is time for historians and cultural critics to consider that Native Americans have their own history of exchange with the racialized work ethic of the industrial economy, an exchange that continues to construct ideas of race long after the heyday of industrialization. Martha C. Knack and Alice Littlefield have helped by editing a collection of essays on the history of Native American wage labor. Unlike whites and blacks, American Indians have seen their most rapid movement into wage labor in the twentieth century. But the great depression put particular pressure on socialization into the national economy and the ways that it constructed Native American ideas of race, work, and gender. It is one thing to draw Indian men or women into the white-dominated economy and another to relegate them to the subordinate place that that economy sets aside for its under- and unemployed, especially in the 1930s when unemployment assumed so threatening a role in the wider cultural imaginary. With mass joblessness pressuring ideologies that link masculinity to market-valued, public employment, the depression reshaped Native cultural dilemmas and economic suffering in wider national and international terms, inviting radical critiques of work-contingent notions of masculinity and of market-contingent notions of the value in work. Writing independently of, yet in some ways congruently with, the 1930s experiments in socialist and proletarian fiction, both Mathews and McNickle invite readers to rethink the conflation of work, masculinity, and the market. While they do not offer a socialist or any other systematic alternative, they encourage a suspicion of the systematicity that threatened to collapse work, masculinity, and market value into a machine of colonization and assimilation, with—for Mathews and McNickle's purposes—local Indian culture as its target.

As *Sundown* has received relatively little critical attention, a brief summary may prove helpful. Mathews's second book and only novel, *Sundown* tells the story of Chal Windzer as he grows up amidst the gusher of Osage oil wealth in northeast Oklahoma, goes on nervously to the university (transparently the University of Oklahoma, though never named as such) and fraternity life,[3] quits school to join the Army Air Corps in World War I, returns home to an aimless life of wealthy dissipation, and then watches helplessly as the depression dries up oil income and most Osages find themselves suddenly impoverished. Chal can never resolve his attraction to Osage culture with his embarrassment over its appeal to him, just as he can never resolve his attraction to the bustle of economic "progress" with his horror at the encroachments of white culture and modernity. His male acquaintances, especially the Osage men, try out a variety of failed options that pose them as foils to Chal's sense of superiority and his on-again, off-again desire to assimilate. While the men's lives crumble, the women of *Sundown* stay disturbingly in the background. If Mathews paints the men as melodramatically but profoundly uncertain, mostly he paints the women—Osage and white—as mere airheads, reference points for the novel's men and their uneasy pondering of their own masculinity.

Sundown joins together two fixed but competing models of thinking: the nostalgic construction of an imaginary Osage world free of worry or progress, versus a worried sense that such an imaginary must give way to busyness and competition in the economic marketplace. From that second worried perspective, the novel's Osage imaginary—constructed as pure and whole, a world without work—must give way to a white symbolic structured in difference and deferral, where exchange value (money, wealth) rules, where men (again, the focus is decidedly on men) prove their worth through work and aspire to linear, progressive advancement. As the *Daily Oklahoman* put it in a troubling description of Mathews's first book, *Wah'Kon-Tah,* in 1939 when he won a Guggenheim fellowship, Mathews tells the "story of the absorption of his carefree people by a money-minded people" ("J. J. Mathews"). In *Sundown,* Mathews sets these fixed, contradictory models in Chal, partly sharing Chal's thinking and partly retaining a critical distance, although readers—especially if they have not read Mathews's other books—may feel tempted to identify the novel with its focalizing protagonist.

To Chal, these two fixed models of thinking seem like opposites, but each tangles into the other. The Osage world never could have been so escapist or so merged with childhood as Chal imagines it. Again and again, he keeps identifying his childhood memories with being Osage, drawing on the regressive desire that anyone might have to imagine purity or authenticity in the cultural past and in one's own earliest experience. He also draws on the wider white culture's link between boyish play and Indianness (as in toy Indian headdresses, or Boy Scouts adopting bogus Indian rituals),[4] merging the nostalgic fantasy that children represent an early stage of freedom in the evolution to adulthood with the racist fantasy that Indians represent an early stage of freedom in cultural evolution. At the same time, in a closely linked illusion, Chal collapses adult work with whiteness, banishing Indian-associated activities from his notion of work and banishing white-associated activities from his imaginary realm of psychic comfort, despite enormous evidence to the contrary for each side. Indian men (like Indian women) have always worked, but the dominant culture that catches Chal in its assumptions separates what it understands as work from what it recognizes as the activities of Indian men. Chal thus tries to prop up a false binary between Indian and white, between work and Osage identity. The binary always threatens to topple over, yet its threat to fall intensifies the frightened, defensive desire to prop it up.

Chal identifies his Osageness with the people, rituals, and material culture of older Osage ways, as we might expect, and also with a specific set of behaviors and images: lying on his back; taking off his clothes; seeing himself as an animal; Indian silence; the Osage hills and their blackjack oaks; the color red (Louis Owens, *Other Destinies*, 51–52); birds; and flying. Over and over, Chal nostalgically identifies these motifs with his childhood, as he identifies his childhood with his Osageness.

Meanwhile, the novel uses these motifs to organize its plot through Chal's two models of thinking: dreamy nostalgia versus the worldly demand to "do" things. "There is not much of a story to *Sundown,*" says Charles R. Larson; "plot has, in fact, given way to character development" (56). Larson's comment mixes insight with distortion. On the one hand, he is right that *Sundown* does not offer a typical plot. It raises expectations (about characters, events, and plot) that it later seems to forget, letting them fade into red herrings and plot feints. And it trails off into what Andrew Wiget calls a "tiresome" pace (*Native American Literature,* 77), until the story suddenly stops with no sense of closure. One otherwise favorable review complained that the novel "goes dark every now and then . . . because of a rigid and . . . unnatural exclusion of dramatic incident" (Constance Skinner), and another lamented that "in places it sags a bit" (Maxine Barrus).

The dominant American culture that this novel both critiques and participates in tends to condense and distort its plots into stories of individuality, and we can read Mathews's focus on a single character as complicit with that tendency. On the other hand, we can also read critics like Larson who condense the novel to character as perhaps themselves complicit with the ideological assumption that individuality is the foremost gauge of cultural value, and as underestimating how the novel uses its single protagonist for a larger cultural and economic plot that continues on even as the protagonist runs out of energy.[5] In the intimacy of form and content, the question of plot addresses not only whether we read the novel as one protagonist's story or as cultural history (or as both), but also how we read its cultural assumptions about what makes a story. Larson's mainstream model (56) anticipates a teleological bildungsroman with Aristotelian beginning and middle pointed to a particular end, the story of Chal's stage-by-stage growth culminating in maturity and insight, congruent with the premodernist European novel. Alternatively, we might look to this Osage book as remixing a culturally mixed Osage imagination with a culturally mixed modernist imagination.

Indeed, the years portrayed in *Sundown* brought intense Osage self-consciousness about cultural mixing and change within tradition. For during these years the most traditional Osages, while holding to their identity as traditionals, also gave up their traditional religion in favor of peyotism, a syncretic practice drawing on new ideas as well as traditionally Osage and Christian ideas. By the time Mathews wrote *Sundown,* "the complex social and ceremonial system in place just forty years before was all but completely supplanted."[6]

But the overdetermined pressure for cultural simplification and false binaries conspires against Chal, pressing him to imagine a singular notion of what it means to be Osage, even while the flaws in such a notion always loft it over the horizon of his capacity to imagine it. As the intricate density of Indian life and traditions remains almost invisible to non-Indian culture, so it can seem almost invisible even to the protagonists of *Sundown* and *The Surrounded,* partly because of the pressures to assimilate to the surrounding world and partly because it is sometimes hard for Chal or Archilde to see what they grow up in and take for granted. As fictional characters, however, Chal and Archilde depend on their authors' invention, and the density of Native culture can be hard even for Mathews and McNickle to pick out and objectify in narrative explanation. Perhaps for the same reasons as their protagonists, Mathews and McNickle seem to hold something back from their representations of Native culture. But while the fictional characters merely think in their own minds or speak with a few acquaintances, the novelists produce a public document. Writing for a wider public puts the novelists in position to consider that much of Native culture is not necessarily the business of outsiders, and that outsiders might not care about or might misconstrue or condescend to what they have difficulty seeing. Writing just after *Black Elk Speaks* sought to explain traditional Sioux beliefs to the non-Indian world in 1932, Mathews briefly introduces an old Osage traditional named Black Elk, only to poke fun at the old man's inability to understand modernity (80–83), as if to spoof Black Elk and John Neihardt's effort in *Black Elk Speaks* to package ancient ways for a wider audience.[7] Nevertheless, Mathews and McNickle's greater reticence helps prop up some of the cultural mystery that in other respects their novels often seek to unmask. The effort to show the routine of Indian, Flathead, or Osage cognitive life, to bring out its unexotic ordinariness, thus gets caught up in preexisting cultural narratives that remystify its demystifying.

In *Sundown,* we see a good deal of public, political Osage culture, with discussion about the council and local economics, but we see little of private Osage culture or specifically Osage ways. Chal's thoughts allude to Osage ways pervasively, yet in general terms. He thinks of dances and songs (once even giving the lyrics), clothing and villages, buildings, gestures, and silences, but he gives little of the cultural histories and associations they evoke. In some ways it would make no sense for his thoughts to explain things he takes for granted, except that he is an outsider as well as an insider to traditional Osage life, a nostalgic observer more than a participant. Yet that makes him an insider to the position of many, perhaps most Osages in his own time.[8] Chal never participates in ceremonial life. Since Osage clans are inherited patrilineally and Chal has a white, patrilineal great grandfather, he would not belong to a clan (though Mathews never says that).[9] Indeed, beyond a few passing references and one episode about peyote religion, the novel tells little about Osage approaches to what Europeans see as religion. More broadly, it tells nothing of the cultural integration and meaning of story, belief, clanship, kinship, cosmology, ritual, material culture, and behavior.[10] (The episode about peyotism is the exception, but peyote belief is new to Chal, not traditionally Osage, and nothing in the rest of the novel draws on that one isolated scene.) At the same time, little as we see of these things, we see much of their meaning to Chal. He thinks of his Osageness not continuously or in detail, but still repeatedly and passionately.

The pattern begins early in his childhood:

> Evenings when there were no lights in the house and his parents sat for two or more hours in the silence. From his mother's lap with his head on her gently heaving breast, he could hear the singing on Wednesday evenings come from the lone frame church in the valley. The little church to which the few white people of the Agency came. . . . For an hour or more he would lie thus, without daydreaming, lulled by the bread and milk in his stomach and the sleepy, murmuring night. He would sometimes concentrate on the bass chirruping of the cricket, out of harmony with the rest of the chorus and much nearer, per-

haps under the porch. . . . A veil would come over his thoughts, smothering them in sensuous torpor, and he would be conscious only of a very slight squeak in his mother's corsets as she breathed. Even this squeak was soporific, and soon . . . he would pass into sleep. (14–15)

Here, early on, we see a pattern of comfort, interruption of comfort, and return to comfort, whether we take up loosely Lacanian terms and think of it as the infant's imaginary continually interrupted by the symbolic and yearning to recover the imaginary, or, without necessarily holding to Lacanian models, think of it as a merging with the maternal or with a comfort that the maternal can evoke, continually interrupted by the world's fuss that distinguishes Wednesdays from other days, white people from other people, the cricket's bass chirrup from the night's harmonious murmur, the squeak in his mother's lap from her lap's deeper inducement to sensuous torpor. That back and forth between comfort and interruption models a yearning struggle to recover a dark, speechless, boundaryless comfort more complete than the child could ever really have known. (And more complete than the child's mother could accurately represent: Chal may associate comfort with his mother's body, but her squeaky-tight corset suggests her actual constricted condition.)

Through the rest of the novel, Chal—concerned with his own condition and oblivious to his mother's—reenacts that early struggle between comfort and the world's fuss, lying alone on his back and daydreaming, escaping to a geographical imaginary where the blackjacks and the hills imprint themselves on his mind as a definition of comfort in being Osage.

Sometimes he was a panther lying lazily in his den and blinking in physical contentment, or a redtail hawk circling high in the blue of the sky. Often at night, when he heard the raindrops on the tin roof of his bedroom, he would be an animal; an indefinite animal in a snug den under the dripping boughs of a tree. Sometimes real pain would be the result of these dream-world metamorphoses; pain caused by the desire to fly over the green world high in the air, like the turkey vulture and the hawk. Unhappiness would descend on him as he lay on his back in the prairie grass, watching the graceful spirals of the redtail. (9)

As I have suggested, he repeats the same actions and emotions over and over: riding his pinto or walking off alone to recapture the feeling of the Osage hills and the blackjacks (11, 68–72), whether at the university (101–3, 133–37, 152–54), back home during vacation (170–71), or after he returns from the Army and drinks and speeds around in his red roadster (e.g., 294–302). Often, he breaks into Osage song or dance (70—

twice, 71, 136, 296–97); strips off his clothes (11, 70—twice, 71, 103, 222) as if trying to recover an elemental, infant originality; envisions himself as an animal; retreats to or relaxes in comforting silence; contemplates the color red; or enviously contemplates birds—as if (in a stock symbol from the literary repertoire) birds' capacity to fly could evoke freedom from the symbolic and the law.[11] Or he contemplates flying itself, culminating in actually flying a plane in dreamy nighttime escapades—against the rules—that seek to convert flying into escape from rules and law.

He associates such actions and feelings with comfort and his Osage childhood, but he also fears that other people, especially white people, will catch him in the act of his Osage identifications: "if there was no one in sight, he would resume the role of wounded buck and run home" (56). He "chanted an Osage song, but . . . then got up and looked around as if he expected to see someone spying on him" (71). "Sometimes he took an eagle feather with him to wear in his hair, and one time he took some paints and painted his face, and for a short time felt the thrill of the eagle feather spinning in his hair. But he did this only once. He had felt so mortified that he could scarcely bathe the paint off fast enough. He almost sweated when he thought of the possibility of a cowboy having seen him" (72).

> He threw off his coat and unbuttoned his collar, but his hands stopped. . . . He decided he wouldn't go into the water—what if someone should see him. Of course there was only the remotest possibility, but if someone did see him, they'd think he was crazy. . . . It would be humiliating to have anyone know that he walked out here by himself, but to undress and float around in the water, that would be too much—they'd know he was crazy, and he was not quite sure that they wouldn't be right. He wasn't a boy in the Osage hills any more. As he buttoned his collar and drew on his coat, he decided that he was going to be like other people. (103)

And yet more: "Suddenly he had an impulse to trot, but before he did so he looked back to see that no one was in sight, then he broke into a trot down the road. . . . Soon he was dodging about and bending low as he ran. Then he stopped suddenly. He looked around to see if anyone had seen him. . . . He felt his face grow hot as he realized that for the last few minutes he had been imagining himself a coyote. . . . Then he said aloud, 'I guess I am crazy, all right'" (133). "He dreamed most of the time, and looked out of the windows. His clothes became burdensome. . . . When he became too uncomfortable, he would walk out into the country by himself, but was ever careful to take paths . . . where he would not be seen. He didn't want people to know that he walked out into the country"

(152). "He could walk out very easily, but he was ashamed of walking; people might think he was crazy . . . , and someone would be sure to see him" (167). "He began taking off his clothes, without thinking, and stood naked in the moonlight. . . . Suddenly he wondered if by any chance Meyer might have seen him" (222–23).

Silence works much the same way, as both a haven of security for his Indianness and a threat to expose his Indianness to the wider, skeptical world. On the one hand, Chal identifies silence with his mother, his Indian friends (68, 93, 98, 99, 111), and Indians more broadly. He remembers "the silence, the tranquillity of his home. Always he remembered the silence. . . . He had a reverence for it as long as he lived; even when he had assumed that veneer which he believed to be civilization" (13). His father notes "the Indian silence of his wife" (53), and Chal admires how she proceeds "silently, in her Indian way" (165). White teachers and students find themselves baffled at Indian students' silence (25, 54, 88, 93, 98, 129, 149, 198, 215), but Chal associates Indian silence with the comforting imaginary of the secure and familiar, the personally early and the culturally ancient. On the other hand, he wants desperately to escape his silence and fit in with noisy white people (98, 135, 139–43, 148, 157–60), but he cannot find his way out of it. Or once, when he manages to join the guys' talk about "coeds" by remarking that the girlfriend of one of his fraternity brothers "had beautiful breasts in her evening gown" (140), he gets himself into trouble for reasons he cannot understand.[12]

If Chal imagines the Osage world as a haven of comfort in continual danger from the conquering white world and its cultural contagions, he imagines the white world as a treadmill of discomfort, of never feeling satisfied and always wanting and seeking more. Of course, Chal is wrong on both counts. If nothing else, his very fear of exposure as an Osage—even to other Osages—proves that the Osage world is not identical with self-satisfaction, any more than the white world is inevitably anathema to comfort, relaxation, or dream. For in this novel and its surrounding world white and Osage life partake deeply of each other, even in their most antagonistic relations, with whites appropriating Osage lands and minerals, and with Osages like Chal all too often judging their own worth by its reflection in the mirror of white colonialist values. It tells us something that Chal's Osage imaginary depends mainly on moments when he is alone. If he did more to integrate his sense of Osage identity with the social world, he would find it harder to sustain his notions of isolated Osage ways or dreamy Osage impracticality and escapism, and *Sundown*, in turn, would rely less on an isolated protagonist. But *Sundown* can hardly paint a broader picture of Osage social life when so much of it remains invisible to outsiders, and when many Osages may want to protect their ways from appropriating colonialist eyes, even though they themselves may be susceptible, like Chal, to looking at their culture through those eyes. Hence Chal's need and the larger cultural imperative to drive a wedge between ideas of Osage culture and ideas of white culture.

For Chal, white culture is everything that being Osage supposedly is not. (I say "being Osage" rather than "Osage culture," because Chal's Osage imaginary is so lonely, so nonsocial.) Instead of the imaginary comfort of being Osage that Chal nostalgically constructs, with no difference and no absence, with only fullness and immediacy, in his construction of the white world (and it is not only *his* construction, of course), everything depends on difference, absence, and deferral, because people want most to gain what they do not have (that's what the novel mockingly calls "progress"), so that, in the market economy's familiar spiral, if they get it, they then want yet more. Money itself is a system of representation and deferral, Derridean *différance.* Money can purchase the metonymies of satisfaction, the flashy autos of Osage oil prosperity, yet their very flashiness advertises their incapacity to fulfill the desires that they represent. If Osageness for Chal is being, then whiteness is wanting, without being.

Of course, Chal's binary between white and Osage cannot hold up, and Chal wants a great deal. He tries to corral wanting into whiteness, because (like anyone, some of the time) he wants to escape the responsibilities of adult desire. But his Osage imaginary has less to do with actual Osage culture, which the novel paints rather thinly, than with the colonialist need to write off colonized cultures into dreamy and nostalgic impracticality, into cultural childhood. In that way, Chal's dream of being Osage, attractive as it can be in its sense of oneness with animals and the landscape, is partly complicit with the colonizers' romanticizing delusions of Indian simplicity. Thus, however much Chal tries to define white people by their culture of economics, business, money, frenetic activity, and compulsive talking, at a circle wider than his own point of view *Sundown* defines white culture by its defensively self-protective, colonialist pressure on Chal, and on Indians and whites more broadly, to define whiteness and Indianness as utter opposites: to see Indians as the dreamily regressive people of the past, whom things are done to, versus whites as the ingeniously progressive doers, the agents of modernity and change. The colonialist project depends on its capacity to prop up that illusion as truth and common sense, and to most people, that's probably what it is.

To Chal, Indians do nothing, or nothing that counts as anything, and whites cannot stop doing. But his descriptions never match his ideologically driven interpretation of them. Much as he associates talk with white people (16–17, 24, 36, 83, 87–88, etc.) and silence with Indian people, he also repeatedly thinks of Indians as talkers, not least his own orator father,

John Windzer. The difference is that he credits white talk with doing things, even when he doesn't much credit the doing, whereas he credits Indian talk with doing nothing. "It was plain to him that Sun-on-His-Wings and Running Elk lacked the spirit of the times—lacked 'get-up,' as John expressed it. They seemed contented just to sit in the village and talk, like many of the other young [Osage] men" (68). Sun-on-His-Wings, he laments, "just sat in the village all day, talking. . . . Chal was disappointed in his [Osage] friends because it seemed that they didn't have any ambition. Their incomes were large and were getting larger as the oil production increased; he couldn't see why they didn't have some ambition and get into some business" (162). The full-bloods talk in the village, and the mixed-bloods talk in the town: "The mixed-bloods would stand in groups at the corners and discuss" the new oil wells. "There was nothing to do except talk. Their incomes were so large now that they didn't think of working at anything; in fact, they had never worked except by spurts when some enthusiasm came over them" (74–75).

Desperate both to observe and to magnify difference between whites and Osages, Chal identifies whites with business and practicality, and he pushes away those interests from anything he can imagine for Osages, which leaves him at sea about where to imagine himself. When he walks off into the country, lies down to daydream, and some cattle happen by, "he felt very foolish and said aloud, as though to prove to the staring cattle that he was there on some practical business like any sane person: 'Well, what th' hell d'yu want?' The word 'hell' always seemed practical and forceful to him" (138). He learns to make excuses. He "told the tenant that he was gonna see if there was any fence needed fixin'. He didn't have any intention of riding the fence. He had learned long ago to have a purpose, and that a practical one, to hide his purposelessness" (170). He "always liked to appear that he was busy" (254), but he never is busy. Asked what he figures on doing, he responds "with embarrassment. 'I'm not doin' anything,' he said. 'I uh—I'll—uh—probably go into something, though, I guess.' Chal believed that if you weren't in some business you didn't have the respect of the community" (241). As Mathews puts it when the narrative accelerates into summary, "The years went by fast for Chal, though he did very little except ride around in his long, powerful red roadster" (245). He drinks steadily more, until he can hardly "sober up, but he didn't care—there wasn't anything else to do" (264). "His thoughts would become practical sometimes, and at such times he was sure he was going to major in economics, to prepare himself for business. He decided that he would be a business man and amount to something in Kihekah. . . . Chal was sure that if he didn't go into some kind of business he would be like the other Osages" (153–54). He thinks that he must be

like the whites or like the Osages, imagining the two as opposite and exclusive rather than relational, fluid, or even mixed or overlapping.

> He wished he had something to do—some business, but there wasn't anything
> for him to do. He couldn't get a job. No one would give a job to an Indian. . . .
> He felt that he could get more respect if he had a job or was in some business
> for himself. He knew in his heart, however, that he wouldn't go into business
> or get a job if he had a chance. There seemed to be another dignity some-
> where that would be hurt if he worked. Then he had a thought that made him
> smile; he guessed he must have two dignities, one tellin' him to do something,
> and one tellin' him not to do anything. (263)

Such a binary makes it impossible for Chal to imagine his own Osage position because it reads Osage action as inaction, as a mere negative of a
gullibly read white activity, an interpretation of white activity that takes
that activity's ideological presumptions at face value.

Moreover, this passage about two dignities seems dangerously made to
order for the kind of critical intelligence (soon to organize loosely into
the new criticism) that might seize on polarized dignities or identities as
profound moments of paradox, ambiguity, and tension. In that way, the
dialogue of dignities can start to look like the clash of essences that so
much of the novel sets out to undermine, much as with Faulkner's portrayal of Joe Christmas in *Light in August* (1932). Some critics have leaned
toward reading Chal as "caught between two worlds,"[13] "caught between
the red and white cultures as between two millstones" (Priscilla Oaks, vi),
"a victim of a bi-culture identity" (Carol Hunter, "Protagonist as a Mixed-
Blood," 320). As Hunter puts it, "Osage and white cultures created two realities for Chal so that . . . he became psychologically crippled, emotion-
ally stunted and incapable of expressing his own character which resulted
in alienation from his own self-worth and identity" ("Protagonist as a
Mixed-Blood," 324). That makes it sound as if Osage and white cultures
are stable entities entirely independent of each other, and as if all Osages,
or even all modern Indians, would inevitably turn into pathetic case studies in helplessness. But it is not as if full-bloods and non-Indians are
monocultural. With much more cultural insight, Robert Allen Warrior
notes that, unlike in most other novels about Indian mixed-bloods, Chal's
mother and father are both Indian. He argues that *Sundown* challenges
Hunter's "language of victimization, tragedy, and alienation," that it is not
about "the conflict between white and Indian values, but a nuanced description of what Mathews saw as the weaknesses of two internal political
and social strategies" (56, 54). Even Chal's would-be Osage imaginary is
not exclusively Indian. Like Chal, Blo Daubeney, the white sorority god-

dess, strips off her clothes to glory in her nakedness (128). As Chal identifies with animals and the purity of nakedness, so the narrator notes one of his white future fraternity brothers running out of the shower, "leaving great, wet tracks like a bear on the polished floor" (98). Such moments teasingly critique the temptation to draw impermeable lines between Indians and non-Indians. And even though Mathews—like Faulkner in *Light in August*—may sometimes succumb to the language of stable, polarized binaries, it behooves us as readers to sort the drag of received language from the forward motion of cultural criticism.

This sideshow of falsifying binaries can deflect scrutiny from Chal's desperate effort to make Osage work and action invisible and naturalize white capitalist frenzy as the only model of work or action. "He felt that he had been silly, mooning the way he had, and he felt ashamed of his emotions. He knew that he ought to be more practical about things. . . . The talk he had just listened to was the talk of the strong, practical men who did things, while the Osages dreamed silly things in a mystical dreamworld. Men like Doc Lawes didn't sit around and dream; they got out and did things" (280). But Osages may follow another law than Doc Lawes, whereas Chal's zeal to take up white-identified cultural blindness exiles Osages from law itself, an exile that he can carry off only because of the distance he keeps from Osage cultural and ceremonial life. The narrative's skepticism of Chal's fears invites us to see past the thinness of its Osage cultural representation, but its reliance on Chal's view keeps Osage ways almost invisible. In turn, that near invisibility lets the novel itself delicately embody Osage difference. And in a circular logic of projection and introjection, Chal's dream of taking up white-identified cultural positions acts out the dreamy inactivity he attributes to Osages, making his unrepresentative self the novel's purest representation of supposedly moony Osage ways—ways that may bear some relation to Osage ontology but that distort it so much that Mathews knows better than to confirm so sullen a view of Osage life.

But if he can't or won't join either his Osage friends or his white acquaintances, and he can't imagine living outside those binaries, then Chal turns into a Joe Christmas figure who can imagine no terrain for himself in the polarized cultural landscape. "There was no one to talk with," he thinks. "He was the only person not doing something except the mixed-bloods and the fullbloods, but he believed that there wasn't much interest in them—he certainly didn't want to be like them. He knew that he ought to be doing something. Of course he had never in all his life done anything. Not even as a little boy when the little white boys were delivering papers or telegrams, or working in their fathers' stores and offices. It seemed to him that it was a disgrace to sit around and do nothing" (162).

These thoughts encapsulate a great deal of the novel. If "he had never in all his life done anything," then everything he has done counts as nothing. While sometimes he feels pride in his Osage identity or enjoys the way his "bronze complexion" attracts (white) women (230), more often he stews in self-hate and yearns to be white. "He had succeeded . . . in associating himself almost entirely with the white boys" (68). He "had wondered if he wasn't too dark. He had often wished that he weren't so bronze. It set him off from other people, and he felt that he was queer anyway, without calling attention to the fact. It was embarrassing to attract attention, and when people looked at him he became shy. He thought he still might have black eyes and straight black hair that shone like patent leather when he put grease on it, if his face were only white" (117). "Other people" are white, he assumes, naturalizing whiteness. "He didn't want to call attention to the fact that most of his blood was of an uncivilized race like the Osages" (153). He wishes that he "'didn't have a drop of God damn' Indian blood in my veins,'" as if the default alternative were necessarily white, and when Lou Kerry notices his dark skin and asks if he is "'Spanish or something,'" he says "'Yes, Spanish'" (160, 203). She cannot imagine his Indianness, despite her excited fear of and attraction to "or something." But in desiring to be white he does not simply deny that he is Osage or Indian. He also denies the possibility for any place outside the yo-yo of racial binaries.

Hence the jarring feeling at those rare moments in the book when other racial categories come up, when Lou's stereotypically "large negro chauffeur" (202) summons Chal and then Chal goes along with her suggestion that he himself is "Spanish or something," or when he tries to lord it over a "slovenly negro" worker: "'You know you're treated better when you work for an Indian than when you work for white men in town—why don't you appreciate it?' The negro had become quite frightened, and he said, 'Yes suh, Mistuh Chal, Ah knows' at—Ah sho knows 'at.' Chal felt better" (265). At such moments, both the character Chal and the stereotyping novel pass up the chance for solidarity among African Americans, Native Americans, and Latinos in favor of a desire to identify with white people, like the Irish and other immigrant workers that Roediger and historians of labor and popular culture have described. In this last case, however, Chal's identifying with whites takes the form of imagining that he is so white that he is better than whites.

Chal's binary-driven whining also naturalizes an identification between whiteness and masculinity. Although he thinks a good deal about white women, from his priggish white cousin to Blo Daubeney, his comparisons between whites and Osages set purportedly white, masculine business and work against the dreamy inactivity he attributes to Osage young men. In his view, inactivity threatens to feminize men, for he cannot recognize either women's or Osage men's work or activity. When he thinks of white "women and girls who had nothing to do" (202), he may be sneering at middle-class female privilege, but he also takes inactivity as a natural characteristic of white females. He never realizes how he sees white females and Osages in the same category, merging his inability to see the activity of women, whatever their color, into a corresponding inability to see the activity of Osage men.

Much as he feminizes Osage men by seeing women in general and Indian men in particular as having nothing to do, he infantilizes Osage men by seeing them as playing rather than doing. But the novel's epitome of Osage play in relation to masculinity comes in a passage not about men so much as about boys: the magnificent early scene about Osage boys at a swimming hole. In a perfect homosocial imaginary, the boys play water tag and watch a father introduce his son to the water, while the narration pays tender attention to the father taking off his breech clout and later putting it slowly back on, to the boy's "copper-colored bottom" emerging from the water, and to the father's "body and his long hair" (35). Then a group of white boys barges in and punctures Chal's idyll:

> The little Indian boys went on playing but Chal felt very annoyed with the intrusion, and he told little Running Elk and Sun-on-His-Wing[s] that he was going because the white boys stared so much and made so much noise. As they undressed they began to shout at each other, saying "Huh" when they didn't hear what was said. The little Indian boys believed that they said "Huh" so much because they were all talking at the same time; talking like blackbirds bathing in a mud puddle after a rain.
>
> The Indian boys pretended not to see them, but were so fascinated by some of the things they heard that they lost interest in their game. One of the little boys on the bank used words like a freighter, and Chal thought he used them because he wanted to show the others how big he was. As they undressed and revealed their white, glistening bodies . . . Chal wondered what [their fascinating words] meant, and as he watched them come up to the bank one at a time and dive in, or push each other in and roar with laughter, he had a feeling that their white bodies were indecent in some inscrutable way. (36)

Chal objects to the noisy white boys staring at his own nakedness and activity, as if their stares introduce a subject-object relation into the imaginary stasis of his pleasure with Indian boys, a pleasure he has imagined as comfortably complete without difference or absence. When the white boys crash the Indian boys' party they seem to introduce difference, but we might suppose that difference is not so new as it seems, and that the white boys only add to it and make it undeniable. After all, the Indian boys' game of tag already acts out a shadow drama of likeness and difference as they hide from the boy who is "it," trying to blend their nakedness into the watery dark to escape becoming the next "it." And the narration, like a shadow of Chal's gaze, has already stared at the Indian father's nakedness. Chal may resent the white boys' staring, but in his more discreet way, he stares back, because they fascinate him. Still, his gaze at their "glistening bodies" also frightens him. It feels indecent, so that he expels his sense of contamination by projecting the indecency onto the white boys' bodies. His heightened alertness seizes on one boy's desire to seem different and bigger and on the insecurity that such a desire enacts, and then in effect finds itself unwittingly measuring his own position in relation to the white boys' glistening whiteness and their suddenly different and hence more visible masculinity.

The Indian boys decide to leave, and then suddenly they "see Sun-on-His-Wings' pinto stallion break loose and consummate an amorous flirtation . . . with a little sorrel mare that one of the white boys had ridden":

> The little white boys swam to the bank and crawled out shouting, "Oh-oh!" and "Hot doggie," and looking at each other with expressions burdened with secretiveness as they gathered around. Several of them looked around at the undergrowth as though expecting someone to come and catch them in some crime. Two of them shouted and hugged each other and danced in circles.
>
> . . . Chal was mystified. He couldn't understand what made those white boys act that way. He believed that only crazy people acted that way, but he was sure they weren't crazy. The impression of that day was deep and he remembered the incident the rest of his life; that impression of the white man making so much over the very unimportant matter of the possibility of another horse coming into the world. (37)

The white boys' hysteria at equine sex yet further interrupts Chal's imaginary sense of completeness without difference or absence. Here is difference indeed, needing the protection of "secretiveness," as if the horses' act were a crime and as if the white boys' themselves, finding their own silenced desires and curiosities acted out by the horses, cannot help feeling that they themselves are the criminals. Two of the boys react in the opposite direction. Instead of harboring their desire, they celebrate it, but their showy expulsion from secrecy seems no less defensive than secrecy itself. The horses figure sex between men and women and between whites and Indians, both because an Indian owns one horse and a white owns the other, and because the Indian pinto couples with the white sorrel. And in the context of the white and Indian boys' half-repressed stares at each others' glistening bodies, and the two white boys' eager desire to deny their repression by nakedly hugging and dancing, the horses also figure breaking the taboo against sexuality between men. Immediately after this moment the Indian boys try to reconstruct their homosocial imaginary community by working together to play tricks on Indian girls and an old Indian woman, as if to defend against the white boys' interruption of their swimming-hole, masculine idyll and, more subtly, to reconstitute their homosociality as a bulwark against the earlier scene's unconscious intimations of homosexuality.

Beginning with this moment between horses, Chal repeatedly puzzles over how white people worry so much about what he calls "mating." Whites treat it as "strange or unusual," whereas he takes it as "natural" (139, 229). Yet Chal's relation to sexuality isn't simply natural and unanxious, as he supposes. He usually isn't interested in sexuality, although he sometimes goes through the motions of obligatory heterosexuality. One reviewer remarked cynically that *Sundown* doesn't have "enough sex" to become a best-seller (Barrus). Chal's lack of interest in sex worries him, and over this and other matters he often wonders if he is "out of step" (89, 90, 98, 100, 101, 138, 208) or "queer" (89, 90, 92, 104, 107, 148, 172).

I am not arguing anything so straightforward as that Chal is an unconscious homosexual or that the word *queer*, which Mathews uses frequently in a variety of contexts, snaps Chal neatly into 1930s or later sexual usages of that term. In today's lingo the term *queer* can carry a resistance to the confining binary of homosexual versus heterosexual, and I am arguing that Chal fits into a similar pattern of resistance to dominant sexual categories. *Sundown* is no story of boy meets girl. It ends with Chal in his early thirties (he's a university freshman in about 1916–17, and the novel ends during the depression), and he never shows any interest or disinterest in marriage, not even other people's marriages, or any interest or disinterest in having children. He dates a bit, goes to dances, and hangs out, but only at other people's behest. Late in the novel, women chase him, but he chases no one. He daydreams of Blo Daubeney, but only from an abstracting distance; he never pursues her. Blo (148) and Chick, his curiously named fraternity brother, set up dates for him because he is "the only safe one around the house" (155), someone they trust not to pursue his date. Meanwhile, Chal "admired Chick's physique, but he wouldn't admit the fact to himself" (114). Chal goes along when sought out by Lou Kerry, with her masculine first name and androgynous last name, but he quickly grows bored with her. If he feels attracted to anyone in the novel, it is the sexually ambiguous geology instructor, "Goosie" (191) Granville, who twice invites Chal home to his "digs" (186, 190). "Because of Mr. Granville's reticence and his queer actions, Chal had been drawn to him.

They said at the University that he was queer because he took long walks by himself, wouldn't accept dinner invitations, and lived by himself. . . . Students laughed at him. . . . He wore short pants like the old knicker-bockers the boys used to wear, and gay stockings, and his shoes were thick-soled things. Students thought he was crazy because he rode a bicycle to classes" (172). Like Chal, Granville is "out of step." He keeps to himself, vaguely asexually and asocially, stays silent when others would chatter, and seems to reserve his passion for flora, fauna, and geology, suggestively worrying, as he sits on the ground with Chal, over whether to call the Osage hills "virginal" or "untouched" (175). Such patterns can make either of them look "crazy," and we have already observed Chal worrying that he seems crazy (on 103, 133, and 167; similar passages appear at 138, 157, 168, and 220), because he doesn't fit in.

He especially feels the pressure of not fitting in at school, where the others taunt him on racial and gendered grounds. At the agency school the older boys tease him, calling him a girl and then a little white girl, until finally one boy steps up and pushes him, leaving Chal humiliated (28–29). When he changes to a private school, the white boys make fun of him for being Indian, and again the most obnoxious boy pushes him, which Chal "knew . . . was the greatest insult" (54).[14] At the university, his fraternity institutionalizes the ritual, formally paddling the freshmen, which horrifies Running Elk and Sun-on-His-Wings, as well as Chal, who "remembered his first day at the Indian boarding school" (108). The point is not that anyone treats Chal differently about gender, for the others might go through similar initiations. Rather, the point is that these moments speak to his uncertainty about masculinity and masculine touch, yet they suppress questions about gender by displacing them with more admissible questions about race.

Chal seeks out masculine companionship, but he runs away from it as well. He joins the football team, then quits it. Then he returns to practice with the football team and run with the track team. He also makes up to his fraternity brothers for quitting football by joining the "Iron Men," who "affected . . . the raiment of dock wallopers or stevedores." They gather at football games "with hands on each others' shoulders," chanting "We're hard, we're mean" (144). Sports offer the possibility of intense physical contact between men, which attracts and frightens Chal. At football practice he finds himself fascinated by the quarterback's body, yet reacting grotesquely against his fascination: "He kept looking at the back of Carson's freckled neck. . . . Chal wondered what would happen if he were to cut it with a sharp knife; he wondered if there would be blood coming out of the wound" (109–10). With the Iron Men he finds himself watching the "thin-bony-shouldered fellow" (144) in front of him. "Sometimes when he looked at that thin neck closely, he had a desire to put his hand up and choke this fellow. An overwhelming impulse, which he hurriedly put out of his mind. . . . One time he almost sweated, the desire was so intense, and he immediately looked away so that he wouldn't be tempted. He had nothing but the friendliest feeling toward this fellow" (145).

Later, Mathews fills out a cultural context for Chal's interest in choking and throat-cutting. Chal begins to dance and wonders "why that emotion which had begun to choke him did not come out through his throat. He was an Indian now and he believed that the exit of all spirit and emotion was the throat, just as the soul came out through the throat after death" (297; cf. 257). Chal gives the cultural dimension a personal pattern. Repeatedly, he feels an attraction to another man, an attraction not simply erotic or unerotic, and then reacts against his attraction. The urge to violence suggests an urge to punish himself for forbidden desire, a punishment that Chal displaces onto the objects of his desire, as if those objects were to blame for the desires that he resists, and as if the fictional Chal were to blame for or could represent desires that Mathews resists or wants to criticize. Chal looks at Metz, his kindly flight instructor, with a gaze that recalls his fascination with the quarterback and the spindly Iron Man: "He remembered for years the back of Metz's head and his thin neck" (197). Then, as if the novel needs to punish Chal yet again, a new instructor immediately appears, objectifying Chal's revulsion: "he shouted . . . 'I said Metz was killed yesterday—some student of this stage froze the controls on 'im.' He . . . looked at Chal as though he would like to choke him" (198). Similarly, when Chal goes off to meet Lou Kerry for his first sexual encounter, he sees a couple kissing in the dark, blocking his path to Lou, and the sudden mix of surplus and suspended sexuality overwhelms him: "As Chal watched, he was suddenly suffused with . . . a wild anger which urged him to run up to this man and pull him away, and choke him if he resisted" (226–27).

Through all these instances, Chal's pattern of attraction and defensive revulsion ties together a cluster of homophobic anxieties that reinforce and overdetermine each other: anxieties about affection for men or about masculine company and about heterosexuals' fear of being associated with gays or queerness or being gay or queer, together with anxieties about the cultural pressures to conflate the feminine with the colonized and to cast doubt on colonized, native masculinity.

Native American cultural criticism has not usually attended to gender as much as I am trying to in this book, nor has it much taken up discussions about gender and colonialism or shaped such discussions through Native American concerns. In part, I am trying to encourage students of

Native American culture to join and to redirect these discussions. As the epigraph to this chapter signals, I would like to discuss the relation between gender—in particular the casting of doubt on masculinity—and what we misleadingly call unemployment, a term that suggests that people without paid work do nothing at all. Across the population, ideologies of unemployment were magnified during the depression, and for many Indian peoples, over decades or centuries, similar ideologies of unemployment grew in influence as Indians' movement into the large-scale market economy accelerated. The depression thus offered a special possibility for concerns about unemployment in the broader culture to converge with such concerns in Indian communities, at the least through the unwitting dialogue of mere analogy. Such concerns include the desire to spread the so-called work ethic, which labor historians like Roediger associate with the growth of white workingmen's self-conscious sense of whiteness, and the resistance to such an ideology. During the depression, masses of non-Indian Americans lost the means to value themselves that they once found in wage work, and through the gendered biases of ideology and the economy that loss was seen to fall more heavily on men than on women. Most men—some historians seem to imply especially most white men—had seen work as a defining activity, as their answer to questions about what they "do." But when they lost that work, many men and those who knew them had to see or at least sense the work and value in other activities, including typically women's activities that had not been granted the honoring label of work or the practical compensation of wages. Of course, ideological reactions and shifts never proceed that simply; I am addressing only one of a multitude of reactions, regressive as well as progressive. But suddenly huge numbers of non-Indian men who based their value on "jobs," on market-based labor for wages, had no jobs or had lower-paying jobs, and in that limited way they gathered a likeness to a large proportion of Indian men, however unwitting the likeness and however diverse its sources and cultural settings.

Not much came from this opportunity for alliance, just as relatively little came from emerging depression alliances between black labor and white labor. These alliances foundered partly because demagogues stirred up racial divisions between whites and blacks who shared economic interests, and perhaps because the depression threw more white workers into competition with black, brown, and Indian workers for the same low-paying jobs (Knack and Littlefield, 18). But I am arguing here that in their novels, much-traveled intellectuals like McNickle and Mathews saw the connection between European or Euro-American and Indian ideologies of work and the opportunity that the depression provided to think critically about that connection. To be sure, to say that they thought about it critically is to offer a modest claim. They were not ready to formulate a positive theory of an Indian work ethic, along the lines of those put forward about African Americans by Du Bois and Genovese and undoubtedly by a great many African Americans in popular culture, as well as by a great many ordinary Native Americans. The working-class Indian poet Chrystos, for example, in a poem called "Why Indian Unemployment is *So* High," writes that Indians are good at lots of things, and she risks stereotype— sometimes with tongue in cheek—to name a number of particulars, such as honesty, dancing, singing, cooking "on nothing," liking to live with friends and relatives, but "The main things Indians / are good at," she adds, "have absolutely no market value" (89–91). The enormous range of Indian cultures and the limits to any sense of pan-Indianism probably make it even harder to ground broad claims about Indian workers than it is to ground such claims about African American workers—and it is already hard to make such claims stick for African Americans, although Genovese attends diligently to variations across region and across different kinds of work. McNickle and Mathews were still swept up into the business work ethic that they sought alternatives for, and that kept them from formulating or even just describing a fully fledged alternative. But they got so far as to imply a critique of that work ethic and a need for an alternative, one that attended both to continually changing Indian traditions and to the ongoing mutual influence between those traditions and the changing dominant economy.

To be sure, the economic setting differed greatly between the Flatheads and Osages. Even before the Osage oil boom, the Osages fared better economically than most other Indian peoples. They negotiated a sizable quarterly payment when they were forced to give up their first reservation in Kansas, and they set up lucrative grazing leases for their lands in Oklahoma. In the 1880s, one federal agent went so far as to call them the "richest people in the world" (Garrick Bailey, "John Joseph Mathews," 207, and *Changes,* 92). Still, despite Osage wealth, Osage attitudes toward work share a pattern familiar across many reservations. Indian people had not organized their economic life in terms of jobs until their movement into the white-dominated economy led them increasingly into that frame of mind, but even then there were few jobs for Indians, fewer high-paying or year-round jobs, routinely lower pay than whites received for the same work (Knack and Littlefield, 29), poor preparation for many jobs, an unreceptive climate (and often outright hostility) among non-Indian employers, and poor preparation for Indians to make themselves their own employers on a profitable scale: in short, for much of Indian America, a state of permanent depression.[15] Until the national depression, the Osages' wealth protected them from local depression, but otherwise it solved none of these problems and did not integrate the Osage people into a national work ethic. Indeed, with their large incomes, Osages had no economic need to work, frustrating federal agents committed to assimilating them into the dominant work ethic (Bailey, *Changes*, 79–83; Terry P. Wilson, *Underground Reservation*, e.g., 34; Lucy B. Gayler). In 1885, Laban J. Miles, the agent who left Mathews his papers—leading Mathews to write *Wah'Kon-Tah* about Miles—wrote condescendingly about Osage men: "The full bloods . . . are indolent in their habits, the men lounging about their lodges or houses most of the time, allowing the women to do most of the work." They "look upon work as degrading, and to plow and hoe only fit occupations for poor white men who have to work for a living, and they are careful to impress this idea on the minds of their children." He didn't have much kinder words for mixed-bloods, granting that they "are all *to some extent* engaged in farming and stock-raising" (89, emphasis added). One of his successors reported in 1902: "The full-blood Indians, as heretofore, have the past year been engaged principally in looking after their farming operations, visiting back and forth among their relatives and friends, lolling around camp, hunting lost ponies, and deporting themselves much as they have for the last forty years, and as they probably will for the next forty years" (O. A. Mitscher, 293). Federal agents are far from the most reliable source, but they can help represent how Osage attitudes looked when viewed through the dominant culture's expectations, which in turn increasingly influenced Osage attitudes, as they influence Chal's. Instead of provoking new Osage ideas about work, therefore, the oil wealth filtered and reduced the pressure to change attitudes. By the time the national depression dropped the oil boom into a bust (euphemistically described in *Sundown*, 303–5), wealth had not broadly changed the Osages' economics or culture of work (Wilson, *Underground Reservation*, especially chapter 7).

Nationally in the 1930s, bad conditions on reservations got even worse, propelled by the general collapse of the economy, by the return of unemployed urban Indians, and by plagues of grasshoppers and drought (Calvin W. Gower, 5; Knack and Littlefield, 18). Even before the stock market crashed, Osage oil income began to sink ominously. In an ironic voice, the *New York Times* reported in 1928 that "comparative poverty has come to the Osage Indians, for the last quarterly distribution of oil royalties gave each member of the tribe only $1,400" ("Oil Royalties for Osages Are Beginning to Decline"), still a substantial income. Just before the crash, the *Times* noted with a smirk, "The Osages, once the wealthiest of all Indian tribes, may be forced to abandon their idleness born of luxury. . . . If the money flow stops, it will mean that many Osages must work—a thing most of them never have done" ("Osage Indians Face Loss of Oil Wealth"). For most Osages in the 1930s, oil income no longer brought enough money to live on (as the *Times* also noted in 1931 ["Going Back to the Soil"; "Some Osages Broke"]). Those not on or not descended from those on the 1906 tribal roll did not even share in the dwindling oil income (Wilson, *Underground Reservation*, 173–74; "Proceedings," 18 December 1935, 8). A 1936 survey found no employed full-bloods, despite a drop in tribal oil income from $29,600,000 in 1925 to $1,700,000 in 1931,[16] or, in figures Mathews cites in *The Osages* (775), from $13,000 of royalties per capita in 1925 to $712 in 1932. (Both figures represent about a 95 percent reduction in oil income.) Even as the absorbing national economy pressed Indians more toward Euro-American gender patterns,[17] with men asked to take up the role of family breadwinner, hard times cut back Indian men's already small chances to play that role.

Mathews was elected to the Osage Council in 1934, the year of *Sundown*'s publication, and he led several Osage delegations to Washington to argue that even the once wealthy Osages suffered from the depression as much as their white neighbors (Wilson, "John Joseph Mathews," 160; Mathews, *Talking to the Moon*, 212–13). The next year at a council meeting he addressed the onset of federal relief for young Osage men through the Indian Emergency Conservation Work program (the IECW, later called the Civilian Conservation Corps [CCC]—Indian Division): "It occurs to me that it is an emergency strictly, absolutely, to give these young men work now. In that type of work [emergency conservation work] I don't know that they have any particular future. . . . I don't see what it would fit them for unless it would be for manual labor and the Indian is not a good manual laborer. [But t]his kind of work he likes. I talked with quite a few of them. They rather like this. It is not like being in foundries and factories and laying bricks and that sort of thing" ("Proceedings," 18 December 1935, 10). In Mathews's eyes, at least, Osage men like those he observed through Chal or described rather glibly at the council meeting did not necessarily value job-work, and the work wasn't available ("No one would give a job to an Indian").[18] As his comments indicate, even the IECW was hardly more than a thumb in the dyke. The wages were set with young, single men in mind; they "were not sufficient for the Indians to develop working capital or become self-supporting, and day laborers do not usually acquire skills that can be sold subsequently for high wages" (Cardell K. Jacobson, 165–66). But the IECW introduced Osage men—not women—to a wage-work economy that they and many other Indians had

Fig. 1. "Indians at Work on Soil-Saving Dam, Osage Agency," 1935, from *Indians at Work,* the Indian Emergency Conservation Work (IECW) magazine. Subjects and photographer not identified.

Fig. 2. Winter humor: cartoon by Bill Standin' (presumably a pseudonym) from *Indians at Work,* 1936, showing that the IECW could poke fun at itself.

lived apart from, and across the country it provided many Indian men their first wage labor (Parman; Gower; Knack and Littlefield, 18–19).

My point is not to praise or fault the IECW but to use its history as an index of the crisis it addressed: Indian men's (and here in particular, Osage men's) relative separation from the larger economy of men's wage labor. In line with Mathews's remarks, other and differently positioned observers also saw the IECW as addressing a crisis in Osage men's unemployment and attitudes to employment. Charles L. Ellis, superintendent of the Osage Agency, praised the IECW's effect on Osage men in terms that drip with scorn for what he saw as Osage attitudes toward work before the onset of federal assistance. "When IECW was started the Osage Indians who were employed . . . were soft and flabby, with too much flesh and almost no muscle. The work caused them to develop physically—weight in general has been reduced, some few as much as 40 lbs." As Terry P. Wilson recounts, Ellis "also praised the 'moral effect' of the work, which had convinced some Osages that they could compete successfully with whites and learn 'the value of a dollar earned.' Many Osages, Ellis reported, now believed working to be 'much more pleasant . . . than to be *doing nothing*'" (Wilson, 163, emphasis added). As superintendent, Ellis can hardly provide the most reliable testimony. But his view matches Mathews's remarks at the council meeting, as well as a short piece penned in 1935 for the IECW magazine, *Indians at Work*, by Sylvester Tinker, an Osage IECW sub-foreman who, beginning in 1970, would be repeatedly elected principal chief (Wilson, 202):

> Many of our Osage boys had never had any experience and never were accustomed to work. . . . The shovels felt clumsy to us and our hands were soft. . . . However, not a man quit the job. . . . The IECW . . . has not only meant the conservation of the soil, but in a large measure has been the conservation of the Osage boys who have been connected with the IECW. The men have all developed a sense of responsibility and know what constitutes a good day's work. Their morale is high, and everyone of them are able to take their place in any job and make their way if given an opportunity.

In the national ideology that Tinker's rhetoric makes concrete, without work they are boys, but with work they are men. Without white help, therefore, Indian males were in some ways seen as boys with nothing to do, at least until the white-led government socialized them into the habits of doing that its economy required but had given them little chance to absorb.

When the economy crashed, the depression so familiar to many Indians suddenly became, in effect, an equal opportunity unemployer. With jobs scarce across the social spectrum, the hindsight offered by later critiques of gender relations might make us imagine that cultural critics and ordinary people caught in the depression looked for and perhaps even theorized ways to anchor masculinity outside of market-valued public employment. No doubt many people took up that kind of cultural pondering, even if not on a massive scale, and if we searched through public commentary and the archives of daily life, we could probably find indirect, perhaps unwitting or half-witting evidence of such thinking, and perhaps direct statements as well. Here I find such evidence in fiction.

In the 1930s, perhaps more than ever, American fiction writers explicitly committed their writing to cultural example and criticism. Although McNickle and Mathews left no sign of connection to the movement for proletarian fiction, both were avidly political writers on the liberal-to-radical left. McNickle finished *The Surrounded* while working for the Federal Writers Project and then joined John Collier's Office of Indian Affairs (OIA, later known as the Bureau of Indian Affairs or BIA) in the Roosevelt administration, and Mathews supported the New Deal and Collier's Indian Reorganization Act[19] while also criticizing local capitalist intrusions (Wilson, *Underground Reservation,* 155) and, in *Sundown* and *Talking to the Moon,* critiquing capitalism more broadly.[20] In *The Surrounded* and *Sundown,* McNickle and Mathews critique dominant notions of work in Indian and white culture and discourse. In some sense, white-associated assumptions make easier targets, because they deny that Indians have any discourse of work beyond what gets misread as lazy disinterest, and because white liberalism and the thirties' interest in socialist writing made Euro-American economic assumptions familiar targets for criticism.

Both these novels, however, sniff out something subtler than the familiar attacks on rapacious capitalism. By showing the resistance to job-work as part of an active culture rather than merely a passive nay-saying, they pit the capitalist conflation of work, masculinity, and market value against an equally formed if still hardly visible alternative—hardly visible, at least, to outsiders or even to would-be outsiders like Archilde and Chal. Rather than arguing that one culture must assimilate the other for its own good or that both can happily coexist, these novels lament that the two systems cannot coexist. Their pessimistic lament draws dangerously on the myth of the vanishing Indian that later Indian novelists sometimes make fun of (e.g., Louise Erdrich in *Love Medicine,* Thomas King in *Green Grass, Running Water*). What was needed was not some sense that two separate systems would duel to the death until the last Indian died at the end of the movie, but rather a sense that each system was reshaping the other even as each continued to shape itself, and that Indian people can envision their cultures as agents of change, rather than as static emblems of a noble past now doomed to extinction. McNickle and Mathews shaped their views in the twenties and thirties, before the heyday of the African American civil rights movement made it easier to think programmatically about minority cultures in dialogue and exchange with majority cultures. But the political rethinking in McNickle and Mathews's generation, combined with the civil rights movement and the centuries-long legacy of local, tribal, and reservation-based resistance, helped make possible the last several decades' resurgence in Native American politics and literature. In the thirties, however, McNickle and Mathews could hardly envision the later activism, though they helped make it possible.

In *Sundown,* Indians, and especially restless young Indian men, don't know what to do—at least so far as Chal can see, which isn't very far. In Chal's imagination, the only thing they can do is work (as he understands work—getting a job), but work is a non-option, not only because, as we have seen, whites don't want to hire Indians, but also because no one wants to reimagine the work that Indians do—least of all women's work— into the form of jobs. Until the depression, Osages have oil wealth, but no means to institutionalize their wealth under their own long-term control. "There were no factories, no mills, no industry except the cattle business which had flourished for years. There weren't even any oil refineries" (77; see also 240). As a social worker noted in 1936, "there is little occupational possibility for the unskilled laborer in Osage County" (Ruth Boutwell, 79). Yet even so, and even if Chal cannot see it, Indians have things to do. The novel focuses on town life, mostly evading the villages but still showing just enough to imply village ceremonial life. Chal worries that Sun-on-His-Wings and his friends just sit in the village and talk, without setting out to fulfill anything that Chal recognizes as ambition, but he also sees Sun-on-His-Wings ride out from the village with a group of men to defy a storm with "ancient ritual" (81), and Sun-on-His-Wings takes Chal to the peyote ceremony. These moments show considerable "doing" in village life that doesn't register as doing for Chal, just as, apart from one passing reference to Sun-on-His-Wings' wife (266), neither Chal nor the narrative ever notices her or even their marriage. To Chal, such things as village life, ceremony, or a love life don't signify progress, ambition, moving onward. Even the novel itself, following the story of Chal's life, hardly moves onward and never concludes, in that it keeps repeating the same pleasures and worries, and then simply stops.

In that way, *Sundown* implies a broader critique of the concept of doing and progress that Chal identifies with white people and that he yearns for but cannot commit himself to. Later, in *Talking to the Moon,* Mathews expands his critique of work routines and economic progress, echoing Thoreau's *Walden* as he describes his life alone in a one-room home through the year's cycle of seasons.[21] While the white, practical activity that Chal envies so much in *Sundown* eventually comes apart in the depression, it has always already disintegrated from within. For throughout the novel, Mathews paints such activity as so frenetic that its vaunted practicality starts to seem like a defensive façade, covering up white people's— especially white men's—desperate need to prove themselves, as if all their confidence finally amounts to no more comfort with their own mode of doing than Chal can muster with his.

Unlike Sun-on-His-Wings, Chal can never sustain a comfortable sense of his own doing. He wastes away his life in a lost generation dissipation that recalls Hemingway's *The Sun Also Rises* (1926), despite the two novels' curiously inverted titles.[22] When Chal thinks, as we have seen, that "he was the only person not doing something except the mixedbloods and the fullbloods" (162), he erases both the actual doing of mixed-bloods and full-bloods and his own presence as a mixed-blood, so that not to do finally becomes, in Chal's imagination, not to be.

Not doing thus leaves Chal vulnerable to others whose doing usurps his potential to do. At the end, having failed to live up to his romantic masculine imaginary with his Osage friends, university acquaintances, and Army acquaintances, Chal also fails to live up to his father's vision of a masculine imaginary. He cannot take the pride that his father seeks in oratory or citizenship and cannot live up to the name that his father gave him, Challenge ("'He shall be a challenge to the disinheritors of his people'" [4]), until finally he degenerates into the oedipal horror of a two-week drunk with bank robbers (308), implicitly (though Mathews never says so) the same robbers who killed his father (237, 246). He is too drunk even to remember whether he joined in the robberies. Running Elk's father cannot stop thinking about Running Elk's murderers (270), but Chal never thinks about his father's murder or murderers. At one point, Mathews calls attention to Chal's culpability when, soddenly drunk, Chal hears jays in a tree. "He felt that they were accusing him of something and he became unreasonably angry," hurling his empty bottle at the jays until they fly off, "each screaming 'murder!'" (302). At this point, the novel's concern and Chal's guilt focus not only on his father's death but more broadly on his failure to stand up for his own and his people's life, his failure to follow through and become "a challenge to the disinheritors of his people."

Chal's repeated failure to follow through governs his impulsive claim, at the end of the novel, that he will go to Harvard Law School, because, fresh from his escapade with bank robbers, Chal hardly seems like a plausible candidate for Harvard or any other law school. He hasn't finished a bachelor's degree, and his life has collapsed into drunken aimlessness. To most critics, Chal's sudden plan seems hopeless, a grim confirmation that he has lost contact with practicality, and a grim ending to the novel. Class-room experience teaching the novel, however, suggests that many readers want to take Chal's plans at face value and even read those plans as a sign of optimism at the novel's conclusion. In a similar vein, Louis Owens strains to read the novel's closing nature imagery as a sign of hope (*Other Destinies*, 59–60).[23] I believe, nevertheless, that such optimistic readings tell more about what we typically look for from endings and how attitudes toward Native American possibility have changed since Mathews wrote this novel, which, after all, is un-optimistically called *Sundown*. Mathews wrote within and in dialogue with Osage traditions, but he wrote apart from any established tradition of or dialogue with Indian writers. There is no evidence that he knew of the few Indian-written novels before *Sun-down*, Yellow Bird's (John Rollin Ridge's) *The Life and Adventures of Joaquín Murieta, The Celebrated California Bandit* (1854), S. Alice Callahan's recently rediscovered *Wynema: A Child of the Forest* (1891), Simon Pokagon's *O-gî-mäw-kwî Mit-i-gwä-kî (Queen of the Woods)* (1899 but probably not written en-tirely by Pokagon), or Hum-ishu-ma's (Mourning Dove's) *Cogewea, The Half-Blood* (revised by Lucullus Virgil McWhorter and published in 1927). He may have known of John Milton Oskison's Oklahoma novels, *Wild Harvest: A Novel of Transition Days in Oklahoma* (1925) and *Black Jack Davy* (1926), but they don't have much to do with Indian people. Working therefore more or less alone, Mathews brought a brooding pessimism to his novel that can seem out of place in our own time of assertive identities (which may themselves oversimplify no less than Mathews's grim sense of no place to go and nothing to do).

Hence *Sundown* has much to say about Chal's failure to follow through and about his restless generation's failure or unwillingness to follow through on what its cultures expect; and in another sense *Sundown* has much to say about its own failure, unwillingness, or insight in not follow-ing through on its own plot. The novel is riddled with plot lines that it picks up and silently drops. At the beginning Chal has sisters (6–7), but we never hear of them again. The beginning also hints that John will be-come an alcoholic, but he doesn't. Chal seems destined for football fame, but he quits the team. He seems destined to fight in World War I, but the Army never sends him overseas. Red Feather (6–7), Little Flower (254–55), and Jean (252–61) get introduced as if they will turn into sub-stantial figures, but they never reappear. Blo Daubeney plays a large role for a while, making readers expect more, and then the novel drops her. When Marie Fobus appears for a lengthy episode (247–61), it sounds as if she were a major character earlier on, but she has shown up before for only one forgettable sentence (161). The later chapters are rife with hints that Chal will kill or maim himself and perhaps others in an alcoholic car crash, but he never does. Twice he thinks ecstatically about suicide (218, 264), but the novel never develops that urge, unless we see his inability to do anything as no less depressive than suicide. The peyote ceremony prepares Chal for profound, peaceful transformation, and then the novel forgets about it in the leap from one chapter to the next.[24] Indeed, the peyote chapter ends suspensefully as Chal falls asleep to a hint that he is about to kill or hurt himself smoking in bed, but the next chapter ignores the hint and takes up other events (278–79). Chal never becomes the great leader of cultural pride and recovery that his name and dramatic birth promise. Of course, we can take broken plot strands as art. For example, we can chalk up Chal's failure to live up to his name as irony. But again and again, it seems as if Mathews changed his mind or cooperated with an editor's suggestion, cutting or adding without troubling to make the rest of the novel fit. The culminating dissonance comes when the novel stops abruptly without concluding.

Whether deliberate, careless, aesthetically fulfilling, or aesthetically inept, all this connects to everything I am arguing about *Sundown*. Late in the novel, by the time we get to a chapter that begins "Chal didn't know what to do with himself" (262), we may wonder whether the novel knows what to do with itself or Mathews knows what to do with the novel. That he gives so many indications he doesn't know what to do and persists in not knowing ends up suggesting not so much aesthetic carelessness—though we're not in the realm of objective evidence that can rule carelessness out of the picture—as it suggests an aesthetic alternative to the well-wrought urn, the aesthetically organic whole, the teleogically driven unit of beginning, middle, and culminating end. If Mathews couldn't decide how to end the novel, or didn't care, or didn't even notice the feints and dropped plot lines, that's all to the point. The over-practical, snap-tightly organized, progressive, teleological culture that so attracts and appalls Chal requires a well-wrought novel that builds up through climax and culminates in closure, and Mathews refuses that mode, like many of his modernist contemporaries, and like Thomas King, though unlike his contemporary McNickle. The *New York Times* reviewer, under an astonished headline declaring "An Educated Indian," concluded that although Mathews, "himself part Osage . . . writes very ably, the book has a decidedly inarticulate quality, as if the problem he is trying to state had been only half comprehended and is hence not susceptible of clear statement. Perhaps this very quality, which mars the book as a novel, makes it an even more effective social study" (20). To this reviewer, being part Osage, half comprehended, and inarticulate seems all of a piece with being less literary and more social. Another reviewer, by contrast, concerned less with plot and more with mind and expression, concludes that Mathews "has gone deeper into Indian consciousness and set down his findings more tellingly than any

other writer of fiction known to me. Moreover, he is an artist with words"
(Kenneth C. Kaufman). It hardly matters that Mathews later described
the novel as an uninspired chore he didn't care much about and never
reread, or that a photograph of him at home defies that story by revealing
the dust jacket framed and prominently displayed on the wall behind
him.[25] I am not making an argument about intention or purpose so much
as an argument about the shape of Mathews's aesthetic, and reading that
shape as a formalist allegory of the cultural debate that ensnares Chal.

The point is not that white guys are bad and the novel refuses their aesthetic imaginary in favor of an alternative, Osage, aesthetic imaginary.
There is much that may press us to put it that way, but I am trying to argue
something harder to express in our paltry language of aesthetics and of
the relation between form and content. Such oversimplifying, binarizing
expressions as "the relation between form and content" are themselves
part of the obstacle. The novel depends heavily on Chal's focalization, but
Chal never convincingly grasps what an Osage imaginary might be. As we
have seen, his ideas of it center on inactivity, feminized passivity, an indifference to job-work and the market economy, and on dream, song, and
dance, and he incorporates these ideas into his own behavior, even as he
tries hard to resist and resent them. Some of his interests, especially
dream, song, and dance, surely play a large role in other Osages' imaginary and not just in Chal's, but the novel never entirely adopts Chal's binary of white masculine work versus feminized Indian passivity. For all
around the borders of Chal's observation *Sundown* allows us to sense that
other Indians have plenty to do, sometimes satisfying things and sometimes tragic things, but that Chal sees their plenty to do as nothing to do
while they, nevertheless, continue their doing under the enormous, assimilating pressure to interpret it through the same skepticism and binarizing that so plague Chal. The barely glimpsed ability of other Indians in
the novel to continue on other paths, in the university fraternities (not all
the Indians quit school like Chal and his friends), in traditional and not-
so-traditional ceremonies in the village and at John's funeral, in Chal's
mother's understated persistence, or in Mathews's own writing of the
novel, suggests many models of Osage and Indian ideals and activities beyond those that Chal has room for in his imaginary. Like the vision of so
many of his cohorts, Chal's vision is much narrower than the novel's. Absorbed in internalized self-hatred and self-doubt, Chal, when he looks at
Indians, sees the restless young men with nothing to do who would continue to haunt the Indian imaginary and play so large a role in Indian
writing after Mathews's novel.

CHAPTER 3

Who Shot the Sheriff: Storytelling, Indian

Identity, and the Marketplace of Masculinity in

D'Arcy McNickle's *The Surrounded*

Critics of D'Arcy McNickle's acclaimed novel *The Surrounded* (1936) have focused on its pondering of Indian identity and its rooting of that identity in oral storytelling. McNickle, who would later take over forty years to write *Wind from an Enemy Sky* (1978), spent nine years writing and rewriting *The Surrounded*. He finally chose its storytelling scenes, John Purdy implies, as a way to Indianize the modern novel, a suggestion that picks up the concerns of the novel and the culture it represents with cultural and racial identity and neatly focuses how McNickle translates those concerns into narrative structure. In a sense, even on that broadly cultural scale, McNickle's innovation worked—eventually. For many of the patterns laid down by *The Surrounded* and its immediate predecessor, Mathews's *Sundown,* reappear over three decades later in such landmark novels of the American Indian renaissance as Momaday's *House Made of Dawn* and Silko's *Ceremony,* especially the angst-filled, mixed-blood young man (often—though not in *The Surrounded*—a war veteran) returning to the reservation and struggling to find his place among its traditions and the pressures to acculturate.[1]

Even in the short history of Indian novels, *The Surrounded*'s interest in storytelling was not new. It resembles Mourning Dove's *Cogewea, The Half-Blood* (drafted by 1914, revised by Lucullus Virgil McWhorter and published in 1927), a western romance probably unknown to McNickle though set on the same Montana reservation as *The Surrounded*.[2] Yet, although many critics have fixed on the role of oral storytelling as a defining interest of Indian written literature in general (see chapter 4) and of *Cogewea* and *The Surrounded* in particular, not only Indians tell oral stories. Even *The Surrounded* juxtaposes scenes of white storytelling to scenes of In-

51

dian storytelling. And the Indian oral stories in *The Surrounded* usually tell about contact with whites—an unsurprising choice but hardly an adequate model for the future of Indian novels. Indeed, as Mourning Dove and McNickle turned to oral stories to pin down the Indianness of their novels, other American novelists were also turning to oral stories to pin down—or unleash—into written fiction the roots of other American identities, from Mark Twain, George Washington Cable, and Charles Chesnutt to many of Mourning Dove and McNickle's more immediate contemporaries, such as William Faulkner, Zora Neale Hurston, and Henry Roth. Anthologists of the 1930s, just after the heyday of the Harlem Renaissance, took a similar turn, connecting non-Anglo ethnicity to storytelling and the "folk," while anthropology—then at the academic center of what has since been reinvented as American Indian or Native American studies—approached the apogee of its rush to "salvage" a supposedly vanishing Indian America, not least through transcriptions of oral storytelling.[3]

Salvage anthropology and the modernist fascination with ethnicity and the folk encouraged and responded to the two most momentous legislative initiatives in the history of post-removal federal Indian policy: the Dawes Act of 1887, which tried to enforce assimilation, and the anti-assimilation Indian Reorganization Act of 1934. As the Dawes Act assumed that Indians would die off or fade away and tried to speed up the exit by hurling Indians off reservations and into a voracious, white-dominated market economy, salvage anthropology tried to preserve the supposedly vanishing cultures, but to preserve them in formaldehyde, as museum relics disconnected from the present. Then, as modernists rediscovered and reimagined the contemporaneity of non-Anglo ethnicities and folk culture, reformers put through the Indian Reorganization Act, trying to reverse the Dawes Act by recognizing reservation sovereignty and the ongoing life of indigenous cultures. The IRA often imposed federally sponsored reorganization, so that in the guise of putting an end to enforced assimilation reformers sometimes substituted one kind of assimilation for another. In these ways, Mourning Dove and McNickle's investments in ethnic particularity tie their work to a broader cultural project, a project that was laid out for them to choose at the same time that they had to choose it themselves.

In this context, while continuing the interest of Purdy and other critics in *The Surrounded*'s portraits of oral traditions and changing Native identities, I want to build on the discussions of labor, economics, and gender in the previous chapter to argue that *The Surrounded* links those concerns to other, related sites of cultural contest, in particular to changing gender identities and the effects of the expanding market economy. After all, McNickle wrote *The Surrounded* not only when comprehensive Indian suffrage was new (it came with citizenship, in 1924), but also when women's suffrage was new (1920), and he wrote in the midst of a depression that challenged men's ability—including his own—to find the work that most Americans identified with masculinity. While finishing his novel, Mc-Nickle vainly sought hard-to-find employment in the market economy that would not support his ambitions as a novelist, wrote detailed discussions of depression-era economic policy in his diary, desperately borrowed $25 from the Authors' League to pay the rent, and then moved to Washington to work for the Federal Writers Project and apply to join John Collier's Office of Indian Affairs.[4] Amid such concerns, he cast his novelist's eye on reservation men's masculinity, their frequent indifference to the labor market, and their uneasy relation to the federal government and the OIA. To see these preoccupations in *The Surrounded* can expand our sense of the legacy that McNickle's novel leaves for later Native fiction. And that, in turn, draws out Native precedent for the keen eye on gender roles of such recent novelists as Janet Campbell Hale, Thomas King, and Betty Louise Bell, as well as encouraging us to distinguish among different traditions in Native fiction.

SHOOTING THE BUCK

Well into the novel, in a scene that hasn't attracted much critical attention, Archilde Leon finds at the last instant that he cannot shoot the fine buck he holds in his rifle sights, and the knotted twists of plot and ideology in this slow, understated scene rehearse the crisis that crashes down minutes later to reconfigure the novel. Archilde's refusal to shoot the deer, although overshadowed by the pivotal killings that it leads to, condenses four fascinations that the novel keeps trying to knot into one: storytelling, Native identity, gender identity, and the market economy. I begin by studying this unlikely scene in detail, as an introduction to a larger reading of McNickle's novel and its place in the tradition of Indian novels. The pivotal scene that comes next, with its sudden burden of corpses, jolts events out of control, but the earlier scene sets up that pivotal scene by a defining momentum of events that show Archilde at his most deliberate. Archilde's refusal to shoot the buck becomes a decision about the representation of cultural and gendered identity, a decision made possible by the market but one he must contextualize and then justify in oral story.

Hunting stories had always excited him, giving him a feeling that he would like to be envied for his good shooting and his hunting sense. But it was clear that he had not understood himself, he had not understood about killing. The excitement was in matching one's wits against animal cunning. The excitement was increased when a man kept himself from starving by his hunting skill. But lying in wait and killing, when no one's living depended on it, there was no excitement in that. Now he understood it.

He remembered then that he would have to give his mother a plausible story. It wouldn't do to say that he had been mistaken about the deer coming there to drink. He didn't want to lose credit for being that much of a hunter. It would be bad enough to say that he had missed. Oh, well—

He pointed the gun against the mountainside and pulled the trigger. When he opened his eyes the deer were gone. . . . His mind was at rest about the fact of his failure as a hunter.

On the way to camp he met his mother. She was coming quickly, a short knife in her hand. "Did you pick a fat one?" she asked at once.

He could not explain it, but he felt like a fool. . . .

"Something scared them just as they came to the water. I waited too long, and when I shot there was nothing but air." The explanation sounded weak.

"A young man waits for a better shot and hits nothing. An old man makes the best of it and gets his meat." It was her way of teaching a lesson by talking in generalities.

"When the smoke clears away the women are still talking." He knew how to respond in her style. He felt satisfied again. (121–23)

Up to this point, Archilde has procrastinated decisions that he imagines might solidify his identity. He wants to travel, but he also wants to return home, and so he returns home planning only to visit, but then he keeps extending his stay through an improvised series of reactions and excuses. Then suddenly, onto the once ordinary act of shooting a deer he projects a capacity to define his Indianness and his masculinity.

Definitions promise completeness, but they are part of history, continuously changing. To produce definition, therefore, whether in search of fixity or to emulate its elusiveness, requires narrative. Until this moment in the hunting trip, Archilde reluctantly pursues an old story of masculinity and Indianness. His mother Catharine presses him to take the trip so that she can shore up that story. She associates hunting in the mountains with a defining core of identity, the pre-contact past of her ancestors and early childhood. And so Archilde rides with her into the mountains and dutifully goes off to play his allotted role in the story: the male hunter. Indeed, "hunting stories had always excited him."

But the past perfect ("had always") and the generic idea of hunting stories, rather than his own hunting stories, contribute to his sudden sense that now the story has changed. He feels a futility in going off into the mountains, and his slow-witted, clumsy brother Louis disgusts Archilde by trying to tell the old story of stealing horses and running off into the mountains.[5] Archilde competes with Louis over their claims to masculine confidence. When Louis shows up hungry, Archilde refuses to let Louis hunt with him: "'I'll go alone. Louis is no hunter. His feet get tangled in the brush and he falls down.'" Even the obtuse Louis hears the aspersions cast on his masculinity, vindictively conceding Archilde the place next to their mother in the small, two-person tepee, as "he didn't care to sleep like a squaw" (120). Now Archilde, in the luxury of proving his skill according to the old story, by finding the herd and holding a buck in his sights, suddenly feels that the old story no longer fits, and that he will need a new story to replace it. Through old and new, he continues to negotiate his identity through stories, and much more imaginatively than Sheriff Quigley, who—having read and "heard stories" about Old West sheriffs—"was intent on being all of them in himself" (117).

Earlier, as the novel opens, Archilde already tries to negotiate identity through stories, but with little success. He comes home and tries to explain his absence to his mother, but the word "Portland" means nothing to her.

"I had a job. I played my fiddle in a show house. I can always get a job now any time I go away."

She looked at him. . . . So he could go away any time now? He did not have to be fed at home?

"They paid me this money. Look!" She barely glanced at the offered money. It was all strange, she could not make it into a picture. An Indian boy, she thought, belonged with his people.

They sat in silence for some time. It was useless to think of fiddle-playing, and for a while Archilde could think of nothing that was not equally useless. When you came home to your Indian mother you had to remember that it was a different world. Anyhow you had not come to show your money and talk about yourself. . . .

"We will make a feast and my friends will see you again."

That was something he had forgotten to include in his visit—the old lady and her feasts! You gorged yourself on meat until you felt sick, and a lot of old people told tiresome stories. He frowned. (2–4)

He tries to tell a new story of his identity, with new terms for masculine pride ("I can always get a job," "They paid me this money"), but she—indifferent to jobs and money—can hear only the old stories that he finds tiresome. Swelled with his newfound modernity, Archilde feels embarrassed by the stories, like the jaded moderns whom Walter Benjamin described in 1936 as embarrassed by traditional storytelling (83). Still, when the feast comes and Archilde finds himself captive to the old oral tales, he listens with interest "for the first time" (74). Soon he finds himself staying home longer than he planned and then agreeing to ride into the mountains with his mother and play by her notion of masculinity and Indianness. He will fire his gun. He will shoot not just a deer, but a buck. But he cannot do it. The old stories no longer produce the confident identity that they promise.

In a sense they never did. One generation's old story is an earlier generation's new story. The rifle that he and his mother associate with the old ways is a recent, post-contact technology—yet no less Indian for that. Indianness, like any other identity, continually redefines itself, just as, in the post-contact world, it continually redefines the whiteness surrounding it and within it. Archilde himself is not only the "Indian boy" of his mother's fantasy, but also the child of a white father, mixing biologies and remixing already mixed cultures. Even his French and Spanish name, Archilde Leon, blends cultures, suggesting the burden of his role (our shield, our child, our childe—in the archaic sense of a noble youth like Childe Roland—and our lion) and advertising itself as an overdetermined site of representation, identity, and heavy-handed literary "symbolism."

But the less the old stories apply, the greater the pressure to reinvent their urgency. In *Wind from an Enemy Sky,* Bull and Pock Face cave in to that pressure. In fits of impulse, they try to prop up their shrinking masculine and cultural power by firing Bull's gun at the visible crust of white dominance: the dam that kills the water, the engineers who build and run the dam, and finally even the understanding BIA superintendent. *Wind from an Enemy Sky* revolves around the futility of anger, violence, and guns as mechanisms and sanctuaries of masculine, Indian meaning amidst modernity, but it also revolves around the apparent lack of coherent alternatives. Thus, it is one thing for Archilde to decide not to shoot the buck, but it is something else to explain that decision to his mother, and—with increasing urgency as the novel moves on—to explain it to himself and to explain the bizarre but fateful quicksand of events that it leads to. He needs "a plausible story." He cannot tell her that he has reinvented his masculinity, and he can hardly tell her that he has reinvented his Indianness. To say he has decided that times have changed would only draw her scorn. The lie he finally reaches for does not help, for no plausible story would check her frustrated expectation. There seems no escape from her scorn, no way not to "lose credit." He thinks he can manage that; he thinks his "mind" is "at rest"—until he hears her eagerness, so oblivious of alternative ideologies or even of the possibility that he could shoot and miss ("Did you pick a fat one?") that, at least for readers, Archilde's pain achieves a rueful comedy.

His feeble lie evokes a question about compromise and "strategic essentialism,"[6] that is, about pretending to accept stable, singular identity roles gauged to audiences (in this case, his mother) not ready to comprehend a more fluid, contingent sense of identity. Archilde feels a pressure to stick to the old, great-hunter standard of masculine and Indian invulnerability, even after he revises his own standards from hunting to preserving. If we try to reinvent the criteria of pride, we risk speaking to ears that remain tuned to another scale, like Catharine's, and inevitably like much of McNickle's audience. We risk insulting—or being thought to insult—the old criteria. And since no such reinvention proceeds in a vacuum without accommodating itself, at least partly, to the potential criteria invented for us by the surrounding culture, we risk capitulating—or being thought to capitulate to—that surrounding culture.

Hence much is at stake when McNickle has Archilde pit the deer's beauty against its potential role as just more meat in a market economy. As Archilde rides up the mountain, he imagines that it looks the same as "years ago" (115). "Nothing would have been much different," he thinks; "he would have felt the same sway of his horse." He seems not to mean a time before rifles and horses, yet rifles and horses are too new to fit the implicitly lengthy, pre-contact past he romanticizes. Then he turns skeptical: "But it was different. The mountains were empty of life, that was the difference. This ride with his mother was no more than a pleasure trip; that was the difference. If they returned without fresh meat, no one would worry; at home there were canned peas, potatoes in the cellar, and meat could be had at the butcher's; that was the difference" (116). That is why he finds "no excitement" at the prospect of shooting the buck.

It may be crudely unfair and reductive to ask what is the "Indian" thing for Archilde to do when faced with that buck, but *The Surrounded* is exactly a portrait of unfair and reductive questions that will not go away. In one sense the traditional Native thing would be to shoot the buck. In another, often romanticized sense that today we call ecological,[7] the traditional Native thing would be to let the buck live. And if the figuration of "shooting" and "buck" suggests that Archilde's masculinity is at stake, it can also suggest economics. Here the market, ironically, makes possible the very environmentalism that tries to resist the market's ravages. Yet the ecological choice that the market makes possible for Archilde would be impossible to explain as Native to Catharine. She does not think in ecological terms or in terms of money and markets. She cannot understand her son's pride when he shifts to the market economy. With the earnest bluster of a small-time parvenu, he boasts that he held a job and earned a salary, and can get another job when he likes, while she sees him as deserting his Indianness.

When he returns to his mother after deciding not to shoot the buck, she scolds him in a syntax and diction that remind us she is speaking in Salish. Archilde's ability to respond in kind with a wisecrack about Indian women restores his satisfaction with his own identity, both masculine and

Indian. But by now that satisfaction seems fragile, and it turns out to be a novelist's feint, a lull to set up the pivotal storm that soon overtakes Archilde and the novel, as suddenly everything happens almost at once.[8]

SHOOTING LOUIS

A swirl of events surrounds Archilde too quickly for him to do more than lament his impotence. Louis returns, carrying a yearling doe. Archilde, insulting Louis's meager trophy and riding the momentum of his lie to Catharine, now lies to Louis, claiming to have shot a grander deer and hung it in a nearby grove. Then a game warden rides up and sees the illegal doe, provoking Louis to tattle about the deer Archilde supposedly shot. When Archilde denies it and the warden gets angry, Louis and Catharine talk to each other in Salish, panicking the warden. Catharine convinces Louis to cooperate, but when Louis picks up his rifle to go with the warden, in a flash the panicky warden shoots him and—before Archilde knows what has happened—the shocked Catharine has buried a hatchet in the warden's head.

In cautious deliberation, Archilde decides not to kill, and then suddenly Louis, the warden, and Catharine each kill without thinking, with the warden shooting Louis in a reflex of what we now call racial profiling. Archilde's controlled decision to shoot into the air, in effect to lie— though considered and not reflexive at all—soon cascades into a series of lies that sweep all events to destruction. Trying to tell the improbable truth that he has not killed a deer, that he only played a joke on his brother, Archilde thinks "The situation had grown baffling" (125). When the warden shoots Louis, Archilde blurts out "'You're wrong! It's a mistake—'" but then thinks "Explaining was useless. It only added to the stupid confusion" (127). Then, with two corpses on their hands and a snowstorm brewing, Catharine and Archilde have to go home. Once they return, explanations may seem useless, may only add to the confusion, but again and more than ever, Archilde needs to tell a story.

By making Catharine kill (or murder?) the warden, McNickle refocuses and magnifies some of the novel's most perplexing questions. He pushes Archilde into ethical and ideological quicksand, for any story Archilde tells will only sink him deeper. Because he's an Indian, the authorities will doubt his word, yet if he tells the truth they will also doubt him because he's a man. He can hardly go to the Indian-hating Sheriff Quigley, infamous for always getting his man, and say "My momma did it." But it hardly seems better to lie and say that *he* did it. Just when Archilde has been groomed to become the next great hope of his people, the Big Paul of the future who, unlike the earlier Big Paul, can negotiate between two worlds, he suddenly looks even worse than the hopeless horse thief Louis. He and

Catharine ride into the mountains in romantic escape from the market economy, and then the market economy's warden rides in on them and their world collapses.

Not only Archilde's masculinity is at stake in the story he tells. Catharine's femininity, as the novel's world conceives it, is also at stake, both in whatever story they might tell and because the novel seems to take for granted that only Archilde and not Catharine will need a story. But as McNickle renders the pivotal event, Archilde plays no role:

> There was no accounting for what happened next. Archilde saw only the final action, not what led up to it. He was near the warden, watching him stoop to examine Louis. Then he saw the officer bend at the knees. His face was twisted with pain. The old lady had hit him in the head with a hatchet.
>
> The way he remembered the scene afterward, Louis was lying face upward with blood on his shirt front. He had been shot in the back of the head. The warden had plunged his face into the dirt and lay still. The old lady had covered her head again and was wailing for the dead. That was how he remembered it, and he could not explain how his mother had been able to move without being seen or heard. That was inexplicable. (127–28)

And there the chapter ends, in the inexplicable. We have already seen that Archilde cannot explain his job or his stay in Portland to Catharine, and he "could not explain" that he shot his rifle into the air. When he tells a feeble lie instead, he thinks that "the explanation sounded weak," as if his strength were in doubt. Before the suspicious warden, "explaining was useless." Now, "there was no accounting for what happened." Indeed, as focalized by Archilde, "what happened," as he thinks of it evasively, not naming the "what," is narrated after the fact, in the past perfect, and sometimes in the passive voice, as if it were already done rather than as if Catharine actively did it or Archilde actively colluded in it. Catharine didn't hit the warden; she "had hit" him. She didn't move; she "had been able to move." Archilde is left with no choice—or at least he can imagine none. In an earlier draft, he even loses bodily control, fainting, then needing to lean against a tree in nausea "with no strength to move or speak," feeling "ashamed of being an Indian and part of" his mother (McNickle, *Hungry Generations,* 71). With Archilde helpless, here and later in the final scene that echoes this one, women do the killing. And Catharine kills with a hatchet, recalling the iron ax in the story at her feast, "the thing that would make life easy." All too ironically, the thing that would make life easy actually makes death easy and life difficult, even inexplicable, unnarratable.

The inability to narrate has much to do with ideologies of racial and gender identity. Archilde feels crushed into the prefabricated narrative of

Native masculinity that has already swallowed his brothers into bitter disappearance and early death. "He would wind up," he fears, "like every
other reservation boy—in prison, or hiding in the mountains" (150), a
more impoverished version of the young men with nothing to do in Mathews's *Sundown*. While Archilde does more or less nothing, or no more
than acts of omission—shooting into the air, not cautioning Louis to stay
clear of his rifle, not keeping an eye on his shocked mother in the seconds
after the warden shoots Louis—the dominant ideologies that surround
him like the air he breathes write onto his passivity the narrative of the
wild young no-good Indian murderer. This is the masculine side of the
prefabricated narrative; we later hear the feminine side applied to Elise
and her sisters as "'those La Rose sluts'" (228). As George Beckwith, a
merchant and possible model for the novel's Moser, told a reservation
reader who wrote McNickle about the novel and its local reception, "he
has seen so many of them come and go, each ending in just such fashion
as did Archilde. And too—that there are girls in the Mission today just like
that La Rose girl. The Sisters, according to Mr. Beckwith, . . . can teach
them everything but character" (J. Verne Dusenberry). So many of *them*—
just like *that La Rose girl*—can teach *them*—the prefabricated narrative
comes down hard. Under such pressures, the novel seems uncertain
about its own resistance to stereotypical expectations of gender, for its
plot privileges an ideological resentment of women's growing agency by
making its Indian killers women. Archilde's vaguely thought-through,
procrastinating efforts to invent a new model of Salish masculinity are
overwhelmed by the limited models that he can recognize or envision in
his surrounded state. As in *Sundown*, that has to do with the novel's comparatively thin portrayal of Native reservation culture, notwithstanding
Archilde's moving rediscovery of value in traditional culture, which some
critics have focused on, fittingly enough. He sees other, less stereotypical
models of masculinity, but they hardly seem appealing or accessible, at
least not on the reservation. The priests range from benevolently naive,
patronizing colonialists to sadistic child abusers. The almost too scrupu-
lously asexual Mr. Duffield, Archilde's violin teacher at the boarding
school, seems part of another world, with his Sunday teas. Meanwhile, the
example of McNickle himself looms over the narrative horizon, but it offers far more hopeful a model than this novel's plot will contemplate, and
perhaps too distant and assimilated a model—with McNickle writing in
New York—to make much difference in depression-era reservation life.[9]

   No critic seems to have noticed that McNickle models the killings at the
center of his novel on an actual event in local history. In October 1908,
when McNickle was four years old, a white game warden and deputy shot
and killed four Flathead hunters, three men and a boy, who shot and
killed the warden and wounded the deputy. Three Flathead women and

one girl escaped. A garbled story dribbled out to the *Daily Missoulian* from the deputy and other white male sources in a series of frenetically revised versions ("Game Warden Killed," "Story of Peyton's Murder," "Peyton's Body," "Rudolph Arrives"). According to the deputy, when the warden "advised the four bucks that it would be necessary to bring them to Missoula they, with one accord, seized their rifles and fired a close range volley at the officers, who returned the fire dropping two of the bucks" ("Game Warden Killed"), as if the warden and his deputy, instead of regulating hunters, were hunting Indians. While the newspaper and its white sources spoke of the Indians as animals, they celebrated the warden as a hero. Meanwhile, in a tone that matches *The Surrounded*'s worries about feminine agency, the paper and its sources seemed terribly anxious about the "squaws" who got away.

But when the warden's notebook turned up, it must have raised doubts even among ordinary whites, since it listed hunting licenses for three of the Indians. Then the *Daily Missoulian* printed a letter from a white reader who supported the Indians, along with sworn testimony from the two uninjured Indian women who witnessed the killing. Backed by the federal agent from the reservation, the women's detailed statement told how the warden fired first, even though two of the Indian men and the boy were away from their rifles. A third Indian man explained to the warden that they were leaving, as the warden had asked, and "was tying a rope on his horse before mounting and had his gun under his right arm." One of the Indians, the women said, was shot through the back ("Indians Tell"). Chastened by the women's testimony and the agent's description of the dead Indian men as "a peace-loving band of fellows" who "had never had any trouble of a serious character" ("Squaws Return"), the newspaper cast suspicion on the warden, saying that it "holds him responsible" and taking the women's account as more reliable ("Indians Tell"). Fifty years later, the girl who got away, Mary Stousee Finley, told her version of events after growing up with the story and interviewing and consulting "many of the old Indians . . . as well as many white men who are still alive that had contact in some way with the story" (2). As she put it on the title page of her narrative, "This . . . is the way that I saw my father and my brother killed." She had the story translated into English and "decided to have it printed for the benefit of the many people who tell their version of what they think happened, adding many parts that is untrue" (1). Finley's concern reinforces the sense that McNickle would have heard the story growing up. Her account corroborated the women's testimony in more detail, even explaining that the lone Indian man without a license had a special permit from the federal agent. But the changing series of white-produced newspaper reports and the noxious, shoot-now-and-look-later racism of the earlier reports underscore the hostility of most of the non-Indian au-

DELIVERS ST TALKS

est and Enthus-
Farther East.

RTAIL ITINERARY

mpaign, Republican
oncerning Par-
ord—Tells
ng.

GAME WARDEN KILLED BY FLATHEAD INDIANS

Charles B. Peyton, While Attempting to Arrest Four Redskins at Holland Prairie, Near Ovando, Is Shot to Death—He Manages to Slay All of Assailants.

Herman Rudolph, Companion and Brother Officer of the Dead Man, Was Witness of Shooting and Took Part in the Affray, Escaping With Slight Injuries—Squaws of Party of Illegal Hunters Escape and Posses Are Scouring the Country in Their Pursuit—Coroner Is Notified.

MOST IS R

Welcome
All Simil

MEN OF W

Yankee Unif
diality c
to J

Word was received in Missoula yesterday morning of the killing of Deputy of Ovando by Indians on Sunday afternoon. From meager reports of the affair it is understood that the deputy and his assistant, Herman Rudolph, found a band of Flathead Indians encamped on Holland prairie, about 40 miles northeast of Ovando, and attempted to arrest them for the unlawful shooting of game. In the band were four bucks and three squaws, the latter fleeing at the approach of the officers. When Peyton advised the four bucks that it would be necessary to bring them to Missoula they, with one accord, seized their rifles and fired a close range volley at the officers, who returned the fire dropping two of the bucks. Peyton was struck in the breast, and, as he staggered, called to Rudolph that he was shot, but to keep after the redskins. Peyton dropping on one knee continued to pour a hot shot at the remaining Indians, and as the last of the quartet threw up his hands, the warden fell forward on his face and, without uttering a groan, died.

Pursue Fleeing Squaws.

Rudolph, who was uninjured save for a slight scratch, ran to the assistance of his chief as soon as he was sure the last of the redskins was unable to renew the fight, but found Peyton dead as the result of rifle wounds through the breast and abdomen. Hastily carrying the deputy to a secluded place, Rudolph ran to a nearby ranch for assistance in carrying for the dead deputy and the bodies of the Indians, after which he started for Ovando, which place he reached yesterday morning. Here he advised the people of the town, who organized several posses, which started immediately in pursuit of the squaws belonging to the band.

Authorities Notified.

Coroner Marsh was notified, as was also Indian Agent Samuel Bellew of Arlee, who telephoned instructions to the Ovando authorities relative to the burying of the dead Flatheads after the coroner's inquest. The body of Charles Peyton will be brought to Missoula as soon as possible, but arrangements for the funeral are being withheld until the return of relatives who left here yesterday morning for the scene of the tragedy.

Family of Peyton.

The murdered deputy leaves a wife and three children, who left Ovando last Saturday for Grantsdale, about six miles from Hamilton, where they were to have spent a week's vacation with Mrs. Peyton's parents, Mr. and Mrs. Tip See. A sister, Mrs. Leslie Wood, lives in Missoula. Mrs. Peyton was in the city Saturday on her way to Hamilton. Late reports of the bloody fight indicate that there were some members

LAWYERS QUIBBLE IN THAW CASE

LEGAL QUESTIONS ARE ARGUED IN PITTSBURG BEFORE JUDGE YOUNG.

Pittsburg, Oct. 19.—After hearing the motions and arguments today in the proceedings having for their ostensible object the bringing here of Harry Thaw, the slayer of Stanford White, to testify in the voluntary bankruptcy petition filed several months ago, Judge Young of the United States district court late today reserved until 1 o'clock tomorrow his decision in the points raised in today's proceedings. These are, first, whether Judge Young shall accept jurisdiction or whether the matter must be presented to Judge Archibald of Scranton, Pa., by whom the writ of habeas corpus id testificandum was issued. Judge Young having been in Europe on vacation when the application was made, and, second, whether Thaw shall be brought here to testify in the bankruptcy proceedings. A libel Gardner, special deputy attorney general of the state of New

of the band of Indians who were well known in Missoula, one of them being Yellowhead, who was the first to fire at the wardens and the first to fall from the effects of a bullet from the weapon in the hands of Peyton. It is also rumored that Louis Ashley, another well-known Flathead Indian, was a member of the party, but this story lacks confirmation.

Holland Prairie.

Holland prairie, where the shooting took place, is located on the Swan river, about 40 miles from Ovando, and is a most beautiful natural park and a favorite run for deer. It is about three miles from the Howland ranch, but well removed from wire or rail communication.

Fearless Officer.

Among his acquaintances and co-workers Peyton was known as a man possessing supreme nerve, being regarded as one of Game Warden Scott's most fearless subordinates, and having the reputation of being a dead shot. He was feared by the Indians, having arrested many of their number on previous occasions for offenses against the game laws.

Pays Glowing Tribute.

When word was carried to Game Warden Scott in Helena of the tragedy on Holland prairie and the killing of Deputy Peyton, he expressed deep regret and paid the officer a high tribute, according to the following dispatch:

Helena, Oct. 19.—"Pleasant and affable, quiet and unassuming, yet one of the nerviest and gamest men I have ever met," said Mr. Scott, in commenting upon the case. "He was one of the most untiring men I have ever known, his continued rides of from 60 to 75 miles a day over the mountains being remarkable, not only to me, but to all residents of that section. His vitality was perhaps unequaled, while as for bravery I doubt if the man knew what fear meant. Personally, I feel as if I had lost a brother, so intimate had our relations become, while as an officer he was one of the best I have ever known. Sympathetic to a degree, yet a terror to evil-doers, the department has suffered an irreparable loss."

it prosperity that the pies have given.
ook up the Philippine—problem that we had to result of the war. To-ipino school children are ng and reciting in Eng-given than practical the central government ol over the provincial governments.
ip the Panama canal, years, since the time of ilth, has been the subvestion. Under the present there has been an or-bating, machinery and such a way that in the or six years anyone who the work can promise so that your navy will Caribbean to the Pacific." ot took up what he oral awakening, respect-of large business en-ling in a "quickening of conscience."
think from statements he added, "that no—en made, but the pro—remarkable. Through the rate bill the rail—ors have abandoned the—bonded unlawful dis—nd have taken away the vitality by which unlaw—monopolies have been

dressed this with its in—be combination of cap—ate purposes. He said: ation of capital is in no progress as the a machine, and the ntrol is great and the nfs needed are many denouncing them as they are used for an
The normal, legal ombination is to re-production by induc—a the management of in only when undue to in stifle competition the line of legality, ight to be restrained

Tokio, Oct. corded the Amer the government a conceded by the ers to be the h perfectly carried reptions received mided from th Admiral Sperry officers to the A able to any hon plished, but the fleet and its has been an card ried out to the a lasting impres upon the mind of has witnessed it.

Sailors

The men of th anese fleet are where throughou hama. Every w sailors is anticip jacket finds an ba among the Jap American uniform same" everywher the Japanese ex—tinate of the crew It is impossible ity of the Japan officers and sail ning to understan evident desire on new founded upon finds its source in show that such fri the part of Japan of the Japanese all misunderstand and American and Americans are insip ittude of Japa

FORMER REPUBLICAN ON

Fig. 3. To the *Daily Missoulian,* reporting a 1908 incident that seems to have inspired the pivotal scene of McNickle's *The Surrounded,* Indians killing a white game warden stood out more than a white game warden killing four Indians.

dience for Archilde's story. Much depends, historically and in the novel, on who hears and who tells the story.

All this connects in diverse ways to the novel's scenes of oral storytelling, such as the story of the thing that would make life easy. For in some ways, Archilde's burdensome passivity is the privilege of his (by comparison) easy life, his economic security at home with his father's wealth or on the road with his marketable skill as a fiddler. In that sense, his passivity differentiates him from the other young men in economic limbo on the reservation and makes him more like the oil-rich young men of Mathews's *Sundown*. For, as Mathews shows, to make life easy in one way can make it difficult in other ways.

Purdy's excellent account of oral storytelling in *The Surrounded* describes how the stories teach Archilde to respect traditional culture. In his reading, the ax succeeds: "The story tells Archilde and his people to pay attention to the old ways, for through them power may be maintained. . . . By understanding the ways that people in the past found the knowledge necessary to respond to change, they can find resolutions to their own present quandaries" (*Word Ways*, 57). Still, Purdy finds more optimism in the novel than I do.[10] He reads it more as a bildungsroman, seeing a largely linear plot with Archilde steadily learning and maturing. But the ax story (like the other stories) works in more ways than such an account allows, even before Catharine takes a hatchet to set the novel spiraling to disaster.

When the story ends, Archilde "wondered at it. And the more he reflected on it the more wonderful it grew. A story like that, he realized, was full of meaning" (69), too full, I would suggest, to stabilize in any particular lesson.[11] The story, told by a respected elder, may seem traditional. But it is not traditional in every sense, for the iron ax marks it as a post-contact story about contact, and McNickle curiously names the elder Whitey. Far be it from me to argue against labor-saving technology, nor can anyone escape it; but the history of technological change underlines its diversity of consequences. Indeed, the ax is a metonymy of cultural contact, technological change, and the moral thicket of their consequences in a world where we must somehow blend seeking change, putting up with it, and— like those who refuse to believe in the thing that will make life easy—refusing it. The ax is also a metonymy of money and the market economy. According to the old man in the story, once they have the thing that would make life easy, the people "would not have to hunt or dig for roots or do any kind of work" (66). Buying or trading for the "thing" will deepen their role in the market, where eventually they will buy food instead of hunting or digging for it. In a broader sense, then, the "thing" that relieves people from work can also signify deferral and difference, or *différance*. It is a tool of convenience, not an end in itself. But like any technology, whether the stone ax that the iron ax displaces, or the writing that McNickle uses to render the oral story, the technology becomes not only a transparent instrument but also an opaque object. It partly becomes the culture that we turn to it to produce. That keeps us from controlling it and allows it, in part, to control us ("men have become the tools of their tools," says Thoreau in the first chapter of *Walden* [37]), as Archilde feels controlled by the consequences of its convenience to Catharine's fateful hand.[12]

The story of the ax comes second in a rapid series of four oral stories. The first three recount familiar landmarks in technological history: the arrival of flint, the iron ax, and guns. If the tragic potential of the ax were not already visible in the hint of environmental horror when the old man fells "every tree that stood near the trail" (69), it grows clear enough when we hear Modeste's grieving story of what guns did to the Salish people and their enemies. Then the fourth story recounts the arrival of, in effect, another technology, Catholicism, in a series that moves from the phallicism of flint arrow heads, the ax, and the rifle to the more dispersed gendering of childless yet patronizing "Fathers" who wear robes, "have no wives," and carry "two sticks, one stick across the other" (21, 73). "We thought they would bring back the power we had lost," says Modeste, "but today we have less" (74). In this anti-Catholic novel, McNickle—following the Salish pattern-number of four—organizes history to hint at Catholicism as the fourth in a series of steadily more terrible "improvements."[13]

The Salish stories immediately follow a white analogue, as Father Grepilloux asks Max Leon to recall his early days in the valley and then reads to Max from his journal. McNickle's conspicuous juxtaposition begs us to compare the two storytelling scenes, as does the contrast between Grepilloux's account of the Jesuits' arrival and Catharine's earlier recollection of the same event. Each side imagines the other according to its own credo. The Salish see the priests' arrival as Kolinzuten's answer to their prayers (21), while the priests see the Salish as rejecting "False Gods" in favor of the "True God" (47). McNickle invites us to judge the priests harshly (Purdy, *Word Ways*, 46–50), for unlike the Salish they suppose that only their view carries value. But at that first meeting, as the priests attribute their view to the Salish, so the Salish attribute theirs to the priests, leaving us with a palimpsest of competing stories of the "same" "event," recalling another 1936 novel, *Absalom, Absalom!* For McNickle, however, the contrast points less to a sweeping epistemological skepticism than to a colonialist difference in power. Each side has a different view, but only one side goes on to force its view on the other.

The intriguing contrasts of detail and tone between the two storytelling sessions have already received thoughtful attention (Purdy, *Word Ways,* 46–50). More broadly, each side focuses on its relation to the other, needily poring over stories of contact as if they explained the mystery not of both sides' history and identity, but—for each side—of the Indians' history and identity. This is a novel about Indians much more than about whites. For the American 1930s and for McNickle, then in the midst of deliberately reconstructing his Indian identity, the contest to define whiteness felt less urgent than it felt in the same years for many people in central Europe, and it took the form of naturalizing whiteness by hurrying its contingency onto nonwhites. In that spirit, an emerging liberalism was reshaping federal Indian policy, moving from the Dawes Act's coerced assimilation toward at least an effort to recognize reservation sovereignty, a movement highlighted in the 1920s and 1930s by the work of John Collier, eventually Franklin Roosevelt's commissioner of Indian Affairs and McNickle's boss, and by the Indian Reorganization Act, passed in 1934 as McNickle completed his novel. The Indian Reorganization Act sometimes demanded assimilation nevertheless. It led, supposedly, to local reservation rule—and in 1935 the Flathead Reservation was the first to ratify a constitution and by-laws—but it defined local rule according to dominant notions of "democracy." Whites were not asked to govern themselves by Indian models, but they invited (and pressured) Indians to govern themselves by predominantly white models.

The Surrounded's preoccupation with red-white contact can also recall the accent on racial exchange in Mathews's *Sundown*. But *Sundown* focuses on an imaginary fullness of isolated Indian identity, a preoedipal idyll that continues to tug on Chal Windzer's yearnings and shames, whereas Archilde never feels his Indianness pull at him in ways that exclude the dominant culture, even though, like Chal, he finds that dominant culture alternately attractive and repellent. *The Surrounded*'s preoccupation with contact as the spring of identity resembles most early and, for that matter, most later African American novels, though it contrasts with such contemporaneous works as *Their Eyes Were Watching God* (1937) and George Wylie Henderson's fine but forgotten *Ollie Miss* (1935), which mostly ignore white people. The obsession with contact seems to produce the juxtaposition between storytelling scenes, as if one side's stories of the other cannot stand on their own without redefinition in the other side's reflection.[14] Brian Moore's *Black Robe* (1985) and the movie based on it (1991) call on something like the same process, as does so different and popular a product as Disney's *Pocahontas* (1995), echoing, as many reviewers noted, *West Side Story* (play 1957, film 1961). Such juxtapositions between texts and within texts highlight both difference and likeness: in its different way, each side of the racial divide goes through similar rituals.

For each side, the other's quotidian routines of cultural cognition can seem like vacant busyness. Catharine cannot tell what to do with the messages she learns about white femininity. The Sisters teach her "where to find dirt and how to get rid of it" and a long list of other domestic chores such as cooking, washing, and gardening. "Then it seemed that there were only certain ways in which she could speak to the Sisters or to her friends, certain ways of eating, certain ways of opening the door when someone rang the bell, and certain ways of sitting down and saying nothing when visitors came" (170–71). Vapid as all this seems to Catharine, her perplexity at its crowded layerings of code suggests that she does not see the codes in her own customs. She takes Salish ways so much for granted that they do not rise over her cognitive horizon as objects of contemplation. If the scales of power were reversed, if it were she who assumed a self-evident superiority and taught the Sisters her ways, then she could hardly keep seeing her own culture's daily routines with such unconsciousness. Similarly, her husband Max cannot recognize the systemic expressiveness in Native ritual and masculinity: "He saw silent, straight-walking figures; he saw them at the hunt, which they went at efficiently but with an unnecessary amount of ceremonial before and after" (49). Catharine and Max each find the white world more describable, yet for each of them the other side's assumptions stick out as gaudy superfluities.

But Catharine and Max change over the course of the novel. Kept restlessly awake by the distant light and sound of Catharine's feast and its stories, Max finally begins to contemplate the amplitude of Native culture, even as he recognizes his distance from it: "Why was it that after forty years he did not know these people and was not trusted by them? . . . He rolled away from the glow of light, but still the voices reached him. What were they saying? Why didn't they talk to him?" (75). He senses something there, even if he cannot imagine what. And Catharine, of course, returns to traditional ways with new respect.

But the novel's incessant impulse to juxtapose traditions and to study the cultural urge to do so keeps running into the thorns of history: it is too late for either side to continue apart from the other. Among the Indians, "No one could now remember exactly what was punishable with the lash in those [old] days, because after the Fathers came many new 'crimes' were added, such as creating a disturbance at church" (206).[15] "The Church had come so long ago that she really knew nothing of how people lived before it came" (173–74). Modeste seconds Catharine's decision to return to the old ways with a revealing story:

He also had turned back to that world which was there before the new things came. . . . He told how his *Somesh* (his guardian spirit) had rescued him from a snowslide in which he had been caught when hunting in the mountains. First he had prayed a long time and it did no good, and then as he was about to die his *Somesh* came to him in a vision and just after that somebody saw his gun sticking up through the snow and they dug him out. . . . Since then he too had been going back to the old things. (210–11)

His *gun*: Modeste himself has earlier told the terrible story of what happened when whites sold guns to Indians. His earlier story intensified guns' double identity both as all too Indian, after they arrive, and as the resented instruments of colonialism and its devastating markets. By now, the very concept of "old things" is an imaginary reification of post-contact desire.

The vaunted old stories themselves are post-contact fantasies as well as inheritances. Despite Purdy's argument that McNickle drew on childhood memories of oral storytelling on the Flathead Reservation, McNickle was an outsider on the reservation, as the son of a Métis woman and a white man. We can track most of those stories' sources not to McNickle's reservation memories, but rather to his reading in libraries (Purdy, *Word Ways,* 20–21; D. R. Parker, *Singing,* 43, 50–51). He even cites his written sources in a "Note" appended to the novel. It is easy enough to take McNickle's reliance on books as a soiling inauthenticity made awkwardly public by the regimen of copyright law. Late in the composition of *The Surrounded,* McNickle wrote William Gates, the leading scholar of pre-contact Mayan writing, to ask about "any separate tales or episodes" that he could draw on in his own writing. "Understand," he continued, "I have my own resources as to material. I am not looking for a 'field' to exploit. I have never taken a step for the sake of finding 'local color' nor pried into one person's affairs for the sake of getting a 'character.' If writing does not emerge naturally from one's experiences it can serve no purpose except to ungulf people more profoundly in the meaninglessness in which most of them live" (25 March 1934). Those same concerns, it seems, lead Purdy to insist that McNickle drew the oral tales in *The Surrounded* from memory (as indeed he may have) and to cover the paucity of evidence and the inconvenient fact of printed sources with an insightful discussion of how McNickle improved on his printed sources.

But perhaps the binary of memory versus print is not so cleanly cut. Just as guns became an integral part of Native cultures, so too, by the time of *The Surrounded,* print was emerging as a crucial medium of oral traditions (as I discuss in chapter 4), and oral traditions, as Derrida argues, are not so antithetical to writing as many people suppose. McNickle in effect designed his book to intensify the merging of the oral and the written, to reinvent the novel in Indian terms, negotiating and confirming a new space for Native identity, much as Archilde tries to do by not shooting the deer. McNickle's source citing, therefore, like his correspondence with a scholar of Mayan *writing*, can flaunt the modernist, written continuation of oral traditions even while it sighs over his cosmopolitan distance from them. The dispersions of cultural reproduction send the stories from orality to print and back, continuously. The process is recursive, not linear.[16] Grumbling about the need to get permission from the "authors" of his printed sources, McNickle complained to his agent: "It is difficult to see how a myth or folktale can be copyrighted, especially when it comes so close to yourself as this does to me." McNickle's complaint about intellectual property rights allows us to see his "Note" not only as a submission to copyright rules but also as a protest against colonialist theft of property rights in the name of their preservation (a focus of *Wind from an Enemy Sky*). He doesn't object to writing the oral; he objects to owning it.

In that sense, intellectual property, as represented in the oral stories, suggests an analogue to the history of allotment, which underlies the novel. The Dawes Act, known officially as the General Allotment Act, sought to carve reservations into private land and distribute patches to each enrolled Indian. Unallotted lands were declared "surplus" and put up for sale, which meant sale to whites. The supposed goal was to detribalize the economy and culture and to vault Indians into the "free" market where private enterprise would assimilate Indians and convert them into prosperous "citizens." The upshot was disaster for reservations and for communal land ownership, as even allotted lands easily slipped (or were stolen) out of Indian ownership. By McNickle's estimate, the number of Indian-owned acres shrank from 140 million in 1887 to 50 million in 1932 (*Indian Tribes*, 49). (Since then, some land has been recovered through purchase, legislation, and legal claims.) Amid controversy and resistance, allotment hit the Flathead Reservation in 1906, and in 1910 the federal government opened the reservation to "settlers" (John Fahey, 279–307; Ronald L. Trosper; Flathead Culture 15). In 1925, McNickle himself sold his allotment to finance his studies at Oxford (D. R. Parker, *Singing*, 26–27). In *The Surrounded*, he sets up the allotment story through the puzzled focalization of Moser, the white businessman ruined in the speculation surrounding the distribution of land, whose unthinking exclusion of Indians from terms like "Everybody" and "people" tells much of the story:

> Everybody had expected that great benefits would result from throwing open the Reservation to white settlement. Even the Indians would gain by it, people said. At bottom, if you looked closely, there was a question of justice to

the Indians. Years before, in the middle of the last century, as Mr. Moser understood it, the Indians had agreed to give up their hereditary claims to all of western Montana and northern Idaho in return for a fixed reserve—which was to be set apart for their exclusive use—and additional compensation of money. The money disappeared into quicksand. . . . And finally, at the opening of the new century, each Indian was given a separate piece of land, a "garden plot," of eighty acres, and the remaining area was opened for white settlement. There was a theory behind all that; he had heard it expounded but he couldn't have repeated it now. It had something to do with civilizing the Indians. (30)

On many newly allotted reservations, most Indians were not interested in or ready for the market, and so it plundered them. By the time of allotment, though, Indians on the Flathead Reservation had adjusted to the market well enough to prove themselves profitable ranchers (Trosper, 144–97). No doubt, limited experience with the market made things tougher, but worse still, especially after allotment, the market was rigged against them: "Families could not receive their lands as contiguous parcels, and so, many had to sell off their livestock and reduce their herds to a size consistent with their small tracts of land. Ranching provided less than a subsistence income; farming was virtually nonexistent because of a lack of irrigation facilities. The people were forced to near-starvation conditions. Congress had destroyed a successful ranching community" (Kirke Kickingbird and Karen Ducheneaux, 96–97). Under the cover of allotment, white officials, accustomed to working the system, unleashed a multitude of ruses to sell off Indian lands to whites, both "surplus," unallotted land and allotted land (Trosper, especially 32–66).

In *The Surrounded,* the aftermath of allotment takes shape partly along generational and gender lines, as well as racial lines. Catharine, as we have seen, is indifferent to markets and to money, the flashy metonymy of markets.[17] Immediately after Catharine barely notices the wad of bills that Archilde waves at her, Max, perplexed that Archilde's nice clothes show signs of an employment he cannot imagine for Indians, even for his own son, pummels Archilde with humiliating questions, asks to see the money he claims to have earned by "working, as you say," and then gets angry when Archilde prefers to keep his money, because Max cannot imagine that Archilde will do anything but fritter it away (6–7). Then Archilde chases down his nephews, Mike and Narcisse. Their first words are

"Let's see your money!"
Archilde laughed. "Just look!"
"Where you steal that?" asked Mike. (12)

Alert to the rumor that Louis has stolen horses—another way that oral story circulates ideology—they cannot imagine Archilde earning his money any more than Max can. They no longer even fish.

> "We got no hooks," Narcisse explained.
> "Make a spear then."
> "You talk crazy!" Mike said. "You got to have a hook to make a spear!"
> "That shows what empty heads you got. All you need is a piece of wire."
> "Buy us hooks! Who wants to fish with wire?" (13)

Archilde teaches them to spearfish. Without reentering the market economy to buy hooks, he recreates indigenous tools in post-contact form, with wire. He doesn't need money, but he can earn it. They can't imagine an alternative to needing it, but they can't imagine earning it either.

The church poses as a refuge from money. There Archilde studies a painting of "Christ driving out the money changers" (105). But the painted pose of driving out the market camouflages the church's role as a mechanism to sneak it in, that is, the church's role as a vaguely unwitting Trojan horse for imperialism. "Grepilloux had shown the way over the mountains and the world had followed at his heels" (139). The church may be fooled, but the Indians are not. When the Jesuits arrive, Father Lamberti says naively that the priests "would not interfere in temporal matters, and wished nothing of them but to be allowed to minister to their Spiritual Health." As Grepilloux notes dourly, "the people looked disappointed" (47).

Archilde can work, and he has caught enough of the market's air to show off his money, but his idea of work has nothing of the market's self-replicating frenzy, the bootstrap pride that Mr. Snodgrass, his boarding school superintendent, tries to lecture into him: "'Always take an interest in your work. No matter how much you dislike a job, or how unimportant it seems to you, if it is your job, do it with a will and to the best of your ability. That is the way to make yourself valuable and to win success.'" The young Archilde listens sullenly, "first on one foot and then on the other" (93–94). To McNickle's depression audience, the Snodgrass motto, "work with a will" (94), could hardly sound helpful when there were so few jobs. McNickle mocks Snodgrass's indifference to alienated labor. To be sure, the Snodgrasses, and their loftier echo in Max, might respond that when the supply of labor exceeds the demand, those who work without a will may soon lose their work. But as we have seen in the previous chapter, on most depression-era reservations there was hardly any paid work to lose. The catch is that, unlike his white, would-be role models, Archilde would not care if he lost a job. McNickle fills out the cultural contrast after Archilde works under Max for pleasure and for reaching out to his father, rather than for money. For the first time Max and Archilde start to talk almost frankly, in a scene crowded with descriptions of thoughtful pauses (replaced below by ellipses) that suggest each side's incapacity to understand the other, even now as they try to understand each other for the first time:

> . . . "I never wanted much from my boys. Just for them to take a man's place, know how to work and do things. . . . A man ought to know how to work for his own good."
>
> . . . Archilde did not answer him. There was nothing to answer. Work was a small matter. One knew about it. It seemed useless to talk about so ordinary a subject.
>
> . . . "When you go away from here the only thing anybody will be interested in is: What can you do? Can you work? That's what they'll want to know. If you know how to do something, why, that's all there's to it. You don't have to worry."
>
> . . . "There's lots of things a fellow can do. I never have trouble. Sometimes I work washing dishes, or I press clothes in a tailor shop. It doesn't take much. When my luck is good I get a job playing the fiddle."
>
> . . . "You have money coming from me for your work. We'll have to settle."
>
> Archilde protested quickly. "That's nothing. I didn't do that for money. No, you don't owe me anything for that." (86–87)

Max's last word on his deathbed is the imperative "work" (166). He thinks that Indians "don't know how to work and maybe never will. They gamble away their horses and their tools," and yet he blames whites because "we killed off their game so they can't live in the old way" (146).

Like Mathews, McNickle totters along a tightrope when he tries to show reservation notions of work, money, and the market economy without repeating the myth of the lazy Indian, when he tries to show economic catastrophe and cultural crisis and not repeat the myths of the vanishing Indian and cultural hopelessness. The surrounding culture tries to channel every portrait of something Indian into praise or condemnation of Indian culture at large, leaving artists damned whether they do or they don't. The tightrope wobbles again when McNickle introduces Modeste's house: "There is a kind of chaos about an Indian's homestead that, however complete and hopeless, is nevertheless not inherent; it does not belong to the man. In the tepee, everything is in place; but when houses are built and farming implements acquired, then nothing is surprising"—and there follows a description of trashed farm equipment scattered across the yard, with a fractured grindstone trestle, "one end of its rusty shaft obtruding, like the upraised arm of a drowning man" (195–96).

The danger comes in the dismal, Eurocentrically scandalized picture this paints of reservation life, versus the new respect for reservation culture that Archilde learns as the novel goes on. Put another way, the danger comes in the transition from the Dawes Act to the Indian Reorganization Act, from phasing out reservations and Indian culture to trying to restore reservations and expecting Indians to govern themselves, a transition that McNickle himself would later describe as perilous (*They Came Here First*, 234–47). To face the reservation's suffering squarely can risk reducing it to its suffering. McNickle's contemporary Richard Wright, facing a similar dilemma, has been accused of reducing African American culture to its troubles with his portrait of Bigger Thomas in *Native Son* (1940) or his lament in *Black Boy* (1945) for what he calls "the cultural barrenness of black life" (45). In *The Surrounded*, McNickle takes a similar risk more softly, remarking the "misery and hopelessness. . . . In years of abundance no less than in lean years, the Indians sat in their dark doorways with no expectations, looking out upon a world of meaningless coming and going" (232).

Farming might seem the likeliest option, but as McNickle (born in 1904) grew up on the Flathead Reservation in the same time he would set *The Surrounded,* federal policy was yanking farming away from Flathead Indians. Modeste's barely active farm is the only Indian-owned farm in the novel until Archilde inherits Max's farm. With allotment throwing open reservation lands to white "settlers," the U.S. Reclamation Service undertook a massive project to irrigate Indian lands—not for Indian farmers but instead for white farmers buying out Indian farmers and ranchers. Presumably, that explains why Max shifts from cattle ranching to farming (15, 27, 177). Many displaced Indians had nowhere else to go and few other options for income-producing work. By 1936, the year *The Surrounded* was published, the Flathead Agency superintendent reported that 70,000 acres had been irrigated. "Of this, 65,000 acres belong to the white man; about 3,000 acres are Indian land which is leased [i.e., to whites]; and only 1,800 acres of irrigated lands are actually being cultivated by the Indians" (L. W. Shotwell, 29). For a while, many Indians managed economically not by wage labor but by leasing unirrigated timber lands to logging companies. Then the depression hit and the demand for lumber went bust, leaving Indians on the Flathead Reservation so hard up that the New Deal Indian Emergency Conservation Work (IECW) program ended up hiring a much higher proportion of men there than on most other reservations.[18] More broadly, while the details and mechanisms varied, the Flathead pattern of increasingly successful farming until allotment, followed by a terrible, allotment-driven economic collapse, proved typical across diverse reservations (see especially Leonard A. Carlson).

McNickle tells the history in *Wind from an Enemy Sky*, a more directly political novel about the fictional Little Elk Reservation. None of the Little Elks will take farming seriously except Henry Jim, who betrays his people to the white authorities and sets himself up as a federally sponsored model farmer. Even when New Deal reformers encourage farming, they get nowhere (36–38, 177–79). One character describes what McNickle claims "actually happened on the Flathead reservation" (quoted in Owens's afterword to the novel, 258; see also Shotwell):

"After the land was divided among the Indians and white men were invited—exhorted, really, with literature advertising the rare qualities of soil and climate and mountain wealth—a grave miscalculation was discovered. The land was really too arid and parched to make a crop oftener than once every four or five years. . . . So Congress authorized the construction of an irrigation system. . . . The mountains were still owned by the Indians—no white man wanted to homestead a mountain peak—and the water flowing out of them was certainly their property. . . . Very few Indians had taken pieces of land in the open valley when the reservation was divided up. They knew about the hot, dry summers, the treeless, unsheltered flats. They made their selections in the foothills, in the timber country, along forested streams. Consequently, when their main perennial streams were blocked off and diverted out to the dry valley, only the white homesteaders benefited. No compensation went to the Indians for this appropriation of their property. . . . The Indians had received money for the land which had been taken over by the homesteaders— at a dollar and a quarter an acre, I believe. This was not a negotiated price. The government . . . just said 'That's what we'll pay, in order to encourage strangers to come and take your land.' This revenue was deposited in the United States Treasury. . . . And would you believe it, . . . this money was used by the government to pay for surveys, soil studies, engineering estimates and all manner of preliminary work that went into the development of the irrigation project, to benefit the government-invited homesteaders." (192–93)

As Max puts it in *The Surrounded*, "People are starving! They're freezing to death in those shacks by the church. They don't know why; they had nothing to do with it" (147). People who do not pay heed to the market economy are not likely to understand how their indifference to the market sets them up as its easiest victims.

McNickle genders his portrait of economic misery, fixing on market-

Fig. 4. A detail from this U.S. Reclamation Service photograph in front of the St. Ignatius mission, model for the mission in *The Surrounded,* appears on the front cover of the current paperback reprint of the novel, with the young boy at the right cropped off. The picture dates from 1909, when the Flathead Reservation was caught in the controversy over allotment and McNickle was five years old. To John Fahey, who reprints the same photo in his history of the Flatheads, the men's "clothing . . . ranges from the western dandy at the left to the fullblood in blanket" at the middle (216). The boy shows his face to the camera, unlike the supposed dandy, while the three men's styles of masculinity loom next to the boy like possible options for his uncertain future. Courtesy of the National Archives—Rocky Mountain Region, Denver, Colorado. Subjects and photographer not identified.

driven work for money as an engine of masculine identity. Women work outside the money economy, following Native and non-Native models, as we have seen with Catharine, and no one opposes either model to the other as an authenticity test for femininity. But in the novel's market economy, the reservation's economic hopelessness opens no place for Indian masculinity. That is why Archilde plans to leave: "'Tell me what you think a fellow can do here—steal horses like Louis? Drink and run around? No. The world's big. I'll find something to do'" (15).

He has no Indian father to frame his impulses and curiosities about Indian masculinity, nor even any Indian father-figure, an absence that points again to the novel's slender portrait of local reservation culture. The blind Modeste may strike us as refreshingly unpatriarchal, but he never strikes Archilde as a model for the future of Indian masculinity. He is the past. In his place, Archilde endures the alternately gentle and cruel

Fig. 5. Set next to fig. 4, this photograph underlines the staged quality of both pictures. Amid the representations imposed by the photographer and the wider photographic event, including the horizontal sense of communal space in the rectangular picture frame, the cabin roofs and walls, and the wheel ruts in the foreground, each man negotiates his allotted vertical space. Meanwhile, someone—the man in the blanket or perhaps the photographer—challenges the notion of separate, predictable spaces by placing the blanketed man's hat on the ground between the blanketed man and his neighbor, echoing the tepee positioned in the center where it interrupts the cabins' domination. Courtesy of the National Archives—Rocky Mountain Region, Denver, Colorado. Subjects and photographer not identified.

paternalism of the white Fathers and of his own white father. But they too are the past. It is no wonder that Archilde wants to go away, at least until he feels the siren's tug of stereotypical roles awaiting him from the patriarchy of the past, two roles that reinforce and contradict each other: his responsibilities as wealthy man of the family after his father's death, and the erotically stirring irresponsibilities of his newfound heterosexuality as a wild young man with a girlfriend, Elise La Rose.

Perhaps the worry over "chaos about an Indian's homestead" and its pressure on masculinity tumbles McNickle off the tightrope and into internalized self-hate, but he spins a variation when he gets to the delightful Elise, the gendered exception that proves the rule. She is the only major character that critics have mostly ignored, perhaps because she finds such fun in tossing around gender expectations, not a topic that American Indian studies has tended to zero in on until recently.

Elise has the attitude toward work that the novel otherwise associates with young Indian men: "She was one of those easy-going people who never cared what they did, just so they didn't work hard or never had to live by rules. Perhaps rules were even worse than work. . . . They could get along with anybody, except a fellow who liked to work or who lived in an orderly manner. For such a fellow they had only contempt" (252). Elise runs around like a guy, riding, driving, swearing, smoking, fighting, and drinking. Indifferent as she may seem to feminine expectations, her indifference itself is also a particular feminine type. With her short hair and tough mouth, she is a takeoff on Brett Ashley of Hemingway's *The Sun Also Rises*, or simply a flapper, Montana version, complete with a "boy's strength" (251)—not a man's—and an indifference to cooking.[19]

If critics have neglected Elise, reviewers did not. The only favorable notice came from the *New Republic*'s Mary Heaton Vorse, McNickle's new socialist feminist colleague at the Office of Indian Affairs, whose review mentioned "an Indian girl, . . . gay, vital, with some essential Indian quality still undestroyed" (295). Elsewhere, even otherwise favorable reviews included such comments as "The Indian girl is profane and reckless, without morals or regard for the law of either race" (*Miami Herald*). "Elise, hardboiled and profane, [is] typical of the modern young Indian who has seemingly exchanged the best of his ancient heritage for the worst of our cynical modernism" (*Oakland Tribune*). The *Camden Post* decried Elise and the dialogue late in the book—presumably Elise's dialogue—lamenting the "blunder" that we must read so far into the novel "before we encounter the heroine. . . . Toward the end the Indians tend to talk with a crude vulgarity which makes us wonder if they really do speak quite so much like a Hemingway novel. In any case such unrestraint brands the book as almost too crude for art." The *Waterville Times* took particular offense, oddly punning on Elise's insistence that she likes "tail" (290): "Your fossilized old fogy of a reviewer frankly did not find this lustful, carnal minded little animal the appealing figure that her creator evidently intended her to be. We must admit that we were more than a little shocked at the language used by this very plain-spoken damsel. In short, her choice of words is hardly that of a Lady Chesterfield. It seems a pity that Mr. McNickle . . . should have seen fit to besmirch the tail end of his novel with such unnecessary filth." To the dismay and—I suspect—to the pleasure of such readers, Elise takes all the initiative with Archilde. They first meet when she gallops after him, bests him in a race, and carries the reversal of gender roles so far as to ride off with his handkerchief. Soon, surprised that he "hasn't got a girl already" (223), she leads Archilde—sometimes literally by the arm—to drink, dance, fight, and make love. Which all says as much about Archilde as about Elise and paves the way for the end of the novel.

SHOOTING THE SHERIFF

The keenly plotted denouement, with its perfect-pitch retake on rituals from the crime story and the western, restages the earlier pivotal scene in the mountains. This second time around, Elise unexpectedly fuses the plot functions of Louis and Catharine. Like Louis, she makes trouble and then rides irresponsibly off into the mountains. As before, when Archilde and Louis get so caught up with each other that they do not notice the warden ride up, so now Archilde and Elise get so caught up with each other (more happily, to be sure) that they do not notice Sheriff Quigley closing in. As before, when Catharine kills the warden while Archilde watches passively, so now, while Archilde watches again, Elise kills the sheriff.

The novel's conclusion turns on its ideological interrogation of a plot issue: who shot the sheriff? Elise pulls the trigger, but does she pull it by herself? Who or what invites her to pull the trigger? How much does Archilde produce the conditions that nudge Elise into pulling the trigger, and how much is whatever pulls Archilde or Elise a broader ideological force? The concluding fiasco depends on Archilde's passivity. Elise can take charge, leading him away by the arm and destroying everything, because for days Archilde blanks out in shock at his mother's death. Catharine and Elise kill the outward figures and instruments of white authority, but ideologically, despite Archilde's objections, they come across as doing what by some frames gets read as Archilde's dirty work. If we can read his decision not to shoot the deer in cultural as well as personal terms, then we can also ask what we gain and lose by a cultural reading of the way Archilde's mother and Elise displace what many in their worlds would see as his role, his stereotypically masculine agency. The women wield the weapons, and Archilde cannot shoot or will not shoot.

In this way, the novel climbs back onto its tightrope. It repeatedly walks to the edge of misogyny and then leaves us with a stew of interpretive questions. We could read Archilde as the victim of women, even of a feminine usurpation of agency that supposedly would better be left to men, or if not to men—since after all the novel's men include a gallery of scoundrels—then at least to men of measured wisdom like Archilde. Meanwhile, Archilde's masculinity is also at issue, perhaps also in misogynist ways, if we see the novel as gradually gathering to critique him as a castrated, intellectualized wimp, the same would-be hero who, after he can't do the manly thing and shoot the buck, walks back to his momma

fearful that his "explanation sounded weak." But such a reading sub-
scribes to a caustic ideology of gender that we can also see the novel as
challenging, precisely because an ideology like that reduces Archilde and
the characters around him to such judgments. It locks characters into the
humorless box of prescriptive realism, which dictates that characters must
be "positive role models," strong sensitive women and strong (but not too
strong) sensitive men.[20] We could see Archilde's promise and failure bio-
graphically, as a condensation of the intellectual McNickle's own pride
and self-doubt, writing far from the reservation in New York and then an-
gling to trade on his probably exaggerated modicum of Indian "blood" to
land a position at the Office of Indian Affairs. Biography and the interpretation of characters may matter, but much else is at stake in the context of a history and mythology suggesting that contact has had a differ-
ential effect on Native peoples according to gender.

As we have seen, it is sometimes said that contact with European peoples did more to displace traditional masculine roles and work patterns
than to displace traditional feminine roles. Whether accurate history or
colonialist and misogynist presumption, that belief deserves more concentrated study. One model comes in Carol Devens's *Countering Colonization: Native American Women and Great Lakes Missions, 1630–1900,* which
does not address the same setting as *The Surrounded* but is suggestive nevertheless. Although Devens may be too quick to suppose pre-contact har-
mony between genders, she builds a fascinating narrative of the way contact divided the genders by drawing men more intricately into the
white-led economy and institutions, thus encouraging women to remain
more traditional, and by circulating missionary ideologies that patronized
women. In response, she sees Native women much more than men as
tending to resist the encroachments of white culture.

All this loosely fits what happens in *The Surrounded* in the sense that,
rather than simply mirroring a history that takes shape in something like
Devens's pattern, McNickle's novel also tries to interpret and resist that
history. It calls out not only for more agency and resistance from men, but
also for more purposeful agency at large, as opposed to the impulsive, un-
meditated reflexes of Catharine's revenge, Elise's private quarrel, or
Louis's petty greed. At the same time, it also critiques Archilde's ener-
vated contemplation, so curiously reminiscent of the more feckless Chal's
wasting away in *Sundown.* Archilde cannot save his people, least of all by
the lonely heroism of mere example that is all he aspires to even in his
moments of ambition. Nor does anything in the novel suggest the alternative of political organization, either locally or more widely. But those are
the default alternatives, and they match the activist shape of McNickle's
remaining career as BIA official and cofounder of the National Congress

of American Indians. Shooting the sheriff, after all, doesn't accomplish much. *The Surrounded* can finally stand, therefore, as a critique of narrow reaction and a call for more imaginative, more organized responses, a call that McNickle and others increasingly heeded in political activism and in Native American writing that carries a wider vision of political and imaginative possibility than such founding works as *Cogewea, Sundown,* and *The Surrounded.*

CHAPTER 4

Text, Lines, and Videotape: Reinventing Oral Stories as Written Poems

The Surrounded turns to traditional oral storytelling to construct Indian modernity in written fiction. Following a kindred impulse, the outside world of modernity seeks to temper the new age of mechanical reproduction by turning to a nostalgically recovered orality. Ironically, it often recovers its ties to orality through mechanical reproduction, through Indian oral stories transformed into writing and printed either as set pieces in novels or as Indian "poetry." Picking up on that notion of orality as a lever for the invention of Native American literature, this chapter looks historically at the transcription of traditional Indian oral stories and the cultural translation of transcribed, translated stories into Indian "poetry"—an invention of an "Indian literature" that happens not to be written by Indians yet remains foundational to many non-Indians' imagination of what Indian writing might be. I address a body of translation and transcription theory that has proved enormously influential in Indian studies and in the wider study of oral literature and folklore. As McNickle's prose fiction captures the dominant culture's growing identification between orality and Indianness, the production of Indian oral stories as literary poetry merges the Indian, the oral, and the poetical.

A remarkable thing has happened over the last few decades in the tortured history of transcribing and translating traditional Native American oral narrative into written English literature. Not everyone is content with oral stories in the form that McNickle follows in *The Surrounded.* Two brilliant scholar-translators, Dell Hymes and Dennis Tedlock, have made curiously similar and extravagant claims for how traditional Native American oral narrative should be put into writing, and their methods have become canonical. Hymes argues that Native American oral story should be written as "verse," and Tedlock argues that it should be written as "poetry." As a particular practice, there is nothing wrong with transcribing oral story as poetry or verse, and in the hands of Hymes and Tedlock it has led to exceptionally good translations. But as a canonical practice or an interpretation of narrative orality, it causes serious problems.[1]

The translation of Native oral forms into written poetic forms has a long history. Although the line divisions of poetry are visual and written, certain forms, especially song and ritual, seem to fit what readers often assume they "hear" when they read poems. For an early example in English, scholars point to Henry Timberlake's 1765 rendition of a Cherokee "WAR-SONG" in heroic couplets: "Like men we go, to meet our country's foes, / Who, woman-like, shall fly our dreaded blows."[2] From Timberlake, to Teddy Roosevelt's endorsement of Natalie Curtis's influential *The Indians' Book* ("These songs cast a wholly new light—on the depth and dignity of Indian thought, the simple beauty and strange charm—the charm of a vanished elder world—of Indian poetry"), to Paul G. Zolbrod's modern edition of *Diné Bahane': The Navajo Creation Story*, admirers have called on the term *poetry* as a generalized figure of praise for Native eloquence.[3] As early as 1815, Walter Channing celebrated "the oral literature" of American "aborigines" as "the very language for poetry." An anonymous 1840 article suggests that "the trochee predominates" in Indian songs and that "the polysyllabic character of the language is adverse to short lively metres" (qtd. in William M. Clements, "Tokens," 37, 39, and *Native,* 98, 100). Such major figures in the history of textualizing American Indian oral art as Henry Rowe Schoolcraft, whose *Algic Researches* (1839) began the large-scale translation of Native American oral narrative into English and on whom Longfellow drew for his 1855 *Song of Hiawatha,* and Daniel Garrison Brinton, who brought out an eight-volume Library of Aboriginal American Literature from 1883 to 1890, repeatedly drew on the notion of poetry as a metaphor for Indian verbal art (Clements, *Native,* 122, 136–46).

In their desire to write Native oral forms into the sanctified status of literature, many nineteenth-century commentators anticipate later scholars. More loosely, they also anticipate novelists like McNickle, Momaday, and Silko, who integrate transcribed, translated oral texts into their efforts to invent a form for Indian novels. Taking prosody as a defining metonymy of poetry, nineteenth-century commentators seem to believe that the discovery of meter will propel oral forms into the mystified status of poetry and literature. In the late 1840s, Schoolcraft published a questionnaire about "Indian Songs" that asked: "Is there any rhyme in them? Are the words collocated so as to observe the laws of quantity? In other words, are they measured, or are the accents in them found to recur in fixed and regular intervals?" As William M. Clements puts it, when Schoolcraft "did not find such features in the [song] material he was translating . . . he added them."[4]

Eventually, many translators produced four texts of the same story: a transcription, a transliteration, a "literal translation," and a "free translation" in more idiomatic or literary English. That practice helped blur—or multiply—the lines between ethnology, folklore, and literature. Washington Matthews, for example, one of the most famous translators, whose "free translation" of a Navajo prayer Momaday draws on for the title of his novel *House Made of Dawn*, welcomed poets who might draw on his translations but warned them not to "garble or distort." Matthews referred to songs—but not to prayers or "legends"—as if they were poems.[5]

As it happens, the reception history of Matthews's translations of songs and prayers conflated them both into poetry almost indiscriminately. First came Curtis's influential collection, where (with an oddly false sense of novelty) she explained: "The songs in this book are written after a new manner in that corresponding musical phrases are placed one beneath another like lines of verse. This system makes the form of the song to flash before the eye like the form of a stanza in poetry" (xii). Curtis says that the songs are *like* poetry, not that they *are* poetry, but several movements in the history of English-language and particularly American poetry converged to overdetermine their reception as poetry. Matthews's unrhymed, metrically irregular "free" translations came out not long before the emerging prominence of free verse made it possible, and even likely, that "literary" readers would assimilate his lineated texts as lines of poetry. The terse, direct language of Matthews's prayer translations, even more than the occasionally poeticized language of his song translations, sounds something like Ezra Pound's *Cathay* (1915), which set a newly dominant model for translating east Asian poetry into English. And because they carry so little narrative, his translations of songs and prayers also sound rather like the imagist poetry that helped lead to *Cathay*. Indeed, Mary Austin and other modernists eagerly likened imagist poetry to translations and "versions" of Native song.[6] *Poetry* magazine, the vanguard journal of the new modernist poetry, came out with two issues devoted mostly to Indian "poetry" (February 1917, January 1920), some of it translated and some made up from scratch by romanticizing white poets, but none of it written by Indians, let alone written by Indians as poetry.

In response, there followed a series of widely publicized anthologies celebrating Indian "poetry," again without including work written by Indians. As the poet Chrystos wrote decades later in the 1990s,

> I'm invisible turn away ticking
> You won't find us in anthologies of american poets

> We forgot to sign that treaty
> Everybody likes to read the whites writing myths of us
> Us telling about us is too hard . . .
> *Hey I'm not screaming since you're not listening*
> (*Fire Power*, 69)

At this point, Indian poets were not even included in anthologies of Indian poetry, let alone anthologies of American poetry. Instead, the anthologized "poems" were spoken by Indians who did not think of their spoken rituals and songs as poems. These texts were then transcribed and translated (with varying skill), often by Indians as well as by whites, but credit was usually given only to whites, who were named individually, or to whites and to entire Indian "tribes" rather than to particular Indian speakers (no matter how learned and skilled), transcribers, and translators.[7] Meanwhile, of course, Indians were writing and sometimes publishing poems, and more Indians would have written if more were published. Yet, in a practice still alive and well, many anthologies appropriated excerpts from Matthews's song and prayer texts and from many other ethnographic texts, silently removing the commentary and apparatus so as to make them look more like the poems that such editors unambiguously claimed them to be. In presenting transcriptions of oral work apart from representations of its cultural setting, editors also depoliticized it, Craig S. Womack has argued, making Indian oral thinking and art more palatable to the dominant audience (51–74).

By the 1960s and 1970s the momentum of colonizing appropriation encouraged a crowd of well-meaning white poets who reworked material from the anthologies and from ethnographic sources in what came to be called the ethnopoetics movement, partly associated with Tedlock and culminating in Jerome Rothenberg's controversial *Shaking the Pumpkin* (1972, with revised editions in 1987 and 1991). By now, although the controversy continues, ethnopoetics has dropped out of favor, owing in part to the proliferation of contemporary Indian writing. Indeed, some contemporary Indian poets have published poems attacking ethnopoetics, including, before Chrystos, Wendy Rose and Ray A. Young Bear. Leslie Marmon Silko ("Old-Time Indian Attack"), Geary Hobson, and Rose ("Just What's All This Fuss") have written essays building the case against ethnopoetics with impassioned detail.[8]

The debate over ethnopoetics has a long history and a telling cultural arc. To his critics, Rothenberg amounts—in effect—to an unwitting and well-intentioned James Macpherson, the fraud who in the 1760s claimed to have transcribed ancient oral Gaelic poems, which he then presented in English translation, though Macpherson largely wrote them himself. In

Macpherson's day, the excitement over bardic revivalism led Scottish, Welsh, and Irish readers to see bardic traditions as historic and national. By contrast the English vogue for bardic poetry, shaped by the colonizers' fears of inadequacy and by their envy of a cultural vitality that they projected onto the colonized, saw the bardic as literary more than as historical and national (Katie Trumpener, 6–7 and passim, especially chapter 3). Similarly, the white modernist vogue for Indian "poetry," shaped—Silko argues in "An Old-Time Indian Attack"—by a white fear of inadequacy and by white envy, projects a romantic value onto Indian culture while nevertheless distorting Indian texts by lifting them out of their cultural settings and transposing them into a traditionally Euro-American literary setting.

All this background suggests that, much as Hymes's and Tedlock's ideas have become associated with them personally, in many respects those ideas and their reception are sites where a broader set of ideologies and discourses interpellate Hymes and Tedlock and their audiences. Romanticized ideas of "the Indian" and romanticized ideas of poetry converge in the reassurance of desperately sought mutual corroboration. To be sure, Hymes and Tedlock seized the moment, innovatively folding Indian oral narrative into the already highly invested space of Indian oral "poetry." But even before Hymes and Tedlock, their claims were already being prepared, and so was the eager and (for the most part) surprisingly uncritical reception of those claims. The point is not so much that if they hadn't come along, they would have had to be invented. The point is that in crucial ways they already were being invented. Thus, when I refer to Tedlock and Hymes, I refer not only to those particular innovators but also to a much broader cultural history that they have come to represent. That cultural history traces a key movement in American poetry, and it also traces the wider (mostly non-Indian) reception of Indian orality, writing orality into a partly enabling, partly repressive metonymy and mythology of Indian identity itself.

My goal is not to diminish Hymes's and Tedlock's translations. Instead, I seek to reinterpret the social ideology of genre implicit in their arguments, as well as the accompanying assumptions about orality and Indianness, and then briefly to look at related issues emerging with the growing interest in video renditions of traditional storytelling. Specifically, both Hymes and Tedlock not only claim that Indian oral story should be transferred to the page as verse or poetry. They also slide quickly into the claim that it *is* verse or poetry. What starts as a metaphor or simile soon takes over as an identification, a "discovery" that traditional Native American oral narrative is really verse. Columbus has been foisted on us yet again.

Hymes and Tedlock read their "discovery" of verse and poetry as a discovery of value, in effect implying that if Native story were not absorbed into the colonizing culture's notion of verse, it would not have as much value. That is to misconstrue the social relation between power, genre, and value, as well as the fluidity of oral genres and the role of audiences. Audiences can choose to hear, transcribe, or read oral narrative as verse, but they cannot discover that it *is* verse. Therefore, Hymes and Tedlock's "discoveries" about the narratives and their value are actually interpretations of the audiences that they write for and represent, the audiences that they argue put more value on oral narrative if it is cast as verse. The real purpose, I suggest, of presenting traditional Indian oral narrative as poetry or verse is polemical and canonizing. In the social ideology of genre, verse and poetry have canonical status and even an elite class status. If their elite status can be claimed for traditional Indian oral narrative, then the status of traditional narrative (and those who study it) can be raised, but at the cost of complicity with a discourse of colonizing appropriation.

Unlike Tedlock, Hymes does not often work with tape recordings or storytellers. He retranslates other translations, usually texts made long ago in languages that he has studied but that no living person speaks, such as Melville Jacobs's transcripts and translations of Victoria Howard's Clackamas Chinook tales, told in 1929 and 1930. Here is how Hymes begins his landmark argument for transcribing and translating Native American oral narrative as verse, in an article and book chapter titled "Discovering Oral Performance and Measured Verse in American Indian Narrative":

> I should like to discuss a discovery which may have widespread relevance. The narratives of the Chinookan peoples of Oregon and Washington can be shown to be organized in terms of lines, verses, stanzas, scenes, and what one may call acts. A set of discourse features differentiates narratives into verses. Within these verses, lines are differentiated, commonly by distinct verbs. . . . The verses themselves are grouped, commonly in threes and fives. These groupings constitute "stanzas" and, where elaboration of stanzas is such as to require a distinction, "scenes." In extended narratives, scenes themselves are organized in terms of a series of "acts."[9]

The hedges here straddle the Grand Canyon. The acts, for example, are not acts; they are "acts" or "what one may call acts," although the quotation marks and qualifiers will soon evaporate. The question is whether Hymes's claims are indeed a discovery, or whether they are, as I will argue, an interpretation. The difference may seem minor, not only to poststructuralists who see everything as interpretation anyway but also to positivists who stand by Hymes's distinction. Either way, however, the difference between discovery and interpretation grows vast because the rhetoric of discovery so pervasively runs away with the ongoing argument and practice of Hymes and his followers.

The metaphor and simile (now one, now another) of "verse" run away with the argument, because once Hymes and his followers decide that a narrative divides into acts, scenes, stanzas, verses (in the narrower sense of the term, as opposed to the broader sense of *verse* per se), and lines, then the mere process of figuring out where to make all those divisions takes over the discussion. For example, in by far the most famous text, Howard's "Seal and her younger brother lived there," a story that far more than any other has carried the burden of representing Hymes's argument and of representing traditional American Indian oral narrative to a wider scholarly public,[10] Hymes divides a 354-word story (in his translation) into 66 lines, 20 verses, 11 stanzas, and 3 scenes (he leaves out acts, apparently because the story is so short, possibly even a fragment). That requires 100 separate decisions about where to draw the line between one category and another (and countless decisions about where not to draw it, plus Hymes's decision to separate the title and the last line into categories by themselves). It is no wonder, then, that the translators' commentary for Hymesian texts reads like an account book. Visually, the numbers and letters that track the divisions stand out to the eye almost as much as the words. A given line, for example, can get tagged in Hymes's format as act II, scene [iii], stanza (B), verse (47), and line 216, a veritable thesaurus of categories that Susan Hegeman calls "intimidating" and "bizarre" (275). Sometimes Hymes makes acts part of a larger category he calls "parts," as if he has run out of terms from prosody and drama. And along with all these parsings out, he divides things on the page visually, starting each stanza at the left margin and then indenting the rest of the stanza one, two, or more tab-spaces per line, a sign that he has been reading William Carlos Williams or his imitators.

Why make such divisions? Because the visual alignments, Hymes explains, are "more attractive" and hence make the work more accessible ("*In Vain,*" 341). Otherwise, Hymes's explanations are labored and inconsistent, except that they consistently dissolve the metaphor or simile of verse into a transparent identification: the oral narrative *is* verse. Here is the paragraph where Hymes most directly explains his general method:

> *Discovery of Verse and Line.* The principle of organization has to do with the initial elements of sentences. Certain initial elements frequently recur in structurally significant roles. In this respect, and some others, Chinookan narratives possess formulaic elements of the sort so important in the work on epic of Milman Parry, Albert Lord, and others. There is a fundamental difference, however, between the two. The formulaic elements of Slavic, Greek, and other

oral poetries occur within, manifest and adapt to, verse that is regulated by another principle. In Chinookan and, I suspect, in American Indian oral narrative generally, the recurrent initial elements represent the regulatory principle itself. They are aspects of the measuring which makes the material verse. (*"In Vain,"* 318)

By this point the markers of division have changed. First they were "discourse features" (a category so wide that it excludes nothing) for verses and verbs for lines; now they are "initial elements."

The wavering argument soon focuses in an astonishing tautology that runs prolifically through Hymes's labored explanations. "The discovery of such a pattern is not arbitrary, because it is governed by the coherence and articulation of the particular narrative, and in addition, by a rhetorical pattern . . . : *onset, ongoing, outcome*" (*"In Vain,"* 320). Later he adds, "The threefold rhetorical pattern of expectations (onset, ongoing, outcome) can be recognized at each level of this organization" (*"In Vain,"* 331). First he uses the pattern to prove the divisions, and then he uses the divisions to prove the pattern. Meanwhile, the criteria of onset, ongoing, and outcome are so general—so close to beginning, middle, and end—that they are typical of almost all narrative, hardly the criteria to evidence a particular and fabulously arcane prosody unconsciously embedded in oral storytelling.

Hymes's followers repeat the tautology. M. Dale Kinkade, for example, one of Hymes's most interesting acolytes, divides his translation of an Upper Chehalis version of "Bluejay and His Sister" into Hymesian units partly by the principle of letting initial particles, such as the word *húy* (*and*), mark off the units. He then uses the recurrence of *húy* at the beginning of the units to make a point about the structure of the units: "The use of *húy* can easily be seen to have major structural significance. A glance down the left edge of the text will show that the most common word to begin a stanza . . . is *húy*" (283). But he has used *húy* to help determine where the stanzas begin in the first place. So much for "structural significance," an inflated category in any case, since Kinkade is too caught up in the Hymesian tautology to say what the significance is. The busywork of Hymesian transcription and translation (figuring out where to divide all those acts, scenes, stanzas, verses, and lines) can easily become an end in itself.

In broader terms, Hymes defends his system by arguing that "verses are recognized, not by counting parts, but by recognizing repetition within a frame, the relation of putative units to each other within a whole. Covariation between form and meaning, between units and a recurrent Chinookan pattern of narrative organization, is the key" (*"In Vain,"* 318). He derives the units from the recurrent pattern, but he derives the recurrent pattern from the units. The "covariation" sounds seriously theoretical, but it is the same old tautology. As Anthony Mattina asks, "if there is no consistent formal marking, then how is there 'covariation?'" (134). Hymes's choice of formal marking proves the covariation, but the covariation proves his choice of formal marking. Hymes supposes that formal organization is simply a characteristic of a text, but that assumption proceeds too innocently of any consideration of readers. The perception of form derives not necessarily from something in the text, but rather from a method of reading. Different methods of reading produce the perception of different forms, even in the same text. That is the difference between interpretation and discovery. Hymes piles elaborate detail upon detail, as if that could prove the system he purports to discover, but he underestimates the capacity of eager readers and determined critics to find system in any arrangement or transcription of any text.

Which raises a question of intent. At first, Hymes did not talk about intent, but his system is so elaborate and so independent of any claim that the storytellers thought or even could think consciously about Hymes's patterns, that it was clear that he made no claims for intent. More recently, Hymes has brushed the question aside: "The underlying patterns revealed by ethnopoetics," he says, "are not available in consciousness [to the storytellers?]. . . . Like the beautiful and complex patterns of the languages themselves, the patterns that make so many Indian narratives a kind of poetry are acquired and employed without awareness" ("Anthologies," 42). The problem is that such highly foregrounded patterns of repetition, and the very concept of categories like act, scene, stanza, verse, and line, are by definition categories of intent. To attribute such "obvious, inevitable, . . . inescapable" ("*In Vain,*" 320), and by definition intentional categories to Native storytellers and at the same time assume that the tellers are unaware of the categories, like the proverbial poets who don't know it, is disturbingly condescending. It is like saying that Shakespeare wrote rhymed sonnets in three quatrains and a couplet—without knowing it. Hymes's discovery is too specific in its multilayered divisions to proceed apart from intent, yet too invisible—before he discovered it—to be intended. Hymes associates his "discovery" with other scholars' discovery of category divisions in Greek and Serbo-Croatian epic, but Greek and Serbo-Croatian singers were conscious of or could recognize the category divisions that scholars had to discover,[11] whereas Hymes never comes near to such a claim for the tellers of traditional Native American oral story. Indeed, there is immensely more formal and cultural variety in Native American oral story than in Greek and Serbo-Croatian epic.

In one article, Hymes goes so far as to expand his argument from

"American Indian oral narrative generally" to all narrative: "My studies of narrative in various languages persuade me that . . . the rehearsal of experience in narrative takes the form of lines. . . . The presence of lines becomes enough to have words called 'poems.'" He continues: "What is the more striking given the commitment of anthropologists not to impose ethnocentric categories on native materials, is the belated recognition that volumes of myths and tales are not in fact sequences of prose paragraphs, but sequences of groups of lines" ("Poetry and Anthropology" 407–8). Beginning with a circuitous paraphrase of "I think" that depends on the claim of expertise rather than on arguments from expertise, this slides to a shifty "enough" and then to a pseudo-logical argument that since anthropologists don't like to project what they look for onto what they see, therefore, when they see it anyway, it isn't a projection; it's really there. Then it concludes with a slipped-in "fact," so that instead of saying plainly that stories come in lines, he makes that claim in an S-curve detour of prepositions and elisions that covers up its status as interpretation: "but [are in fact] sequences of groups of lines."

The point is not to criticize Hymes as an interpreter of stories. The structures he describes have real interest. But they are structures, rather than *the* structures. They are interpretations, rather than discoveries. Kinkade seems to admit that distinction, but then declines to follow through on its implications: "Different readers react to different features of the presentation, and hence can see different groupings and divisions. Presumably, however, these different approaches will have much in common, and will not detract from the concept of verse structure. In the long run, one analysis should be preferable" (288). These presumptions seem to me exactly wrong. Not only does the concept of verse structure depend on the capacity to identify the particular groupings and divisions, but in the long run, *many* analyses should be preferable to one. If one analysis is preferable, then it is indeed a matter of discovery. But if we prefer many analyses (keeping in mind that many does not mean any—we can still choose selectively), then the act of analysis becomes an act of interpretation. For if we see how translations are constructions rather than discoveries, then that, as Tejaswini Niranjana puts it, "shows how translation is always *producing* rather than merely reflecting or imitating an 'original'" (81; see especially chapter 2). It is easy, for example, to propose alternatives to Kinkade's system of divisions, as Hymes himself has done.[12] Kinkade notes that he begins Act II at a point that allows the beginning of Act II to parallel the beginning of Act I. Such logic shows what happens when we mistake interpretation for discovery. Kinkade's decision produces an artful symmetry. But there are many other principles of aesthetics, so that there is no reason to assume that the story has to be symmetrical. Moreover, if we want symmetry, we could just as well achieve it by splitting Acts I and II four lines later so that, instead of making Act II begin as Act I begins, Act I could begin and end in the same way. Narrative, especially oral narrative, is like pie; there are many ways to slice it. You can prefer one way, but you cannot discover that it is *the* way.[13]

Unlike Hymes, Tedlock worked with storytellers and their spoken language, tape recording Zuni storytellers Andrew Peynetsa and Walter Sanchez. With Joseph Peynetsa, he translated their stories from Zuni to English, producing what is so far the most influential volume of traditional Indian oral narratives translated into English, *Finding the Center: Narrative Poetry of the Zuni Indians* (first edition 1972).[14] As he explains his methods, Tedlock also critiques earlier translators. He shows how they added expressions that have little or no analogue in the Zuni language or in Zuni storytelling, and how they suffered from pre–tape-recorder dictation and transcription techniques and from unimaginative transformations into English. On all these grounds Tedlock's critique of earlier transcriptions and translations seems to me a monument in the history and theory of translation, and on linguistic grounds his translations are a triumph both in the texts they produce and, compared to earlier translators, in the explanations he provides. For Tedlock's explanations advertise the elaborate mediation of the transcribing and translating process rather than disguising it as if the published result were transparent and inevitable, an unmediated equivalent to the oral text: spoken Zuni itself.[15]

Tedlock's great methodological innovation comes in his address to paralinguistic categories and their visual representation in transcription. Rather than giving a generalized version of a story, a generically Zuni version, he concentrates on transcribing the event-specific characteristics of a particular performance.[16] He gives stage directions (although not many, because, he explains, Zuni storytellers are not especially keyed to gesture, and his tape recorder wasn't much help with gestures anyway) and audience responses. He represents the storyteller's changes in volume, rendering louder speech in capital letters, LIKE THIS, and softer speech in smaller letters, like this. He shows a rise in pitch by making the words leap up from the line, like this, and a drop in pitch by making them step down, whether the change is sudden, or g

               r

                    a

                       d

                         u

                          a

l. (One mark of Tedlock's originality—and patience—is that he did all this before word-processing.) He stretches out a word that the storyteller holds for a lo——ng time. Tedlock understands that such distinctions are judgment calls, that, for example, to another transcriber his three degrees of volume—small type, ordinary type, and CAPITALS—could just as well come out as four or five or two degrees.[17] Just as helpfully, he does not let the relativity of such judgments deter him, for such judgments are inevitable, even for the transcriber who renders all speech in a single typeface. The point is not to avoid judgments so much as to make them, as much as possible, with a reflective attention to their meanings.

And most conspicuously and originally, although far less clearly, Tedlock transcribes pauses in the storyteller's speech by breaking the narrative into what he calls "lines," with each line break representing a moderate pause, and with a "strophe break" (*Finding*, 1st ed., xix–xx, xxxiii; 2d ed., xvi, xlv), marked by a dot between lines, representing a longer pause. If that risks confusion, since many readers make a point of *not* always pausing at the ends of poetic lines, especially enjambed lines, it also fills the printed page with an engrossing simulacrum of oral performance. Some readers might object to the way Tedlock's practice freezes the throwaway circumstances of one particular performance into a pristine final version, memorializing the storyteller's stutters, burps, and errors.[18] A pause to scratch is no longer a pause to scratch; it becomes a strophe break. But that is to miss that Tedlock does not presume to give us a pristine final version, nor could he give us one. Even a Modern Language Association–certified edition is never pristine, but always an imaginary snapshot of collated performances. By highlighting the contingency of his text, Tedlock provokes a sharper attention to how any text is a freeze-frame of textuality in process. Tedlock could underline that even more (if he had an indulgent publisher) by giving us more than one performance of the same story, but in lieu of that, his method helps us keep in mind that the single versions we get can never be anything purer than single versions. That is true of all texts, but a collation of many texts into one "authoritative" text can seem to erase its constructedness, versus the way that Tedlock's transcription of an individual performance more frankly highlights and celebrates its own contingency. Even readers who tire of reproducing that performance according to Tedlock's "Guide to Reading Aloud" (*Finding*, 1st ed., xxxiii–xxxv; 2d ed., xlv–xlvi) can pick up on it visually. They can "hear" what they see, as they do in reading the visual arrangement of any poetry. They may not raise their voices when the type turns to CAPITALS, and they may not pause when a line ends, but in each case they still see an imaged difference and its representation.

Having divided the transcript into lines, Tedlock decides that the result is poetry. Or rather, it often seems, having decided that Zuni oral narrative is poetry, he divides it into lines. It wouldn't matter which came first if Tedlock kept alert to the metaphoricity of his comparison between oral narrative and poetry, if he kept in mind that it *is* a comparison. But he soon dissolves the comparison into an identification. In "On the Translation of Style in Oral Narrative," Tedlock keeps the distinctions clear. He refers, for example, to "what I have chosen to call lines" (55). But in his book of Zuni translations, which is much more widely read, not only by students and nonacademic readers interested in Native American literature and culture but probably even by scholars, he is far less attentive to the distinction. Before he has even introduced his radically new system of transcription, he begins to describe what led him to think "that Zuni narrative might *be* poetry" (*Finding*, 1st ed., xviii; emphasis added). One moment Tedlock recognizes his own role in constructing Zuni storytelling into "lines": "I have broken Zuni narratives into lines," he writes (*Finding*, 1st ed., xix). The next moment, when he explains that "Zuni lines vary constantly in length" (*Finding*, 1st ed., xx), he takes poetic lines as an inherent characteristic of Zuni narrative. Even in the second edition of *Finding the Center* he continues to conflate discovering lines with constructing lines: "The most important step in scripting Zuni stories was finding the lines, and once I did they seemed quite obvious. I treated each definite pause as a line break" (2d ed., xvi). To treat the pauses as line breaks is one thing, but to find them—discover them—is something else and depends on Tedlock's first deciding to "treat" them, to construct the very line breaks that he later supposes he has discovered. Elsewhere, Tedlock insists plainly (in an article written as a poem) that

> anthropologists, folklorists, linguists, and oral historians
> . . . must stop treating oral narratives
> as if they were reading prose
> when in fact they are listening to dramatic poetry.[19]

Even so, when Tedlock transcribes oral narrative as "poetry," and when Hymes transcribes it as "verse," their transcriptions *are* verse and poetry. But the stories they transcribe are oral narratives, whereas verse, poetry, and prose, when defined by the presence or absence of line breaks, are characteristics of written language.[20] Tedlock confuses this issue. "The complications of poetic style," he writes, "have especially strong implications for those who seek to measure the social and psychological content of narrative by means of word counts. 'Killed the deer,' repeated three times in a line . . . , might well have been reduced to a single occurrence in the translations of the past" ("On the Translation of Style," 54). Indeed it might have, but that has nothing to do with whether the translations come as poetry or prose. He goes on in the same vein: "The treatment of oral narrative as dramatic poetry, then, clearly promises many analytical rewards. It should also be obvious that there are immediate aesthetic rewards. The apparent flatness of many past translations is . . . caused by the dictation process [versus Tedlock's tape recorder], the notion that content and form are independent, a pervasive deafness to oral qualities, and a fixed notion of the boundary between poetry and prose" ("On the Translation of Style," 54). None of this has anything to do with the decision to cast oral narrative as poetry. You can use a tape recorder and still transcribe the results as prose. You can write prose and still listen to "oral qualities" and see connections between form and content. And as for decoupling the boundary between poetry and prose, it is Tedlock, and not the transcribers into prose, who insists on the distinctiveness of poetry, who insists on drawing a line between poetry and prose. For Tedlock, poetry offers "immediate aesthetic rewards" that prose somehow cannot offer. But there is no way to show that poetry offers more of such rewards than prose, just as Jonathan Culler's critique (55–74) of Roman Jakobson's famous case for the distinctiveness of poetry argues that there is no way Jakobson can prove that poetry is more patterned than prose. Different ratios of patterning in poetry and prose are a function not so much of any difference between poetry and prose as of the difference between Tedlock and Jakobson's culturally interpellated attitudes to poetry and to prose, that is to say, the difference between the ways they read poetry and prose.[21]

Only if we succumb to the fallacy of technological determinism can we suppose that a given technology—including verbal forms like poetry or prose—produces a given effect: that, for example, radio sophisticates public discussion and TV dumbs it down. It depends on which radio and TV programs we listen to and watch and on how we listen and watch. In the same way, the effect of poetry or prose depends on the particular poetry and prose that we read and on how we read them, not on any inherent distinction between poetry and prose.

In perhaps the most acclaimed article on traditional Native storytelling, Barre Toelken and Tacheeni Scott, working with Toelken's recording of Yellowman, a Navajo storyteller, and inspired by Tedlock and Hymes, reconsider a coyote story that Toelken had earlier published as prose, retranscribing and retranslating it as poetry. Their revised text and commentary make dramatic improvements, which they offer as an argument for Tedlock and Hymes's claims that traditional oral story should be cast as poetry. In short, they change two variables, the format (from prose to poetry) and the words, but they attribute their new and improved results to one of the two variables. We could just as well demystify the difference between poetry and prose and argue that the improvements come not from the switch to poetry but instead from Scott's linguistic and cultural reinterpretation of Toelken's tape recording, which leads to the changed words.

In the same mode as Toelken and Scott, Joel Sherzer, who has produced some of the most distinguished applications of Hymes's and Tedlock's methods (*Native American Discourse, Verbal Art in San Blas*), takes up the dramatizing language of paradigm discovery to say that he speaks in the tradition of Hymes, Tedlock, and "a growing number of others" (he names ten distinguished scholar-translators) who are "breaking with an earlier generation," because they "believe that Native American oral discourse and especially verbal art is best analyzed and represented as linear poetry rather than block prose. In particular, we pay considerable attention to such features of poetic organization as grammatical and semantic parallelism, intonation, pause patterning, and other oral features of the dramatization of the voice. . . . The determination of line and verse structure is central to this enterprise" ("Modes of Representation," 426–27). The slope is slippery from "best" to "as" to "features of poetic organization," especially because not one of these "features" is specific to *poetic* organization. Not one has anything to do with line and verse structure.

The argument for transcribing oral narrative as poetry, therefore, comes not from any discovery that it *is* poetry so much as from the polemical and canonizing effect of reading it as *if* it were poetry. Scholars and canonizers need a legitimation strategy for themselves and for the materials they study. People have always told and listened to oral story, but in the academic and "literary" world—outside the often condescended-to enclave of folklore scholarship—oral story has never held the class status of poetry. Thus, from Hymes and Tedlock through Sherzer and Zolbrod, the claims for oral story as poetry, ostensibly truth claims about oral story, are actually bids for cultural capital. Tedlock contends: "Some of the features of oral narrative which have been branded 'primitive,' on the basis of comparisons with written prose fiction, can now be understood as 'poetic' instead. It has been said, for example, that while most of our own prose narrative is highly 'realistic,' primitive narrative is full of fantasy. . . . Yet when we encounter gross and unexplained distortions of reality in Yeats, for example, we are apt to call them not 'primitive' but 'dreamlike' or 'mystical' and to regard them as highly poetic"

("On the Translation of Style," 51). None of this has anything to do with an inherent difference between poetry and prose; it is only a rebuke to bad readings of prose. People who cannot see value in prose—or oral narrative—can perhaps learn to see that value, but to teach them to see it by clothing the oral narrative in the written dress of "poetry" is to concede the bias against the oral that we are supposedly trying to undermine. For such reasons, some scholars shy away from the term *literature* for Indian oral stories (e.g., David Murray, 13–14, Clements, *Native*, 98–99). Clements characterizes the issue as suggesting a conflict between the desire to see an identity and the desire to see a difference between Native texts and texts from the dominant culture (*Native*, passim, especially chapter 1). Clements's model can help us sustain the sense that we favor any point along that spectrum only by constructing a provisional way of looking at things for a particular set of purposes, not by discovering what Native texts finally are.

In his blunter fashion, Hymes makes much the same canonizing claim as Tedlock: "The discovery of such organization in Native American narratives . . . makes it possible, indeed essential, to regard such texts as works of literary art" ("*In Vain,*" 332). But surely they are readable as "literary art" whether they are organized as Hymes claims or not. It is only that if they are organized in "attractive" verses, then it may be easier to convince some people that they are literary art. But if that is what it takes, then they are canonized at the expense of being assimilated into the very canon that scholars of traditional Native American oral literature are supposedly using them to change.

By contrast, the best polemic for the value of oral literature that I have seen comes in *Toward the Decolonization of African Literature*, by Chinweizu, Onwuchekwa Jemie, and Ihechukwu Madubuike (especially 25–87). They include oral narrative poetry among their examples, but they make no claims that oral narrative *is* poetry. Instead of crashing the elite party of poetry's cultural capital to gild oral literature by association, they argue frankly for the cultural capital of oral literature, with scorn for traditional European assumptions about what literature might—or might not—be taken as elite.

Even so, Tedlock and Hymes are probably right that more readers can be taught to see value in oral narrative if it hitches a ride on the mystified, hierarchical status of poetry. You could argue that the tactic has worked. Hymes's and Tedlock's translations have played a key role in the invention of Native American literature, the elevation of Native oral stories to the elite status of the literary. The question is, at what cost? If scholars draw attention to an underread literature by describing it in terms that replace its distinctiveness with something more familiar as high art, then they subvert what they had meant to respect. If the emergent cultural value of Native oral story (emergent, that is, outside the traditional contexts where it has long been accepted or even venerated) is made to hinge on the already dominant cultural value of poetry, then, as in an eclipse, the value attributed to poetry will screen out the value we are trying to attribute to oral story.

Meanwhile, the overwhelming majority of nonscholarly, commercial, and locally produced collections of traditional Indian oral story, including materials in schools and stores on and near reservations, continue to rely on prose, blithely oblivious to the scholarly canonization of Hymes and Tedlock. Under current conditions, it seems, prose can reach a larger audience. That could make an argument for translating in prose, but the larger audience that those texts reach is mostly not the elite or "art" audience that Hymes and Tedlock often seem to aspire to.

In that context, Hymesian and Tedlockian discourse unwittingly projects a mimicry of itself onto the texts it constructs. For when such discourse argues that traditional Native oral story is really poetry or—to apply Homi Bhabha's formulations—is "almost the same but not quite," or "almost the same but not white,"[22] the "poetry" then strikes back by mimicking and mocking the romance with poetry's mystified status. Meanwhile, the projected mimicry camouflages the mimicry produced by the colonized subjects, the storytellers. When Victoria Howard or Andrew Peynetsa tell "their" stories to Melville Jacobs or Dennis Tedlock, they join the anthropologists and their pursuits, and they also mimic and mock them, and mimic and mock their own subjectification, as well as the subjectification of Clackamas Chinook and Zuni cultures and the very notion that they or "their" intensely hybrid stories can "represent" those cultures. At the same time they appropriate such representations both for strategies of resistance and for strategies that resist the reduction of Native discourse to resistance. Such multiplicities—the detailed cultural politics and histories of oral story—are hard to see or hear through the fog of canonical debates about poetry and where to draw the line breaks.

Previously, the most skeptical responses to Hymes and Tedlock have come from Julian Rice (8–10, 131–40) and Anthony Mattina. Mattina found that publishers rejected his translations from Colville because he worked in prose rather than in Hymesian verse or Tedlockian poetry.[23] He finds Hymes's and Tedlock's theoretical claims "outlandish" and proposes an alternative, which he calls "Red English," on the model of Black English (130, 139–42). Although Mattina is a linguist, he offers no linguistic description of Red English, much in contrast to the detailed linguistic descriptions we have for Black English. He simply explains that his Colville cotranslator liked Red English, and since he liked it too, he uses her English to translate the Colville story "The Golden Woman." His argument for Red English, moreover, cannot provide the alternative he promises to Hymes and Tedlock, because it has nothing to do with the question of whether to translate in poetry or prose. Instead of describing Red English, Mattina simply gives some examples. One is a short piece by Pretty On-Top that concludes, "I was lonesome for you. / Was you lonesome for me when you went away" (141). Mattina's translation of "The Golden Woman" proceeds in much the same fashion, as when at the beginning of the story four brothers tell their father "We're done with this here grade school, and even if we stay here, we'd be staying here with you, and we won't learn nothing that way, just books" (Peter J. Seymour, *The Golden Woman,* 19). Plenty of people who are not "red" speak in such patterns, however, for the style that Mattina calls Red English has to do with class, not with race or literary genre. There may be such a thing as Red English, but you could not tell that from what Mattina says about it.[24] We might think of the Creek English in Alexander Posey's Fus Fixico letters and the related episodes in Craig S. Womack's critical writing, but those are Creek, not pan-Indian. And because we can write Red, working-class, or Creek English with or without line breaks, when it comes to deciding whether to transcribe oral story as either poetry or prose, Red English is a red herring.

Video offers a promising alternative; many viewers even imagine it as somehow truer than written texts. The fantasy—by now more pop than scholarly—that video captures an underlying real comes from a range of overlapping impulses that combine to overdetermine each other. These include an ideological longing to collapse the photographic into the un-mediated, a sense that film and video's movement and duration evoke present-time immediacy, and the tendency of popular film and video gen-res to mask their own mediation, conventionalizing it until familiarity makes it seem invisible.[25] Between many viewers' temptation to read video as a solution and many videotaped subjects' temptation to lament it as a contaminating interference lies video's promise as its own structure of re-mediation, like printed transcriptions and translations in prose or poetry.

In the conclusion to an insightful article, Andrew Wiget proclaims that performance analysis of Helen Sekaquaptewa and Larry Evers's video *Iisaw: Hopi Coyote Stories* (perhaps the best-known video of traditional Na-tive American storytelling, though that may not be saying much), "enables us to appreciate the storytelling experience as the culmination of process—story*telling*—where it lives in all its fullness, and makes available to us the aesthetic delights of performance, bright, vital, and communica-tive, which outshine the second-hand pleasures of the text" ("Telling the Tale," 332). But the point of calling attention to storytelling as process is that no such process is ever culminated. It may *seem* culminated if we slide into the filmic myth of an unmediated real, but not if we attend to the un-rolling contingencies in *Iisaw,* whether the social demands of video itself, the conspicuous editing and camera work, or the embarrassed adolescent in the videotaped audience who keeps scrunching over to hide her face from the camera. Wiget himself notes that "'ideal' or 'natural' perfor-mance contexts probably are nonexistent" (316).

Part of video's appeal is that, like Tedlock's pause patterns, video selects and recodes contingencies from a particular performance rather than culminating the process or making available the delights of firsthand per-formance itself. We never get a performance in "all its fullness," nor can we. (I recommend asking a storyteller if she thinks that video renders her real performance, though of course, different tellers will give different re-sponses.) Any performance, filming, or viewing is partial, contingent, vari-able. In a live audience, what one person sees and hears will differ from what another person sees and hears. A video, by contrast, makes selected sights and sounds repeatable, yet even for video, different people (or the same people at different viewings) see, hear, and interpret in different ways. Even a single audience member, who is never a fully unified subject, can have competing interpretations. From Wiget's perspective Sekaquaptewa's gestures seem extroverted, but compared to some story-tellers she can seem restrained. A video can render "aesthetic delights," and as Hymes and Tedlock have shown so well, and as Wiget shows so well in his transcribed translation of *Iisaw,* so can a written text. Still, neither can render "*the* aesthetic delights." For a given cultural context or set of purposes, a given video can outshine a given written text, but it cannot "outshine the second-hand pleasures of *the* text," as if video were not a text but a firsthand, unmediated signified or stable referent, a pure thing. *Iisaw* itself includes written text in its subtitles. Every storytelling, written, audiotaped, videotaped, watched live, or performed by ourselves, is always already mediated.

Thus video is not transparent, not a warp in time and space that leaps to an underlying real object. Video does not de-mediate. It re-mediates. The continuing emergence of less obtrusive equipment may remove the need for bright lights, big mikes, and a film crew, but video still tunnels vision, shrinking and flattening its gaze into a small (usually), two-dimensional plane and a rectangular frame. Viewers become outsiders looking in while themselves remaining unobserved by the performer, so that their re-sponses contribute nothing to the storyteller's decisions, unlike the re-sponses of a live audience. With its mobile perspective, video also sees from more angles than any one live-audience member. Yet it tends to anaesthetize viewers to the agents of its production. Viewers often forget that someone controls the focus, angles or tracks the cameras, and zooms in or out. Someone edits the sequences and skippings. Perhaps someone translates the words and transcribes the subtitles, chooses how many words to show at a time—much like choosing where to slash a text into lines of poetry—and perhaps, as in *Iisaw,* someone even abridges the translation, helping the subtitles keep pace with the onrushing visual narrative. Someone also opts for or against the on-off, pause, replay, and slow motion, and often someone else goes along with those choices or resists them. For video floats the visualized scene into another social space, usually a domestic or classroom setting, with its own conflicts and community. In short, video, like live performance and print, has its own economies and technologies of production, distribution, and reception.

We could certainly use more videos of traditional storytelling. They will have their own interests and values, but they are no more a panacea than the printed page. Nor do written texts and videos exhaust the re-presentations of traditional storytelling. With the recent emergence of a whole culture of professional storytelling, people can buy tickets to hear—or can even hire—such storytellers as Vi Hilbert (Lushootseed; see also her print edition of stories, *Haboo*), Gayle Ross (Cherokee), and Johnny Moses (Nootka) or can listen to their audiocassettes.

Nothing that I say here should deter translators from transcribing oral story in poetic form, prose, working-class English, or Red English, on videotape, audiotape, CD-ROM, DVD, or in cyberspace or virtual reality. My point is rather, as Hegeman argues, that there is no reason to insist on any one of those methods. And there are many reasons not to insist on them. Oral story can be *like* poetry or *like* prose, but it cannot *be* poetry or prose, nor can poetry be its secret essence, only waiting for the explorer-anthropologist to come along and discover it. It is not a question of which method is more accurate or authentic, because notions of accuracy and authenticity presuppose a static, underlying, discoverable truth consistent across the variations.[26] Some readers may find this argument too negative if they see it as critiquing the most extravagant claims for poetry, verse, or video without advocating enough of anything else. But it seems to me far more positive, and a trustier sketch of orality, to say that oral story in the age of mechanical and electronic reproduction multiplies into more than any method of reproduction can discover or contain. Rather than not advocating any one medium or form for oral stories, I am advocating all the forms without privileging any of them.

When we present printed texts of oral stories, we can help print to represent orality if the commentary surrounding the translation—which could include videotape, audiotape, or other electronic reproductions—calls attention to print's differences from orality, instead of trying to equate orality with the writing-specific features of poetry. In that sense, we need something for oral narrative like what Larry Evers and Felipe S. Molina have done for song in the written *Yaqui Deer Songs/Maso Bwikam: A Native American Poetry* and the video *Seyewailo: The Flower World: Yaqui Deer Songs,* which give the broadest cultural picture of a traditional Native American oral literature in any studies I know of. We need more, indeed, that might also look like what Toelken and Scott began in their study of Yellowman's Navajo coyote story, especially in their attention to oral detail, and we can hope that the growing number of studies by Native scholars such as Nora Dauenhauer, Greg Sarris, and Craig Womack will lead to more such work, sometimes in yet unanticipated forms. If we are going to enlarge the audience for oral story—traditional Native American and other kinds—then let us draw people to the orality of the stories even when we have to or choose to represent it in written form. The task of transcribers and translators is not to discover. Rather, like the task of storytellers, it is to narrate and to interpret.

Many people and cultural forces—including the work of Hymes, Tedlock, and those they inspired—played a role in the invention of Native American literature. Even the ethnopoetics movement, overlapping with the work of Tedlock (*Finding,* 2d ed., xv–xvii), helped make audiences receptive to Native writing. But to the extent that the Hymesian, Tedlockian tradition conflated Indian imagination and invention with poeticality itself, that confusion of categories, histories, and identities threatened to displace the work of actual Indian poets. And so we now turn to actual Indian poets, represented especially by Ray A. Young Bear and Leslie Marmon Silko.

The Existential Surfboard and the Dream of Balance, or "To be there, no authority to anything": The Poetry of Ray A. Young Bear

> how long can we keep balance atop the existential surfboard?
> —Young Bear, "From the Land of the Red Earths"

The Wordsworthian preoccupation with individual identity, targeted by writers as diverse as Robert Pinsky, Jacques Derrida, Kathy Acker, and Charles Bernstein, takes another kind of hit in the poetry of Ray A. Young Bear, deep-image surrealist, Meskwaki, cultural isolato, and—at the same time—communal cultural nationalist. Young Bear's first two books, *Winter of the Salamander: The Keeper of Importance* and *The Invisible Musician*, have a contemplative intensity that often risks the undecipherable. *Winter of the Salamander* even begins with an epigraph in Meskwaki and English that forswears elucidation:

> A gwi ma i · na ta wi · a sa mi
> ke ko · i i na tti mo ya nini · a yo
> shes ki · ne ko qua ta be ya i ke
> There are no elucidations or foresights
> merely
> experiments with words
>
> (viii)

Young Bear's third book, *Black Eagle Child: The Facepaint Narratives*, explains itself more patiently, integrating cultural exposition with poetic narrative, at times almost like a novel. The blend might recall the way

101

some of Leslie Marmon Silko's poems displace anthropological annotation by having an elder explain things to a child (Mattina, 146–47), except that Young Bear's irreverence keeps the sensibility more ironic and slippery. In his next book, *Remnants of the First Earth,* a potpourri of mostly prose that comes packaged as a novel,[1] Young Bear often turns to explanation directly—or faux directly, for he continues to reenvision the Meskwaki as the Black Eagle Child people and has Edgar Bearchild, his fictional alter ego who often sounds just like Young Bear but also differs from him, explain that he—Edgar—twists the explanations to keep from revealing what outsiders are not supposed to know (124).

In all his books Young Bear pursues something like a Euro-American surrealism while also writing more thoroughly from within a Native culture than any other Native American literary writer that I know of. Readers often feel lost amid the esoteric reference points; and the abrupt, often dream-inspired zigs and zags do little to accommodate our bewilderment. (A typical title, for example, is "in dream: the privacy of sequence.") The tight, crowded cultural frame is possible, perhaps even likely, for a Meskwaki because the Meskwaki, compared to most other American Indian peoples, have a history of tenacious cultural and linguistic independence.[2] As Richard Hugo put it early in Young Bear's career, trying to characterize Young Bear's fusion of the Indian and the hip, "Ray A. Young Bear is magic. He writes as if he lived 10,000 years ago in a tribe whose dialect happens to be modern English." Hugo conflates Indianness with the past, but part of the fun and the profundity in Young Bear's work comes in its frank commitment to the screeching present of Indian life amid expectations of the solemnly ancient. He writes about star medicine, drums, and adoption ceremonies and about grape Jell-o, Alfred Hitchcock, Hawaiian Punch, and the Jefferson Airplane, and with no hint of or no anguish over clashing categories, for all these things are part of his contemporary world, just as when he stands existentialism on a metaphorical surfboard, perhaps echoing his days as a college student in southern California. In a review of *Black Eagle Child,* Elizabeth Cook-Lynn called Young Bear "an accomplished writer who is dizzyingly complex, hostile and prickly, charming, weird, and brilliant. . . . No one, absolutely no one, tells the tribal story like Young Bear" (*Why I Can't Read Wallace Stegner,* 20). No one—not even other Meskwaki, for though it may seem tempting to attribute his distinctiveness to Meskwaki culture, Young Bear is not necessarily any more like other Meskwaki than he is like other poets. "As the lone poet of the Mesquakie (People of the Red Earth) Settlement," Young Bear has written, "there are days when I feel I have purposely chosen to swim away from the Central Camp of Relatives in Tama County, following a tributary like that of the golden carp, going as far away as possible from

tribal obligation and purpose while still being 'a part'—in name, tribal en-
rollment number and 40–year residence. There is an obvious connection
but there is also a self-imposed, deafening distance" ("Journey"). With the
mix of the Meskwaki, the pop, and the surreal, it is difficult for non-
Meskwaki readers versed in European and American poetic tradition, and
I should think for those Meskwaki readers not so versed, to pick out what
in Young Bear's poems we can usefully call surrealist, Meskwaki, or somehow his own.

Young Bear also writes amid some thorny cultural resistances. The
Meskwaki prefer to keep their culture to themselves. When Fred McTaggart, a white researcher, went to the Meskwaki Settlement expecting to
find people happy to tell him stories to record and write about, the
Meskwaki he met were courteously uncooperative. Young Bear himself, as
noted already, insists there is much that he cannot say.[3] Moreover, he
writes in a larger American and international culture that is mostly too ignorant, impatient, or hostile to anticipate the immensely detailed ontological routine of Meskwaki life and thought. Even compliments can be-
tray. A favorable review of *The Invisible Musician* dwells on the beautiful
cover, praising Stella Young Bear for the photo of a beaded bag without
realizing that the cover credits her for beading the bag, not for pho-
tographing it.[4] Meskwaki culture is a self-reinventing flow of the present,
not a relic of the past.

Meanwhile, as Robert F. Gish writes, "Young Bear is generally acknowl-
edged by poets, critics, and students of American Indian literature as the
nation's foremost contemporary Native American poet," and is "destined
for even wider and more fulsome recognition" ("Retrieving the
Melodies"). Sherman Alexie, whose brilliance as a poet and whose public
persona as a popular fiction writer and performer could nudge aside
some of the audience for other Indian writers, testifies on the cover of
Young Bear's recent collection of poems, *The Rock Island Hiking Club,* that
"Ray Young Bear is the best poet in Indian Country and in the top 46 in
the whole dang world." Still, these are curious claims for a writer who remains almost unwritten about, daunting to read and teach, and much of
whose poetry is out of print.[5] Young Bear's recent move to fiction is enlarging his audience, but until recently his readers have been confined to
the small if growing audience committed to reading Indian poetry, rather
than the still small but much larger audience for American poetry at
large. Even his fiction doesn't seem to have cracked into a sizable audience beyond those already interested in Indian fiction.

Those limits need not be a big problem; many Indian writers are quick
to say that they write mostly for other Indians. Young Bear does not discuss other Indian poets, but two of his poems address non-Indian poets'

and editors' readings of Indians in general and, in one case, of the Meskwaki in particular. The same two poems, "in disgust and in response to indian-type poetry written by whites published in a mag which keeps rejecting me" and "for the rain in march: the blackened hearts of herons" (Young Bear has a particular genius for titles), also address Meskwaki identity and the Meskwaki world with the same suggestive obscurity found in so many of his other poems, but their direction to the non-Meskwaki literary world helps make the obscurity more penetrable to outsiders. For Young Bear's cultural worlds and imaginative universes, like any other writer's or any other person's, are fluidly multiple and rife with competing chances and constrictions, even in his sense of what it means to be Meskwaki.[6]

"in disgust and in response" puts the underlying, existential question of *being* Meskwaki in its first line, "you know we'd like to be there," and then takes up the many things that line struggles to enunciate. "You know" has a casual talkiness, yet also the oracular tone of a culture formally elaborated and reproduced, from generation to generation, through oral tradition. It also sneers at those who only presume they know, those who see Indians as a vanishing remnant (the last of the Mohicans) mired in the past. Yet at the same time, Young Bear's "you know" suggests that Meskwaki *would* like to be there. This is a poem, and in many ways Young Bear's is a body of poetry, about trying *to be* wherever *there* is, there where Meskwaki culture is,[7] or in this case where it once was, since the Meskwaki, like anyone else, can get drawn into the cultural fantasy that displaces a people's identity and essence to a vanished past. Being there promises to mean being in some kind of "balance," to pick out words from later in the poem, "whole and complete." Or maybe not so whole and complete, since to say that "we'd like to be there" is also to say that "we" are not "there," even as the "would like" speaks a dream of balance, of wholeness and completeness, a dream that nevertheless remains—in the poem's final line—"no authority to anything."

Indeed, Young Bear puts so much weight on how "we" "would" like to be there, repeating the expression in a separate line, that he sets up an expectation that such desire will be trailed by a "but we can't." The poem never fills out that expectation, but it nonetheless seems to rely on our sense of the ever receding *différance* between the wish and its object, between the present and the ever receding past that pulls at the present so strongly:

> you know we'd like to be there
> standing beside our grandfathers

being ourselves
without the frailty
and insignificance of the worlds
we suffer and balance
on top of now
unable to detect which to learn
or which to keep from
wearing the faces
of our seasonal excuses
constantly lying to each other
and ourselves about just how much
of the daylight
we understand
we would be there:
with the position of our minds
bent towards the autumn fox
feasts
feeling the strength and prayer
of the endured sacred human tests
we would set aside the year's
smallpox dead
whole and complete
with resignation
like the signs from the four legs
of our direction
standing still
sixty years back in time
breathing into the frosted lungs
of our horses the winter blessings
of our clan gods

(*Winter,* 118)

This is not typical of Young Bear's poetry, for mostly he writes without nostalgia about contemporary life, not about the past that is all that most popular myths can see for Native Americans. Here, however, he opposes "beside our grandfathers" to a "now" of "frailty / and insignificance," of "constantly lying to each other / and ourselves." Then, when he specifies the past he refers to as sixty years ago, the notion of grandfathers hardens into the literal. Rather than referring to ancestors at large, it zeroes in on the specific past of two or three generations ago, repeated in the reference to smallpox, which ravaged the Meskwaki people in 1901–02 (Wm. G. Malin, 213–15). The specificity allows us to suspect that such grandfathers may sometimes have felt as frail to themselves as they now appear strong to their grandchildren, who may in turn gain strength in the nostalgia of their descendants, much as some of the young scamps in Louise Erdrich's novels live long enough to draw respect as links to the old ways and the storied past. In Young Bear's poem, the mythical past shatters before the immediate Meskwaki specificity, more in Young Bear's usual mode, that magnifies through the rest of the poem. Only against the backdrop of that Meskwaki world, in so many ways unintelligible to outsiders, does Young Bear at the end of the poem finally address the disgust and response that his title promises.

On the way, he specifies "grandfathers" even more. It is a masculine term (as the "we" of this poem turns out to be masculine), and here it refers to the men of a group that is "separate and apart," for—as *Black Eagle Child* explains—in those days "the tribe broke into family groups during winter" (166). The horses, Young Bear writes,

> would carry our belongings
> and families to the woodlands
> of eastern iowa to hunt our food
> separate and apart
> from the tribe
> following and sometimes using
> the river to cleanse the blood
> from our daughters and wives
> not knowing that far into
> our lives we'd be the skulls
> of their miscarriages
> as a result:
> the salamander would paralyze
> our voice and hearing
> under instruction
> our sons the mutes would darken
> their bodies with ash and we'd assist
> them erect sweatlodges with canvas
> water   plants   fire   and   poles
> from the river
> the scent of deer and geese
> the hiss of medicine
> against the heated rocks
> belief would breathe into their bodies
> camouflage and invisibility
>
> (*Winter,* 119)

The masculine focalization may seem automatic, but in other poems Young Bear writes more of grandmothers than grandfathers, especially his own grandmother. He opens his first collection with his best-known and most accessibly eloquent poem, "grandmother." Here, in "in disgust and in response," it is not easy to read the consequences of gender distinctions. Like so much of Young Bear's poetry, these are difficult lines to follow through their cultural assumptions and suggestive enjambments, and sometimes they seem to ask us to rest in uncertainties, in "not knowing," and in the paralysis of "voice and hearing / under instruction." Not that the uncertainties can never be diminished so much as that uncertainty itself is part of the intercultural and interpersonal being that these poems labor to represent and to suspend in continuous performance.

Indeed, Young Bear often suspends his lines in opposite notes, as in the haunting "one chip of human bone," which reads, in its entirety:

> one chip of human bone
>
> it is almost fitting
> to die on the railroad tracks.
>
> i can easily understand
> how they felt on their long staggered walks back
>
> grinning to the stars.
>
> there is something about
> trains, drinking, and
> being an indian with nothing to lose.
>
> (*Winter*, 19)

One chip isn't much, but this chip marks a death. It is almost fitting, but it doesn't fit. Young Bear can easily understand the many suicides on the railroad tracks that bisect the Meskwaki Settlement, suicides that multiply through his poetry and prose, because he knows the world that produces them. Yet in another, uncapitulating sense he can never understand such tragedies. He is "no authority to anything." As in "in disgust and in response," it boils down to "being an indian." Or as *Black Eagle Child* puts it, "All this internalized agony led us to hurt / or seriously injure one another for no reason / other than sheer disgust in being Indians," and "All else has been a long uncomfortable adjustment to being an Indian, *E ne no te wi ya ni*, in the world of the white man" (5, 167). In "one chip of human bone," that being provokes Young Bear to wonder whether Indians can know themselves and their cultures when it is so hard to see through the veil of all they have lost. If they decide they have nothing left to lose, then that can make them lose everything.

"in disgust and in response" sets out to define the ontological anguish of that wondering. It describes the ceremonial production and reproduction, in sweatlodges with "the hiss of medicine / against the heated rocks," of "belief" that "would breathe into their bodies / camouflage and invisibility." But invisible belief will not translate easily into a world of schooling disputes and mass-marketed, TV-induced urges to conform.[8] The modesty that even the strongest belief assumes, if its form seems invisible, makes it a hard sell in a world that wants things to buy and that refuses to see or hear such opposite notes.

Part of the difficulty is that at some level of existential challenge, "in disgust and in response" suggests that it is no easier for Young Bear—the "invisible musician"—or for any other Meskwaki to say in a "whole and complete" way what is Meskwaki than it is for outsiders. In some ways, none of us knows who we are. The Meskwaki would "like to be there . . . / being ourselves." But like anyone else, they can always feel as if they are only "wearing the faces" of themselves, can always feel the gap between *being* one's self and the expression of such being without which, in a vicious circle, we can't conceptualize our being in the first place. Thus being is never convincingly being, and expressing can never reach the signified it would express. Identity, as a social narrative shaped by traditions in disequilibrium, is always evolving, versus the cultural myth that Native Americans shape Native identity only by looking to the past. "We would set aside the year's / smallpox dead / whole and complete," as if the only way to be whole and complete were to be dead.

Beyond that grim hint, this may all sound ordinarily poststructuralist, but I am not suggesting that this poem submits to the poststructuralist formulas that spin my discussion of it, any more than it submits to the formulas of cultural fantasy about Native Americans. For in Young Bear's spin on Meskwaki ontology, identities *can* be appropriated. That is not what poets do; it is what witches do:

> somewhere an image of a woman's hand
> would lunge out from the window
> of a longhouse
> and it would grab from our fingers
> the secret writings of a book
> describing to the appointee
> the method of entering
> the spirit and body
> of a turkey
> to walk at night in suspension
> above the boundaries of cedar incense
> to begin this line of witchcraft

    traveling in various
    animal forms
    unaware of the discrepancy
    that this too is an act of balance
    a recurring dream of you
    being whole and complete
    sending the glint of your horns
    into the great distances
    of the gods
    acquainting yourself with ritual
    and abandonment of self-justification
    to realize there is a point
    when you stop being a people
    sitting somewhere and reading
    the poetry of others come out easily
    at random
    unlike yours which is hard to write
    to feel yourself stretch
    beyond limitation
    to come here and write this poem
    about something no one
    knows about
    no authority to anything
                    (*Winter*, 119–20)

There, without a period's closing authority, the poem ends.

The words "this too" signal an analogy. Young Bear likens the secret writing of witchcraft, which tells how to take animal forms,[9] to the transformations of poetic imagination, for each is a "suspension / above the boundaries," "an act of balance / a recurring dream of you"—addressing himself in the second person, as if to make his readers hear their own poetic transformations—"being whole and complete." A romanticizing essentialist might stop at "whole and complete," asserting the organic unity iconized by new critical tradition and still in many ways dominant, even more in the world of belles lettres and poetry "mags" than in literary and cultural criticism. But that would entail a "self-justification" at odds with the personal humility of Meskwaki culture and ritual. And beyond the personal, it would provoke a romantic cultural chauvinism hardly better than that in the white writers of "indian-type" poetry and the editors who favor them.[10] Instead of offering an image of the Meskwaki as whole and complete, Young Bear—whose poems neither shy away from nor obsess over differences between different Meskwaki—musters a Meskwaki resentment to help him take being Meskwaki to more than being Meskwaki: "to realize there is a point / when you stop being a people / . . . / to feel yourself stretch beyond limitation."

But white editors usually take more interest in white-written versions of "Indian poems" than in Young Bear's poems. Silko has critiqued the white poets riding the ethnopoetics wave—especially Gary Snyder—for cultural slumming, for supposing they can be Indian for a time and in the process romanticizing Indian histories from a delusory sense that whites have no histories of their own ("Old-Time Indian Attack"). Similarly, in "For the White Poets Who Would Be Indian," Wendy Rose writes:

> You think of us only
> when your voice
> wants for roots,
> when you have sat back
> on your heels
> and become primitive.
> You finish your poem
> and go back.
>   (*Bone Dance,* 22)

While Silko and Rose critique the cultural history that leads white poets to "play Indian" or "go Native" (Deloria, Huhndorf), Young Bear dwells on their ignorance and presumptuous confidence in their own identity. All three resent the sense of manifest destiny and colonialist eminent domain that lets many white poets take Indianness as their own cultural property or toy. In such company, Indian poets seem invisible. As we have seen, Chrystos notes:

> I'm invisible turn away ticking
> You won't find us in anthologies of american poets
> We forgot to sign that treaty
> Everybody likes to read the whites writing myths of us
> Us telling about us is too hard . . .
> *Hey I'm not screaming since you're not listening*
>   (*Fire Power,* 69)

But the invisibility comes dressed in scathing sarcasm, for Chrystos and Young Bear remind us how much the text of invisibility is written by its culpably blind readers. In the same vein, a poem called "'Native Americans' vs. 'The Poets,'" by Kimberly M. Blaeser (*Trailing You,* 53), laments the way readers classify Indian poetry as folklore or anthropology, unable to see it as poetry.

In particular, the editors that anger Young Bear cannot see the cultural identity of Indian poets. It is hard to see past the clichés of ugh-poetry or noble wisdom, past the ethnopoetic assimilation of Indianness to orality that makes seriously literary Indian writing unimaginable, and past the Wordsworthian assumption of poetic individuality. The questions about writing and individuality have much to do with each other when "Indian poetry" in anthologies often means retranslations by whites who do not know the original language and who work from Indian oral texts, such as songs or rituals, often transcribed or translated partly or wholly by unnamed Indian individuals—yet attributed not to individuals or particular styles or movements but instead to entire Indian peoples in the ethnographic present. (The term *ethnographic present* refers to the unwittingly condescending anthropological assumption that something—such as a song, a dance, a custom, a cultural assumption—emerges within that culture as timeless, complete, and fully representative rather than as a snapshot of individual people's acts in a continuously changing and often self-contradictory stream. See Johannes Fabian, *Time and the Other.*)

From within the mindset that produces such "Indian poetry" in the ethnographic present, it can seem—again unwittingly—that individual Indians cannot represent their people as well as learned white people can. Perhaps the Indians will seem too grittily specific, too individual. Or—in the way that stereotypes often come in opposite pairs—perhaps they will seem too unindividuated, lacking in the romantically individualist literary skill that one supposedly needs to represent even one's own people. After all, writing is not really the medium of Indians anyway, since Indians are presumed to be unlettered and oral. And if they are oral, then they live on the far side of an unbridgeable gulf, so far from the writing-centered world of elite poetry that serious, literary poetry by Indians cannot be imagined. And if it cannot be imagined, then it cannot be recognized even when it appears. Both meanings of the term "recognize" apply here: editors and the poetry audience cannot see Indian poetry as serious literary poetry on the same elite plane they grant to recognized white poets, and they cannot single it out for recognition.

This supposed divide between oral and written culture is the same gulf that Claude Lévi-Strauss takes for granted in "The Writing Lesson" and that Derrida recasts as an ethnocentric delusion. It also shows up in the opposition of the natural and direct versus the sophisticated, as when Richard Hugo explains that he "can imagine a poet reading Young Bear and having a nagging feeling that he too could write this way once but got educated and sophisticated and lost his natural gift for direct imaginative response." But of course Young Bear, educated in Meskwaki culture and a good number of colleges and universities, writes a poetry as indirect, as mediated through systems of representation and cultural accretion as Hugo's poetry. And as we have seen, Young Bear sees his poems as "hard to write," not as effusions of the "natural." Writing, Derrida is at pains to argue, is always already indirect rather than natural. Defining writing more broadly than Lévi-Strauss defines it, Derrida rewrites the Indian world of orality as very much part of the world of writing, even for a people, like the Nambikwara of Lévi-Strauss's *Tristes Tropiques,* who do not write in what Derrida calls "the narrow sense of linear and phonetic notation" (109). Of course the Nambikwara in Lévi-Strauss's tale are a long way from Young Bear. Indeed, even in the sense of writing that Derrida calls "narrow," those who would assimilate Young Bear and his people to orality without literacy, or even just to orality without literary literacy, might be surprised to learn that the Meskwaki people have been writing their own script probably since the seventeenth century, long before Sequoyah invented the famous Cherokee script around 1820.

Moreover, that history of Meskwaki writing looms large in Young Bear's own idea of his role as a writer. Edgar Bearchild mentions that his people "adopted / the alphabet in the 1600s" (*Rock,* 14). As Young Bear says in an interview:

> Writing is very . . . [ellipsis in the original] How do I put it? In the 1600s—it is said—when we first had contact with French emissaries-explorers in Wisconsin, we adopted the English [i.e., Roman] alphabet. For nearly three centuries [actually, more than three centuries] the Mesquakie people have been utilizing the alphabet. But we don't use it in the English context, rather we use it syllabically. Our tribal name, as an example[,] is written out as Me skwa ki proper or The Red Earth People.
>
> Contrary to the beliefs of many, writing isn't new. For me, writing is a personal link to the writings of my grandfathers. I have in my possession their journals that date back to the early 1800s. I therefore believe that "word-collecting" is genetically encoded in my blood. . . . When I look into my roots, reading and translating my grandfathers' journals, I realize that I'm not far off from my late grandmother's expectations. Although she taught me to be wary of The Outside World, she was the one who saw there was a purpose to my work: keeping alive my grandfathers' writings. I bring the journals out on occasion with white gloves in dim light to let them breathe, to remind them we are still here. There is a magic there.
>
> In the novel-in-progress [*Remnants of the First Earth*] I take this a step further. Edgar Bearchild, my alter-ego, is apprised he has been chosen to maintain his Six Grandfathers' journals and to serve as a reminder to his Black Eagle Child tribe of ugly things to come. ("Interview," 38–39)

In some respects at least—and not surprisingly—Young Bear knows more about the history of Meskwaki writing than scholarly experts know. A summary, scholarly account of Meskwaki writing by Willard B. Walker dates it from the nineteenth century, noting that it was "widespread" by 1880 but viewing with skepticism accounts of its use earlier in the century, even though Walker notes that "a possible French source is indicated by the fact that the vowel letters have continental, rather than English, phonetic values and by the shapes of some of the letters" (169). A French source would place its origins in the seventeenth or eighteenth century, corroborating Young Bear's account of oral tradition about written tradition ("In the 1600s—it is *said*"), a blend that explodes the commonplace, Lévi-Straussian assumption of an unbridgeable gulf between oral and written culture. Thus even for writing in what Derrida calls the "narrow sense" of script, Young Bear works from a long tradition. Moreover, he associates writing with his people's history, exactly what the white-led assimilation of Indians to orality would dissociate writing from. And so, while writing for Young Bear may evoke the individual pride of the romantic poet who wants to get his own poems accepted in literary mags, it also represents cultural, tribal, familial, and Indian identity, not in the sense that erases individual imagination by attributing oral "poems" to an entire Indian people, but rather in the sense that the individual poet connects in his or her particular way to a vast history, and that the poet's task is as deeply social and historical as it is romantically individual.

Indeed, Chrystos and Young Bear don't plead to be read predominantly as individuals. Chrystos writes the lines I've quoted in the first person, but mainly in the first-person plural. She makes a cultural argument, whereas the white ethnopoets, Rose suggests, try on their poems like a personal adventure. Silko too critiques the white poets for the very concept of trying on identities not their own. She reads their work as founded on "the assumption that the white man, through some innate cultural or racial superiority, has the ability to perceive and master the essential beliefs, values and emotions of persons from Native American communities" ("Old-Time Indian Attack," 77). Edgar Bearchild complains about "Do-nothing academic types" who "are swift to compile reams of new and old information about our religion, mythology, and current political beliefs. Books about us with hyped-up phraseology and absurd anthropological theories are published," but "we know more about ourselves than they do" (*Remnants,* 89). Rose—herself an anthropologist as well as a poet—recounts the trial of repeatedly meeting whites who erroneously take for granted that they know more about Indians than Indians know about themselves ("Just What's All This Fuss," 14–15).

Though we often have a responsibility to recognize the difference between ourselves and others, in a world where cultures with mixed histories
continue to mix and cross it is not always easy to draw the line between
writing about one's self and writing about someone else. Any self is multiple, fragmented, self-contradictory, and we build our others partly out of
qualities in ourselves that we try to split off and project outward. Rose herself writes poems in the voice of people from groups she does not belong
to, such as a Salvadoran in "The Day They Cleaned Up the Border: El Sal-
vador" and a Tasmanian in "Truganinny." In "Truganinny," she even gets
her history wrong when she works from a story that Truganinny's body
"was stuffed and mounted" (though the actual story is no better—her
corpse was dug up and stripped of its flesh, and eventually her skeleton
was displayed in a museum [see Vivienne Rae Ellis]); yet she still writes a
powerful poem that has (deservedly, to my mind) won wide admiration.
Silko's *Ceremony,* as we will see in the next chapter, narrates the danger of
supposing we can erect absolute borders between cultural groups, and
Silko, a woman, angles the story mostly through the eyes of men.

In these ways, the critiques from Silko, Rose, Chrystos, and Young Bear
tread on thin ice, yet they each get at something that still seems culpably,
appropriatingly false in a great deal of white-written poetry about Indian
people. Wherever the answer may lie, it seems not to lie in the imperial
self that so many white poets assume grants them the ability to know what
they do not know and to become—for the passing moment that Rose describes—what they are not. Indian poets do not inevitably and always
know more about Indian cultures, their own or others, than non-Indian
poets, but of course they usually know more about at least some Indian
culture than practically all white poets. And Young Bear's complaint puts
the force of value not so much in an Indian poet's inevitably superior authority as in another calculus neither opposite to authority nor within its
compass: namely, in modesty, in disavowal of authority.

Thus Young Bear projects a post-Wordsworthian transcendence of identity, yet at the same time describes himself escaping such limits so as to reim-
merse himself in them. For if he would stretch beyond the limits of identity,
it is still his self that he professes to stretch. His insistence that his poems
"stretch / beyond limitation" clashes with his insisting nevertheless that this
poem is "about something." He aspires to "write this poem / about something no one / knows about," which is also to be someone who knows about
it. The two uses of "about" invert each other. The first one affirms, while the
second denies yet remains embedded in the affirmation. That ontological
corkscrew permits Young Bear to open his claim both to be "no authority to
anything" and to have an authority that other poets assume only by fraud.

Whirling out of such an extra-logical stance, the cultural consequences of Young Bear's position evade any neat formula. At the frankest common denominator, it means that he can write about Indians and non-Indian poets can't. The tougher part comes in the why. The writing of such poems is not the province of just any Meskwaki—far from it. Nor can he write such poems simply because he knows what he's talking about while the white dabblers and impostors do not. The difficulty lies, again, in the always receding object of "about," the about *what* (what is a Meskwaki, what is an "I," a self, a "we," an identity, a subject position?). And it lies in Young Bear's sense not only that he can never catch, mount, and display that object, but also that the quest to catch it and the recognition that it will always flutter over the horizon are not the same for him and for someone outside the Meskwaki world, anymore than they would be for him and for another Meskwaki.

"We'd like to be there," then, "but we can't be there. We'd like to be our truest selves, but the limit of "self," "our," and "truth" always disappears over memory's horizon. Still, if it is not always easy for Young Bear or other Meskwaki or anyone else to say who they are, that hardly means they are not anything. Wearing a face is not the same as being a self, but masks can perform self, dramatizing and producing the subjectivity and displacement that they figure. That includes the mask of self-contradiction, the extra-logical cultural stance that allows Young Bear to claim an impossible knowledge about what no one knows about, and to say that his position as a Meskwaki gives him an authority to write about Meskwaki being, even though a Meskwaki—like anyone else—is "no authority to anything." A Meskwaki is not even an authority on "being whole and complete" as a Meskwaki, except in the performative sense that such wholeness and completion are what this poem calls "a recurring dream."[11] Thus in an interview, Young Bear can say "I am extremely fortunate to come from a tribe that is known for its conservative practices. As such, our language, beliefs, history and ideology is unaffected by cultural deterioration." Even his verb, "is" rather than "are," underlines his sense that Meskwaki language, belief, history, and ideology are one and the same. He explains that "self-prescribed, self-imposed geographic isolation has vastly contributed to our stability," yet in the same interview he discusses how Meskwaki music has recently adapted to the "southern style of drumming" and "the latest Northern Plains style of high-pitched singing." He adds: "There is a high probability that Mesquakie song, dance, and drum styles have changed because of cultural change and adaptation. . . . My feeling is, as long as the people who are responding to these subtle idiosyncrasies are Mesquakie—Mesquakie improvising at being Mesquakie—then it is of little concern. Should there ever be a time when the influence of Puccini, Verdi, Beethoven can be heard in our music, then I'd be worried."[12]

As long, he says, as the people are Meskwaki. What then is a Meskwaki? There is no doubt that, compared to most Native American peoples, the Meskwaki have steadfastly kept up their cultural independence. Still, any notion that they have hovered in place flies in the face of everything we know about Meskwaki history. In the eighteenth century, for example, the French aimed an explicit policy of genocide directly at the Meskwaki and came so close to accomplishing it that the Meskwaki could recover only through large-scale adoption from other Native peoples, who brought much from their own cultures, as well as large-scale return of captured Meskwaki, who brought much from the cultures that held them captive. Adoption already played a role in pre-contact practice and ritual, and marriage with people from other Indian nations was not unusual. Marriages between different peoples grew more common under the pressure of Iroquois expansion, which drove diverse western Algonquian peoples west into the central Great Lakes region in the mid-seventeenth century, a time when the Iroquois but not the western Algonquians had substantial contact with whites in the east. In short, cultural mixing and change accelerated with contact, but they accelerated within partly familiar patterns of ongoing change.[13] And like other Indian peoples, the Meskwaki continue to absorb a great deal from widening intertribal contacts and an intensifying, pan-Indian sense of common cultural position. They have stuck it out so successfully (by comparison) not only because of their conservatism but also because of their resourceful mix of conservatism and adaptability, or, in Young Bear's term, improvisation. In *Black Eagle Child,* he describes the resistance to change while concluding, nevertheless, "Change was unavoidable" (60). For Young Bear, conservatism and isolation are not sufficient to explain Meskwaki cultural survival. As his remarks about music indicate, a Meskwaki is not anything we can capture in static definition; a Meskwaki is, circularly and performatively, a "Mesquakie improvising at *being* Mesquakie." Hence, although a Meskwaki has a special authority about such "being," still, since such being is always recreating itself, a Meskwaki is at the same time "no authority to anything."

In *Remnants,* Edgar Bearchild puts the disavowal of authority in historical perspective. "In an earthly realm where the forces of nature are infinitely more powerful than human beings," he writes, "personal and collective insignificance is a given. In our relatively compact tribal society, there was equal standing among everyone other than the chieftain hierarchy. In the ancien régime our people hunted, fished, gathered food, planted seeds, and harvested crops together, making everyone interdependent" (87). Similarly, in the afterword to *Black Eagle Child,* Young Bear writes: "The philosophy that espouses cosmic insignificance, a belief that humans are but a minute part of world order, has shaped my words" (256). In short, even when he speaks of philosophy and cosmic belief or rebukes those who speak with false authority about Native people, he sees himself, again, as "no authority to anything."

Indeed, the anthropological literature singles out the Meskwaki for their lack of interest in authority. Walter B. Miller argues persuasively that European concepts of authority, hierarchy, and leadership were deeply foreign to the Meskwaki social system when astonished Europeans first described it in the seventeenth century. Even after almost three hundred years of change, Miller finds that contemporary practices pervasively reiterate what he finds for the seventeenth century. Things may get done at the Meskwaki Settlement, but the social institutions that accomplish them are so informal as to seem almost invisible. In a similar vein, Frederick O. Gearing describes modern Meskwaki independence and resentment of authority as well as the factional political strife that such a perspective leads to now that the Meskwaki must articulate their social system to non-Meskwaki institutions and expectations.[14] Thus when Young Bear, having already asserted his position as a Meskwaki and Native American authority (beginning right from the comic, resentful title of his poem), then arcs to an anguished conclusion in denial of that authority, his very denial enacts the ontology of authority as it appears—almost invisibly—in Meskwaki performance.

As "in disgust and in response" decries "indian-type poetry written by whites," so "for the rain in march: the blackened hearts of herons" expands to denounce two particular white-written poems that are not "indian-type poetry" but are about Indians: W. D. Snodgrass's "Powwow" and James Wright's "I Am a Sioux Brave, He Said in Minneapolis."[15] Like "in disgust," "for the rain in march" goes most of its length without even mentioning the offending poems; Young Bear may occasionally respond to white poets, but he has plenty to say on his own without needing them to prompt him. He may be their "other," but they are not his.

On the contrary, "for the rain in march" begins with modesty and interiority, begins as "no authority to anything":

> i see myself sleeping
> and i see other ignorant people
> locked securely in their houses
> sleeping
> unaware of the soft dawn-lit
> furbearing animals
> wrapping themselves with the bark

and cone from pinetrees
within each of their thoughts
there is the vision
of the small muskrat's
clasped hands
the struggling
black and yellow
spotted body of a salamander
freeing itself from a young
girl's womb

(*Winter*, 163)

This has nothing to do with Snodgrass's poem (which I will focus on) or with Wright's. This poem is "for" the rain in march, not for the white poets, not even deigning, until it is mostly over, to respond with disgust.

But even while the bulk of this poem has nothing to do with Snodgrass's poem, it also has everything to do with it. For the disconnection shows how ludicrously far afield Snodgrass is when he takes it for granted that he knows the Meskwaki mind. He assumes he has been to the Meskwaki interior, weighed it, and found it wanting, found nothing there but a false consciousness that reflects the ideologies of Snodgrass's own world in degraded derivation.[16] Where, to Snodgrass, do the Meskwaki get their culture? "They all see the same movies," his poem begins, as if that will explain everything, not only for the Meskwaki but also for the Sioux, the Chippewa, and (in a lump) all the rest, which tells mainly about what Snodgrass himself does not see when he looks at the Meskwaki (such meager looking as he pauses for). "The Indians," Snodgrass explains elsewhere, "seemed dreadfully beaten down, poverty-stricken, sodden or didn't seem to know any more than I did about Indians. I really had the feeling that they also had picked up all their Indian lore from Grade B movies. Yet, that was our fault, too, so it just seemed like one more guilt" (qtd. in Gary Gildner and Judith Gildner, 133). Like the whites that Wendy Rose describes, Snodgrass imagines that Indian people know little about their own traditional culture. He sees no Indian subjectivity. To Snodgrass, Indian culture—represented solely by what ignorant eyes can see at a powwow—is a passive product of "our" culture, as if only readers who are part of his "our" were allowed.[17] He does not see the Meskwaki being, the visionary but modest (Young Bear even says "ignorant") being that lives with animals, the furbearing animals wrapping themselves with bark, the muskrat like a fetus, the spotted salamander slithering from a girl's womb. Such things, such being, invisible to Snodgrass, not only do not come from movies, they also antedate movies by millennia and remain utterly invisible within them. They are unparaphraseable in the cultural and linguistic vocabulary of Snodgrass's dominating world, which, to say the least, includes the world of written and English-language literary criticism, as opposed, for example, to Meskwaki oral and written traditions.

In that vein, Young Bear then continues the poem by telling about a certain badger:

> in my dark blue pickup
> i came upon a cigar-smoking
> badger
> who invited himself and
> later came to my home
> gathering chips and splinters
> of my firewood and starting
> a fire
> for an hour we sat
> and then he suddenly stood
> on his hindlegs and walked
> over to the stove
> and opened it
> he took out two narrow pieces
> of burning wood and rammed them
> into his eyes
> he fell on all fours
> and then he made rumbling sounds
> mocking my pickup with its two
> dull headlights
> disappearing into
> the forest
>
> (*Winter,* 164)

Like the opening lines, the story of this trickster badger has nothing directly to do with Snodgrass, but it has the effect of satirizing him by reversal. He reads the Meskwaki through the lens of his own cultural being, whereas Young Bear reads an ill-mannered animal rather like Snodgrass through the lens of Meskwaki being. For like the badger, Snodgrass comes to Young Bear's home uninvited, or if he is invited in the sense that everyone is invited to the annual powwow (a major source of income for the settlement), then he exceeds that invitation in the invasive presumptions of his poem. Before this badgering trickster (echoed in *Remnants,* 287) with his rumbling mockery, the securely locked homes of the opening lines seem exposed and threatened. But the badger's mockery, like the mockery from tricksters through much of Native American oral and written literature, soon turns back on him, driving him from the home he invades and the hospitality he abuses.

Though not always unsubtle, the rampant abuses in Snodgrass's poem make it a ripe target. In language imported from racism against African Americans, he sneers at the dancers' "shuffling," as if to recall that sorry epithet "prairie niggers." All Indians are "the same" to him (he excepts "Only the Iroquois," apparently unaware that there are hundreds of American Indian peoples, most of whom couldn't be represented at even a well-attended powwow), and it almost seems as if nonwhites are all the same to him too. Their ceremonial clothing amounts to "braveries" (he might almost as well say squaw-eries, if that were a word) they are "tricked out" in. As he others Indians as shuffling blacks, he also others Indians—women and men alike (since "They are all the same")—by feminizing them: "They all dance with their eyes turned / Inward—like a woman nursing." To the extent we stop there, at the end of an enjambed line, the feminization might almost appear laudatory, suggesting contemplation and gentleness. But the false pause turns out to be an abuse of late-forties and fifties high formalist play (those are the years when Snodgrass formed his style, and I am supposing that he drafted the poem soon after the 1949 powwow), for nothing else in the poem corroborates such softness. On the contrary, when we cross the enjambment to find that the dancers are "like a woman nursing / A sick child she already knows / Will die," it turns out that we have been set up for another patronizing, infantilizing, misogynist cliché about the femininely impractical and childish red man, vanishing ward of the state, the sort of counterfactual dirge that would help make possible the Eisenhower administration's disastrous effort to do away with ("terminate") reservations.

Young Bear, writing from a conservative culture with its own language, cosmology, and social system, with a body of ceremonial ritual large enough to beggar the Vatican, a culture so private that it finally succeeded in repelling a sixty-year onslaught of anthropologists, skims through most of these insults and focuses with incredulity on the thinness of his culture in the eyes of Snodgrass and Wright:

> coming back I read the poem pow-wow
> written by w. d. snodgrass after
> visiting my people's annual tribal
> celebration
> you can't get away from people
> who think what they see
> is in actuality all they will
> ever see

as if all in one moment they can sense
automatically what makes a people
what capabilities they have of
knowledge and intellect
he was only shown what was allowed
to be shown
what the hell did he expect
out of his admission fee?
and as far as he thinking that he knew
more about indians than they themselves did
he should have thought twice
it's the same way with the poem
i am a sioux brave, he said in minneapolis
by james wright and countless others
he will never know the meanings
of the songs he heard
nor will he ever know that these
songs were being sung long before
his grandfathers had notions
of riding across the ocean
long before translators
and imitators came
some claiming to be at least a good 64th
grabbing and printing anything
in scrapbook form
dedicating poems to the indian's loss
writing words and placing themselves
within various animals they knew nothing of
snodgrass will never know what spirit
was contained in that day he sat above
the feathered indians
eating his hot dog

he saw my people in one afternoon
performing and enjoying themselves
i have lived here 26 years and although
i realize within my life i am incomplete
i know for a fact that my people's ways
aren't based on grade-b movies

(*Winter,* 171–72)

Young Bear, a composer, singer, and drummer with a huge repertoire of songs, like many other Meskwaki spoke only Meskwaki until he went to school. For years he wrote his poems in Meskwaki and then translated them into English ("Connected to the Past," 340–41). From that perspective, Snodgrass and Wright's ignorance of Indian song and ritual, if it were not so stultifyingly familiar, would be as unimaginable as Indian song and ritual are to Snodgrass and Wright. Snodgrass even supposes that the old drummer cannot remember what the song's words mean, just because Snodgrass presumes the song is too ancient and the culture is disconnected from its traditions. Yet Snodgrass thinks that *he* knows it is the "tribe's song for the restless young," as if any Indian song the man sings would have to be a Meskwaki song and belong to the people as a whole. Nor does it occur to him that the song could be contemporary or that it could be rehearsed, with its words part of a patterned genre regularly repeated through diverse variations in ritual or daily life.

As Young Bear has said in an interview,

> I was just amazed at how someone could go to a powwow, pay the standard admission fee, and think that the whole world of the Mesquakie people was going to be revealed to him in one program, when the fact of the matter is that these dances performed by the Mesquakie people are just tribal celebration dances. Snodgrass thought he saw a lot more than he did—especially when he thought he could make it a poetic commentary about the singers, some of the children, the songs. To degrade a form of tribal entertainment was, to me, a great slap in the face to the Mesquakies. I knew that a lot of the Mesquakie people who were the subjects of this poem were not going to read it at all. So I thought I would do an "eye for an eye" sort of thing and write some negative commentary back to him and hopefully he would see it somewhere along the line and know that we weren't as simple-minded and savage, I guess, as he put it in his poem. ("Connected to the Past," 346–47)

And yet Young Bear says that despite the thickness of ordinary Meskwaki life that he knows so closely and that Wright and Snodgrass do not even suspect, he himself does not know, remains "incomplete." Knowing that he does not know, however, allows him to "think twice" as he complains that Snodgrass will not. Ironically, when he visited the powwow in 1949, Snodgrass was soon to win fame as a poet of self-examination, but here he speaks from a position of self-presumed authority, by contrast with Young Bear's sense of himself as incomplete. A smaller-minded poet would take this to the level of children in a sandbox: I know this stuff and you don't. But Young Bear continues to offer his knowledge as "no authority to anything," or, as he puts it in more personal and familial terms in "for the rain in march":

> i will never know who i actually am
> nor will the woman who lives with me

```
know me or herself or the children
we want
i am always surprised at how many
different minds drift across
each other
some resenting everyone
some imitating what they will
never be
others make room for others
and then there are us
afraid of everyone because they
are afraid of us
unable to fit anywhere
                              (Winter, 169)
```

At a level more interpersonal than intercultural, this draws a more delicate taxonomy than any drawn by the anthropologists that Steven Polgar
describes who, sometimes with considerable interpretive resourcefulness,
graph ascending and descending degrees of acculturation, or than Polgar
himself draws when he speculates helpfully about Meskwaki "biculturalism." At Snodgrass's crude level, biculturalism or double-consciousness—
long before described by W. E. B. Du Bois (*Souls*, 16–18)—is unimaginable: Meskwaki culture, in a proto-Baudrillardian parody, comes straight
out of Hollywood. Thus when Meskwaki don World War II "combat issues," to Snodgrass their khaki must be "castoff." He seems unaware that
many Meskwaki would be veterans like himself, and that military service is
a point of special pride for the Meskwaki and for most Native American
peoples. Young Bear, for example, has published poems in honor of veterans and takes pride in singing songs in their honor.[18] Serving in the
armed forces is not simply a way for Indians to move into the dominant
culture; it is also itself a proud feature of contemporary Indian culture.

Beside the ethnic stalemate between Snodgrass's irritation and Young
Bear's mixture of disgust with incredulous indifference lies a conflict
pitched along class lines. In this sense, the first two words of "Powwow" are
key: "They all," soon repeated in the line "They are all the same." Snodgrass's superior tone implicitly pits elite culture and the caressed distinctions of high formalist verse against a patronized mass culture of dungarees, trailers, and "jobs in truck stops and all-night filling stations," a
culture that, he supposes, forgoes fine distinctions to wallow in the undif-
ferentiated morass of "they" and "all" and the "same." Awash in false consciousness, "they" passively take movies as truth, whereas Snodgrass can
watch movies critically—a breathtaking presumption, since Indians of all
people have a perspective for viewing movies critically. The Indians de-

pend on a powwow with hot dogs and bleachers for their income, versus the erudite poet who can afford to go slumming (culturally perhaps even more than financially). He'll even step down for a moment to eat a hot dog, a detail that Young Bear's canny ear picks out, as if to suggest Snodgrass's patronizing humor. Snodgrass can look, but he erects an intellectual quarantine to seal himself off from the Indian world and from the broader culture of poverty and the working class that he consigns it to. He specularizes the powwow, enjoying the cheap frisson of looking at it while sustaining the fiction that he and his family share none of the desires it represents. It is for "they" and them. The real beauty of it, if you can find the way out that those unaccommodating Indians won't explain to you, comes in the relief of escape, the driving away.

Young Bear plays on the class anxieties by having the Snodgrassian badger mock Young Bear's pickup, exactly the kind of vehicle that threatens Snodgrass. Eventually, staggered by Snodgrass's presumptions and fears, Young Bear extends the badger parody into an astonishing ad hominem, as if to bring out how responses like Snodgrass's are beneath arguing with. It remains only to show Snodgrass how it feels to be Snodgrassed, "an eye for an eye," and perhaps even to out-Snodgrass him:

> and i also know that the only thing
> he will ever experience in life
> as being phenomenal
> will be his lust
> stirring and feebly coming alive
> at the thought of women
> crumbs from the bread
> of his hot dog
> being carried away
> by images of crushed
> insects
>
> (*Winter*, 172)

Young Bear mocks Snodgrass by extrapolating from one poem to Snodgrass's whole life, just as Snodgrass extrapolates from an afternoon at the powwow to all of Meskwaki culture. Young Bear even has the insect images (the images, not the insects themselves) from the end of Snodgrass's poem carry away the shreds of his hot dog bun, figuratively castrating him for the wish to make entomological profundity compensate for Indian superficiality. Ironically, Young Bear's response concludes in the kind of "deep image" associated with Wright. The Wrights and Snodgrasses of the world, he suggests, sacrifice their lust to their images. Aesthetically colo-

nizing their denied selves and the cultures they look at and barely see—a
repressed analogy between self and other that only colonizes the more—
they convert their evasions into poetic capital.

Of course, any poem transmutes experience into poetic capital. Young
Bear is not free of that. In "The Dream of Purple Birds in Marshall, Washington," he recounts (to quote his prose summary) that he "realized
through dream or reincarnation that I had once witnessed the brutal
homicide of two white women by two white men" (*Invisible Musician*,
96–97). Two birds, the souls or "once-life of two women / whose body
parts lie scattered / and hidden safely under the dirt and rocks," come
"beckoning" him "from dream, from Iowa, from yourself," but he insists:

> *I refuse to be*
> *their spiritual conduit and release*
>
> .   .   .   .
>
> *in a valley where a large, red fluorescent*
> *cross is physically so much stronger*
> *than I . . .*
>
> (*Invisible Musician*, 88; closing ellipsis in the original)

How to compare Young Bear's transmutation of experience to Snodgrass's? Readers might wonder what provokes Young Bear's dream, and
whether imagined or projected violence against women does not provide
the raw material of his poetic capital as disturbingly as patronizing racism
does for Snodgrass's "Powwow." Indeed, for a poet more readily assimil-
able to the dominant culture, it might seem grandiose to compare one's
powers, even unfavorably, to those attributed to the Christian deity. But
such a reading would entail a colonizing misconception of the routines of
Meskwaki ontology, in which there is nothing so extraordinary about
dream power.[19] And it would miss that, unlike Snodgrass's Olympian
sneer, Young Bear's dream pretends no superior vantage point over the
spirits he describes. Distrustful of authority, he only backs away from the
presumption that he can assume any authority or do anything to resolve
their suffering. Contrary to pop-critical vulgarizations of Freud's ideas,
Freud describes dreams not as wish-fulfillments per se, but as compro-
mises by the dream-work that mediates competing wishes, as congealings
of a dialectic between defenses and drives. Hence we can read Young
Bear's dream of violence against white women as a defense, not just a desire. For he also dreams of resisting that violence, recursively overlaying
defense and desire on top of and within each other. And since such violence, terrifyingly commonplace, is regularly dealt out to Meskwaki by
whites, directly and indirectly, the condensation of dream-work suggests a

still broader resistance to violence, both in the reversal of races and in the urge to rescue the victims. Yet Young Bear, still stirring the stew of competing urges, pleads no thank you to the rescue fantasy (as Freud called it), in his typical, un-pin-downable way of making melody from cacophonous notes: the invisible musician.

Hence Young Bear's universe of poetic authority, instead of converting others' labor into his own poetic capital as Snodgrass does, seeks a communal arena where there is room for his imaginative invention and room for others' inventions, a dream of unlikely balance on what he has irreverently called "the existential surfboard." Not that anything anyone might do is okay. As we have seen, Young Bear is ready to oppose what some poets write, and "The Dream of Purple Birds" reacts against violence. His politics of poetic and cultural authority is rather more like politics on the Meskwaki Settlement, where factional strife proliferates but the factions hold together in their disdain of pressures to distribute land for private ownership (allotment) and in favor of communal ownership.

Mostly, Young Bear writes about Meskwaki, not about whites. Occasionally, as with "in disgust" or "for the rain in march," he criticizes white poets' presumptions about Indians, and in "in viewpoint: poem for 14 catfish and the town of tama, iowa," he lashes out in a blistering critique of local white racism. In another mode, Young Bear can also write of how the modest refusal of authority can make common ground across cultures. In "Quail and His Role in Agriculture," Young Bear goes to the Tastee Freez, drumming on the dashboard while he waits his turn. The beat attracts the attention of several farmers who also wait in line, but they do not chuckle or sneer like Snodgrass. Young Bear imagines that,

> With the constant drone of harvesting
> machinery in their ears, they probably
> thought the tapping was yet another
> mechanical trouble to contend with.
> (*Invisible Musician,* 77)

They allow him to imagine that they imagine his doings as part of their own, even while, when they look, they can surely see the difference as well as hear the rhythmic likeness. Then he completes the poem with these lines:

> It was a hot September day, and we
> had all stopped to have strawberry
> sundaes: I, to celebrate my song;
> and they, to soothe the grain and dust

in their throats. Midwesterners, all,
standing in the monolithic shadow
of a hydraulic platform, which lifted
the semi-truck's cab to the sky
to violently shake and dislodge
its cargo of yellow corn—
the historic sustenance
which was now to some
a symbol of abject poverty.
For others, like myself and all
my grandfathers before me, it continues
to be a transmitter of prayer.
Beautiful yellow corn . . .
                    (78; ellipsis in the original)

Their differences and their likenesses need not always undermine each other, even if they sometimes do. Perhaps, especially in a poem with a national audience, a giddy hint of comic parody creeps into the pride in the corn harvest and heartland solidarity, and yet that pride also sounds a note of anti-coastal defiance. "Midwesterners, all," in their differing ways, differing senses of being, they are not "all the same." But Young Bear and these "horticulturalists" (77), as he calls them half reverently and half teasingly, all produce their evolving, competing, and overlapping cultures in ways he can envision as analogues to all the grandfathers of his past and to each other.

CHAPTER 6

The Reinvention of Restless Young Men:
Storytelling and Poetry in Leslie Marmon Silko's
Ceremony and Thomas King's *Medicine River*

Leslie Marmon Silko's *Ceremony* (1977) and Thomas King's *Medicine River* (1989) bring together the defining issues of this book. Each of these issues served writers as a lever for imagining their own Indian writing and for inventing Indian writing as a category or negotiating the emerging obstacle course of expectations for "Native American Literature."

In diverse and overlapping ways, the four topics I have brought together to describe the invention of Native American literature—young men's threatened masculinity, the oral, the poetic, and Indian cultures' aloof renegotiations of what the dominant culture understands as authority—address a range of issues across gender, sexuality, stereotype, and the appropriation of cultural and intellectual property. Young men's restless sense that they had nothing to do was seized upon to represent the uncertain future of Native cultures in an age before the civil rights movement, Native political resurgence, and (in literary circles) the American Indian literary renaissance helped replenish Indian people's sense of hope. The earlier age gave us depressing titles like *Sundown* and *The Surrounded,* in contrast to more hopeful ones, like *Ceremony* and *Medicine River.* (*Ceremony* even ends with the word "Sunrise," as if opposing itself to Mathews's novel.) Meanwhile, a notion of Native orality and poeticality also came to represent Indian people and offer a means to invent a specifically Indian literature through storytelling and transcribed orality. But the oversimplification in what sometimes seems like a reduction of Indian people to the oral and the poetical, with an accompanying underestimation of Indian literacy and an unwitting sense that therefore white writers and poets are better positioned to represent Indians than Indians are themselves, contributed to an already deep Indian resentment at the appropriation of Indian cultures. When Young Bear responds to such appropriations by drawing on his authority as an Indian learned in his own culture and yet not claiming authority, we can see the argument speak back to its beginning. Which is to say that Chal Windzer in *Sundown* cannot imagine the doing that Young Bear's poetry enacts. *Sundown* and *The Surrounded* nevertheless pose issues and grope toward solutions that anticipate what more recent writers set out to imagine.

With the first canonization of Indian writing in N. Scott Momaday's *House Made of Dawn* (1968), James Welch's *Winter in the Blood* (1974), and *Ceremony*,[1] these issues gathered into something like an agenda directing Indian writers and the reception of their work. Some concerns, such as storytelling, may have been exaggerated in the reception of these works at the cost of attention to these highly politicized writers' anticolonialist rereadings of orality, poeticality, authority, and culturally variable notions of ordinary doing. The widely acclaimed and taught *Ceremony*, while seeming to draw on *House Made of Dawn* and perhaps on *Winter in the Blood*, reimagines this agenda even more than its celebrated predecessors.[2]

Silko can't wish away the anguish-ridden landscape of earlier Indian literature (and probably wouldn't want to). Indeed, she repeats it with an almost loving precision that would seem to come only from a commitment to owning up to history, even to sordid history. But in the process of repeating it she also sets out to transform it through an ethos of ceremony. For Silko, ceremony is not a program for liberal reform, not job training for young Indians with nothing to do. Jobs are not the issue. It is not a matter of giving people—or helping them find—something to do so much as a matter of reconceiving doing, a project that *Sundown* and *The Surrounded* begin but cannot complete. In ceremony, Silko sees another and a recovered way of being. For Silko, ceremony is the direct opposite of the notion of nothing to do, because a ceremonial ethos makes daily life sacred. It makes the ordinary extraordinary, entirely independent of (if not actually hostile to) the business ethos of labor for hire. And so to those—including self-hating Indians like Emo—who would see young Indian men as doing nothing, Silko responds that independently of how they earn their keep, they live—or can live—a life infused with sacred ritual, not in any paint-by-the-number sense of pharisaical piety that requires a slavish repetition of ideas projected onto the past, but rather through an ethos of identification with and respect for what the business ethos cannot see, their people's culture and history. This is the difference between Emo and Tayo, between the dessicated false traditionalists and the respondent traditionalism of Betonie's innovations, between the essentialism of racial and sexual policing and the improvisatory blurs of Tayo's world, between the pious mystification of poetry that drives the theorizing of Tedlock and Hymes and *Cere-*

mony's mix of prosaic poetry with poetic prose, between a rigidly demarcated grid of narrative structure and the amoebic pulsing of *Ceremony*'s resistance to definable form. In short, it is the difference between the cultural pressure to set up boundaries and walls and *Ceremony*'s commitment to replace boundaries and walls with an ethic and ethos of transitions.

In *Ceremony*, again the lens zooms in on restless young men with nothing to do. This time they are Laguna World War II veterans, echoing Abel, the World War II vet in *House Made of Dawn* and anticipating such other characters as Henry Lamartine and Attis McCurtain, the Vietnam vets with post-traumatic stress syndrome in Louise Erdrich's *Love Medicine* (1984) and Louis Owens's *The Sharpest Sight* (1992). In *Ceremony* we find five young men back from the war: Tayo, his friend Harley, and Leroy, Pinkie, and Emo. Compared to other Indian novels, *Ceremony* offers a group of men rather than an isolated individual, yet it also draws a sharp opposition between Tayo and his cohort, enlarging on divisions that recall the less dwelled-on differences between Archilde and his no-good brother Louis in *The Surrounded* and between Chal and his Osage friends in *Sundown*. *Ceremony* splits Tayo from the other men of his generation and experience, casting him as hero while casting Emo and Pinkie (if not also Leroy and Harley) as unambiguously evil: they are witches. Whether readers take the witchery literally or not, *Ceremony*'s sharp differentiation between young men declares what *Sundown* and *The Surrounded* remain too conflicted to assert: that a restless, aimless young man with nothing to do may be restless and aimless for good reason. In Tayo's case, what looks like aimlessness gradually gathers into a project, into a larger way of life that can save Laguna, and even in some sense save the wider community and the entire world through ceremony. Granted, the project remains vague. It may need to stay vague to seem plausible and to respect the independence of Laguna religious and cultural practice. But vague or not, Tayo's project emerges as heroic, culturally valuable, and deeply needed.

Emo represents the other side of nothing to do, the nothing that magnifies into tangible evil, and his view tempts Tayo. Tayo tells Betonie that Emo "says the Indians have nothing compared to white people. He talks about their cities and all the machines and food they have. He says the land is no good, and we must go after what they have, and take it from them. . . . Well, I don't know how to say this but it seems that way. All you have to do is look around. And so I wonder . . . what good Indian ceremonies can do" (132). Here Tayo takes seriously Emo's argument that Indians have nothing, and he defines "having" shallowly, as what you might see just by looking around: cities, machines, food. Times are hard, but nothing in the novel indicates that Tayo's people are starving or even hard up for food, so the reference to food suggests not so much necessities or staples as excess and extravagance. Emo "says the land is no good," presumably referring to the drought, but Tayo's despair at the drought shows that he knows how good the land, his people's heritage, can be. His uncle Josiah tells Tayo that drought is part of the process and not something bad (45–46). Finally, Tayo realizes, if Indians have nothing then their ceremonies must amount to nothing. Emo is like the suicides in Young Bear's "one chip of human bone" who suppose that they have "nothing to lose," echoing Mathews's "nothing to do" and evoking a horrific history of loss. Young Bear's phrase also exposes the in-some-ways deeper loss of denying your culture by believing that it leaves you with nothing left to lose. Emo desecrates the land and the ceremonies that Silko's novel holds sacred, and Betonie responds to Tayo's anguished query by calling Emo's plea "the trickery of the witchcraft" (132).

Betonie tells Tayo that "we can deal with white people . . . because we invented white people; it was Indian witchery that made white people in the first place" (132), and then he tells his story about Indians inventing white people. Betonie's story inverts the assumptions that Indians do nothing and that doing and agency are the exclusive province of white people. In his story whites are the passive objects of Indian doing. In effect his story presents Indians the way the dominant ideology presents whites, and presents whites as soulless, uncivilized killers, gesturing toward if not directly repeating the way the dominant ideology presents Indians. Like a Virginia Slims billboard or other ostensibly feminist or oppositional but still exploitive ruses to make dominated people adopt their dominators' offenses, the reversals in Betonie's story can stir up new problems. In this case the reversals depend on a risky comic effect, as if to say, isn't it funny to tell a story about Indians screwing up and causing their own problems, implying that we take white agency and Indian object-status so much for granted that merely reversing them will seem comic. Moreover, the reversal risks embodying a conservative Republican, Reaganesque ethic, suggesting that since Indians are the agents of their own destiny, they must bear the blame for their problems until they pull themselves up by their own bootstraps. A flirtation with the bootstraps polemic permeates the novel from its beginning, where the poetry announces that "Their evil is mighty / but it can't stand up to our stories" (2). Such remarks could suggest blaming evil's victims for not doing enough to stand up to evil. Indeed, in *Ceremony* Silko is not shy about taking a critical attitude to particular Indians and to troubling patterns in Indian culture that they represent. She offers a scathing portrait of Tayo's false friends, the witches. Like Reagan and the right, *Ceremony* takes evil seriously as a category, unlike many of its leftist or liberal admirers, who often see "evil" as a mystifyingly transcendent label that masks more worldly motives and thus evades the social and political.

If Betonie's story had no humor in its horror, it could suggest conservative Republicanism, but its destabilizing humor suggests outrage at the idea that anyone could deny the terrible agency of European conquest:

> *Then they grow away from the earth*
> *then they grow away from the sun*
> *then they grow away from the plants and animals.*
> *They see no life*
> *When they look*
> *they see only objects.*
> *The world is a dead thing for them*
> *the trees and rivers are not alive*
> *the mountains and stones are not alive.*
> *The deer and bear are objects*
> *They see no life.*
>
> . . . . . .
>
> *They fear the world.*
> *They destroy what they fear.*

(135)

What begins with a degree of comedy ends up as frightening. More largely, Betonie's tale dramatizes the agency of ceremony and story, but not as bootstraps. The ceremony and story he describes come from witches, but their efficacy for witches suggests that in kinder hands ceremony and story, like Betonie's larger ceremony and story of which the tale about inventing white people is only a small part, offer an alternative to the Republican ideology of objectifying commerce (*"they see only objects"*) and the related ideology of European conquest. The point is not so much to blame backsliding Indians for faults in their ceremonialism, though the novel gives us some of that in Tayo himself or in the old stories (e.g., 48), as to put forth ceremonialism as the agency and means for integrating a life into its traditions and earthly setting.[3]

Nor is the point the literal claim that Indians monopolize agency or the ironic claim that, contrary to Betonie's story, we all know too well that, really, whites monopolize agency. Rather, Betonie's story shatters such separations between Indians and whites. Using a "they" that vaguely refers to witches but that has no antecedent and so also suggests more than a single term can contain, Betonie tells Tayo, "They want us to separate ourselves from white people, to be ignorant and helpless as we watch our own destruction" (132). It is tough for anyone who takes pride in Indian distinctiveness to swallow Betonie's implicit link of separation from whites to ignorance and helplessness, but so many years into the history of cultural contact and its hierarchies of power, he argues that separate can no longer mean equal. To say that Indians and whites should not be separated is not to say there is no difference between them, just as Betonie and Tayo's mixed blood does not keep them from being Indian and yet also in some sense being white, different from whites yet also different from many other Indians. Like Betonie's and Tayo's hazel eyes, Betonie's story about Indians inventing white people figures cultural mixing. To be sure, it is an Indian story, told by an Indian as part of an Indian ceremony and as a story about Indian agency. But (and here I dwell on a potentially obvious point, but one that we are trained and pressured to overlook) like the rest of post-contact culture, Betonie's story is mixed, with its expression "in the beginning" from the English translation of the Bible, its allusion to baseball tournaments, its medium of English, and its transcribed rendition of the oral. I am not suggesting that those examples represent whiteness imported intact into Betonie's story. On the contrary, each of those examples, in a routine way, is culturally mixed. The English translation of the Hebrew Bible is part of Laguna Christianity. Laguna has a lively history of baseball tournaments. The English language, as the dominant language of most American Indians and the Laguna people, is now an Indian and a world language, and—despite mythologies that would confine Indians to the oral—writing has long been an Indian and multicultural medium.[4] Betonie's notion of Indians and whites thus depends on continuous process or, in the words of the novel, on transitions rather than boundaries (246), just as he insists that to save the traditional ceremonies he must change them (126). In the same way, Silko rails against boundaries in the form of racial borders, including national borders and walls to keep out undocumented immigrants, in *Almanac of the Dead* and, more directly, in her essays ("Fences against Freedom" and "The Border Patrol State").

Betonie may strike some readers as too readily an authorial mouthpiece. But his agenda doesn't merely cling to safe territory. It may seem safe, because the notion of continuous change happens to chime in with postmodernist platitudes, but those platitudes settled in (where they settled in at all) mostly after *Ceremony* came out. Depending on the Indian culture at issue (and on many other details, to say the least), the idea of unilaterally changing ceremonies may come across as anything from expected to disgraceful. But *Ceremony* as a novel depends not so much on the ideas that Betonie advocates directly as on the ideas embodied in the novel more broadly, including its form.[5]

Formally, *Ceremony* shapes its preoccupation with cultural and literary transitions in a variety of related and overlapping ways. It shifts between poetry and prose. It uses poetry for a set of narratives embedded in the larger prose narrative. It takes up different poetic tones for different poetic narratives or kinds of poetic narrative. And it draws on several different kinds of transitions between sections of prose and poetry and between sections of prose. Apart from the variation in poetic tone, all these structural variations depend on features specific to writing, even as Silko uses those features to represent oral traditions and her weaving of the oral with the written. To look at such a blend of oral and written, prosaic and poetic can also mean to consider the novel's broader use of poetry and its mixing of poetry and prose, including its dialogue with traditions that call on storytelling, orality, or the poetic to legitimize and establish Native American literature.

Thus Silko uses poetry to represent traditional and contemporary oral story and ceremony, drawing on a practice that goes back beyond Washington Matthews's translations from Navajo and that Hymes and Tedlock themselves drew on dramatically in the years immediately before and after *Ceremony*. Hymes's most influential work on verse translations started to come out about the same time as *Ceremony*, perhaps too late for Silko to see it before writing the novel. But Tedlock's edition of Zuni stories, *Finding the Center,* appeared in 1972. With a commercial publisher, it was widely reviewed and distributed. Zuni is close to Laguna geographically and culturally (though not linguistically), and Tedlock's work was much in the air both nationally and in Pueblo Indian studies well before *Ceremony* was published in 1977. Nevertheless, the relevant issue is not the possibility of influence so much as the way that Silko, Tedlock, and Hymes all work in the tradition that identifies Indianness with orality and storytelling, identifies orality with poetry, and sees the confluence of orality, poetry, storytelling, and Indianness as a way to invent and sustain Indian literature.

As in the translations of Hymes, Tedlock, and their followers, the novel's poetry and poetic storytelling can seem to ground Indian writing and make it seem more seriously literary. Silko, however, is actually writing the stuff, as opposed to transcribing and translating it or translating other people's transcriptions. And she is writing it as poetry, which differs from Tedlock's or Hymes's attempts to transform oral storytelling into English-language poetry through the multiple mediations of transcription, translation, and post-facto poeticization. Yet often she is not writing the stuff in the same way that Young Bear or most other poets write poetry, because she often draws so closely on traditional oral stories, including stories that have already been transcribed, translated, and rendered as published prose.[6] Silko's poems are thus written poetry, like the poetry of Young Bear and most other poets and unlike the translations of Tedlock and Hymes or Rothenberg and the ethnopoets, but they also represent oral stories, less like most other poetry and more like those translations. Still, there remains a cacophonous difference between what Silko does and what the ethnopoetic translators do. One writes poetry that continues and extends her people's traditions, signing her name to the work and fostering an identification of the work both with her people and with her own persona as imaginative writer, while the others transcribe another people's stories and write them as poetry because that's what the transcriber-translator—not the storytellers—believes they are already.

But even though Silko often writes poetic prose, her poetry can get prosaic in the extreme, and her poetry inclines to the prosaic more than to the lyrical, even when speaking of things ancient and ceremonially meaningful. Silko's flexible combination of the poetic and the prosaic allows her to challenge the platitudes of Tedlockian theory. She begins deferentially, opening the novel as a poem or sequence of poems (1–3) infused with the ancient creation story as model, as analogue, and even as a beginning for the novel's story about ceremony, thus linking ceremony with poetic storytelling and thus also sacralizing storytelling.

> And in the belly of this story
> the rituals and the ceremony
> are still growing.
>
> *What She Said:*
>
> The only cure
> I know
> is a good ceremony,
> that's what she said.
>
> (2–3)

The repetition of "what she said" makes the storyteller female at least for now, which fits the reference to Thought-Woman in the book's opening words:

> She is sitting in her room
> thinking of a story now
>
> I'm telling you the story
> she is thinking.
>
> (1)

"That's what she said" and variations on that phrase appear prolifically through Pueblo literature, including Tedlock's translations from Zuni, which use the expression over and over: what she said, what he said, what they said, even what the turkeys said.[7] Rayna Green picked out the same words for the title of her anthology of contemporary Indian women's writing, *That's What She Said,* and Joy Harjo uses the phrase to conclude one of her most powerful early poems, "Old Lines which Sometimes Work, and Sometimes Don't" (39). The phrase "that's what she said" underlines Silko's poetry and storytelling as oral, and the link to Thought-Woman underlines the sacralizing quality of the novel's oral storytelling. From that opening, *Ceremony* shifts to prose, intermittently switching back to poetry to describe a ceremony (37–38) or to tell ancient stories that—despite their prosaically casual tone ("The way / I heard it / was . . ." [37])—still reinforce the sense of special deference in the novel's resort to poetic form (13–14, 46–49, 53–54). The casual tone can even suggest the way the novel's ceremonialism integrates a deference to ancient story into its contemporary routine. Then the deference collapses when the novel shifts abruptly to a crass oral story, in poetic form, about the supposed pleasures that World War II made it possible for uniformed Indian men to find with white women.

At first, the story seems to come in Tayo's voice, for the last sentence of prose before the poetry reads "And during the war Tayo learned about white women and Indian men" (57). Though it turns out that Emo tells the story, the transition jars because we do not expect so crass a story either from Tayo or in the poetic form that until then *Ceremony* has approached so respectfully. Suddenly, in written poetry that evokes the oral ("We went into this bar on 4th Ave., see"), we get a boastful story about hitting on two eager white women identified metonymically—by reduction to selected body parts—as a "fat" brunette and a "real blond" with "big tits." The Indian storyteller takes the name of Mattuci, "this Wop / in our unit," and rides home—or at least says he rode home—between the two women, "grabbing titties / with both hands." Next day, he brags to his "drinking buddy" that he "scored," and not with one woman but with both of them:

> "Yes, sir, this In'di'n
> was grabbin' white pussy
> all night!"
> "Shit, Chief,
> that's some reputation
> you're making for Mattuci!"
> "Goddamn," I said
> "Maybe next time
> I'll send him a bill!"
>   (57–59)

Emo's story drives us to reconsider the novel's use of poetic form and orality. For Konrad Groß, through its poetic form "Emo's story assumes mythical qualities and usurps the power of myth" (94). For James Ruppert, the poetic form of Emo's story "emphasizes how myths grow, complement, and structure reality" (*Mediation*, 81). To be sure, early in the novel poetic form evokes the respect Silko expresses through it, but after Emo's story that respect no longer seems inherent to the form itself. Thus Emo's story takes readers through a process like the one that critics have gone through in disputing Roman Jakobson's notion that poetic form necessarily carries particular connotations, or that communications scholars have gone through in critiquing the fallacy of so-called technological determinism, the inclination to read a given technology as necessarily carrying predictable connotations.[8] The notion of technological determinism comes unglued when different web sites or films, for example, express contradictory ideologies through the same style of design or editing, just as poems that invoke competing ideologies might nevertheless use the same poetic technology: the same meter, rhyme scheme, or pattern of alliteration. In short, Silko sets us up, tempting readers to take *Ceremony*'s poetry sanctimoniously, as inherently sacralizing, despite its prosaic sound, because it is prettily carved up in lines that set it apart from the prose. But then Silko turns to a poem so profane—still oral but now spoken by a character so repellent that eventually the book declares him a witch—that it presses us to reconsider the role of poetry in the novel, the differences and transitions between the novel's poetry and its prose, and the role of poetry as a representation of Indian orality and storytelling.

Silko's challenge can provoke a range of responses to the Hymesian, Tedlockian, Jakobsonian formula of technological or poetic determinism. Hymes and Tedlock's theories and Silko's use of poetry in a novel have so powerful an effect partly because they feed off and reinforce the sacralizing, mystifying ideological air so often associated with poetry. To question those theories will not take that effect away; skepticism about an ideological effect might help diminish the effect but won't make it disappear. Moreover, *Ceremony* isn't merely skeptical, just as it isn't merely reverent, as Silko's use of Emo and his story bring out. Putting Emo's story in poetry seems to throw off the reverence of the novel's earlier poetry and deny the ceremonial values it represents, much as Emo trashes Indians by seeing a special value in white women and by denying his own name and with it his name's resonance of personal and cultural identity. On the one hand, when Silko puts Emo's travesties in poetry, the reverence in poetry mocks his travesties. On the other hand, Emo's travesties also mock the supposed reverence in poetry. In turn, that mocking of poetry, despite its corrupt source in Emo, can puncture the unwitting romanticism that undergirds Hymesian, Tedlockian thinking. The point is not that Silko would agree with my critique of Hymes and Tedlock, but rather that she draws on what they draw on (if not also on their work directly) and shows the limits to the broader view of Indian poetry, orality, and storytelling that their work represents.

Poetry thus has more and less in its philosophy than many of its advocates dream of: more because it can do such contradictory things, and less because poetry itself, rid of claims for its particular technologies, for poetic determinism, cannot enforce any particular outcome or ideology. It depends what you do with it. Silko or her interpreters can use it to exalt or to desecrate, and, as in some of the more thematically disturbing episodes in Hymes's and Tedlock's fine translations, the same lines can do both at the same time.

Moreover, Silko eschews Tedlock's visual representation of orality and Hymes's pyrotechnics of prosody. She does not arrange words or lines on the page to represent pauses, volume, or pitch, as Tedlock does; nor does she equate storytelling with poetry, as do both Tedlock and Hymes, since her entire novel tells stories, not only those sections in poetic form. Her use of poetry to integrate oral storytelling into her novel and to multiply the forms of storytelling innovatively extends the tradition that goes back to *Cogewea* and *The Surrounded.* Nevertheless, in *Ceremony* Silko remains a writer, not an oral storyteller. Her poetry is oriented more to writing and print than to sound, with as much interest in visual arrangement as we see in the work of Hymes and Tedlock. She centers her lines on the page, producing an elegant visual effect. On the one hand, the centered lines invite readers to find purpose in the arrangement of particular poems, while on the other hand, the consistent centering highlights the arbitrary and random. Even so, for at least one poem (206), she arranges the centered lines into a so-called pattern-poem, parsing out a hunter's song to look like a Ka't'sina (kachina) and help suggest that the hunter in a mountain-lion cap is himself a mountain-lion Ka't'sina, the same mountain lion that helps Tayo escape the two patrolmen.[9]

Silko also plays variations on the dialogue between her novel and the Jakobsonian desire to sever poetry from prose. She prolifically varies her transitions between poetry and prose, much as she blurs any consistent pattern for transitions between prose sections or between different times, and much as she explicitly thematizes the ubiquity and prolific variety of transitions.

As charted in table 1, the transitions between poetry and prose usually work either abruptly, with no particular link between the poetry and the prose, or by analogy between the poetry's topic and the prose's topic. Offering analogous topics, the poetry tells three tales of drought, and the prose also tells a tale of drought. Sometimes the poetry runs on continuously with the prose narrative, twice to render a song and once even directly narrating the action. Meanwhile, the typographical difference between poetry and prose stays consistent, with the lines of poetry centered on the page versus the left-and right-justified prose. That difference invites us to see a distinction between the poetry and the prose, while the potpourri of continuity and interruption in the transitions between poetry and prose repeatedly bridges the distinction, highlights it, or plays variations on it. In that way, Silko draws on poetry and prose without singling out either for an exalted role in representing orality and oral narrative, even as she continues to take advantage of the long-founded cultural expectation that poetry especially figures the romantic aura of voice and orality. She envisions something to do by building on, absorbing, and superseding the formalist innovations of McNickle, Hymes, and Tedlock while also building on the worry that Mathews brought to Indian literature about young men and old cultures with nothing to do. While highlighting the oral can risk a commonplace condescension to or romanticizing of orality, forswearing the oral would be worse, would be to cave in to the depredations of cultural caricature. Instead, Silko's visual manipulation of poetry and prose on the page underlines print as her medium, helping her extend and even de-binarize the integration of print and orality.[10]

Table 1. *Ceremony*'s Transitions between Poetry and Prose

The first column identifies the sections of poetry in numerical sequence. It also identifies the two continuing poetic series as "a" and "b" and identifies the numerical sequence for each. Thus 5–a2 refers to the fifth section of poetry in the novel and the second section in series a. Series a spreads out across the novel, whereas series b all comes during one episode of the prose narrative and is actually part of the prose narrative.

The second column gives page numbers for each section of poetry.

The third column attempts a concise description of the transitions between prose and poetry by describing the relation between that particular section of poetry and the prose that surrounds it. The abbreviation NPC means that there is no particular connection between the poetry and the prose. I have tried to identify repeated patterns in the relation between sections of poetry and sections of prose without oversimplifying to exaggerate the regularity of patterning.

Sections of poetry, numbered	Page numbers	Transition between prose and poetry
1	1–4	Beginning of the novel; NPC to the following prose; each page seems to work as a separate poem.

2	12–13	Analogy between droughts described in poetry and in prose; first of three analogies between droughts described in prose and droughts described in poetry.
3	37–38	Connected to plot but not continuous with narrative.
4–a1	46–49	NPC, but like Tayo, Pa'caya'nyi "didn't know who his father was" (46). Second of three analogies between droughts described in poetry and in prose.
5–a2	53–54	NPC beyond loose analogy of rough times in both plots.
6	57–59	Continuous with prose narrative.
7–a3	71–72	Analogy between Tayo's loss of his mother and the loss of "our mother" (71) Nau'ts'ity'i (1, 48).
8–a4	82	NPC
9–a5	105–6	NPC
10–a6	113	NPC, but ironic analogy between police driving the homeless from the arroyo and Fly and Hummingbird asking old Buzzard to purify their town.
11	128–30	Implicitly continuous with prose narrative, as a story told by Betonie.
12	132–38	Continuous with prose narrative, as a story told by Betonie.
13–b1	139–41	Continuous with prose narrative and analogous to it, as a part of Betonie's ceremony (its role in Betonie's ceremony grows clearer on 141).
14–b2	142	Continuous with prose narrative.
15–b3	143	Continuous with prose narrative.
16–b4	143–44	Continuous with prose narrative and distinctive in that continues to narrate Tayo's action directly in the poetry (144).
17–a7	151–52	NPC
18	153	Continuous with prose narrative, though not necessarily part of the preceding scene.
19	170–76	Third analogy between droughts in poetry and in prose.
20–a8	180	NPC
21	182	Continuous with prose narrative, as a song within the narrative.
22	206	Continuous with prose narrative, as a song within the narrative, with the lines on the page shaped like the Ka't'sina singer.
23	247	Analogy, in that the poetry is about a witch and ways to restrict witchcraft, while in the prose Tayo runs

		from and thinks about witches, and both poetry and prose suggest that witchcraft can't work "if someone is watching."
24a9	255–56	Analogy, loosely, in the mood of coming to a conclusion, in the remark that "it / sure wasn't very easy," and in purifying the town.
25	257	Continuous with prose narrative.
26	258	Analogy to defeat of evil and witches in prose narrative.
27	260–62	Analogy to conclusion of prose narrative, or can see as completion of and thus continuous with prose narrative, and even as continuing the poetic narrative of 132–38; can also see 262 as separate from 260–61 in the same way that the novel's first four pages each seem to carry a separate poem.

Visually, *Ceremony*'s transitions between sections work as prolifically and irregularly as its transitions between poetry and prose. I count 115 points where a skipped line of some sort marks a visual transition between prose sections. Eighty skip one line without indenting the next paragraph, and 35 skip about five lines and then indent the next paragraph halfway across the page. But I have failed to find any logic for the difference. Similarly, I count 26 transitions from prose to poetry. Eleven skip one line, and 15 skip about five lines, but again, except that the five chants or songs each come after only one skipped line (142, 143—twice, 182, 206), I have found no logic to discriminate between the different-size skips. In the same vein, I count 26 transitions from poetry to prose. Sixteen skip about five lines and indent the next paragraph halfway across the page; one skips most of a page and then indents halfway across the page (5); 6 skip one line and then indent the next paragraph by the ordinary amount; and 3 skip a line without indenting. Those last 3 follow a chant or song (142, 143, 206), but a couple of others follow a chant or song and still indent (144, 182)—and again I have again found no logic to the variations. The lack of such a logic—or its obscurity if after all I've just missed it (though I have read widely through the criticism on the novel and never seen this formal variation even mentioned)—matches both Silko's disinterest in tying any particular arrangement of poetry or prose exclusively to the oral or the written, and her interest in visual and typographical play and variation.

Ceremony's initially bewildering array of transitions between different time periods works even less systematically (see table 2). In part, Tayo's passage through the novel points to his discovery that all times continue in one time: "the world below and the sand paintings inside became the same that night" (145). "The ride into the mountain had branched into all directions of time. . . . The ck'o'yo Kaup'a'ta somewhere is stacking his gambling sticks and waiting for a visitor; Rocky and I are walking across the ridge in the moonlight; Josiah and Robert are waiting for us. This night is a single night; and there has never been any other" (192). From the beginning of the novel, the narrating of that vision of all times as one time structures the book as a web of diverse times in which any single time might at any point percolate up from memory and take over the narrative, much like the narrative structure in the first two sections of Faulkner's *The Sound and the Fury* (the Benjy and Quentin sections) or in some ways like Joyce's *Ulysses* and Woolf's *Mrs. Dalloway,* suggesting a high modernist as well as an Indian or Pueblo affinity for Silko's notions of multiple connections and continuities. The link to Benjy Compson fits Tayo's sense of helplessness early in the novel, including the way that thoughts of his cousin Rocky, or even just hearing Rocky's name, make Tayo cry (27–28), echoing Benjy's cries at the sound of Caddy's name.[11]

Table 2. Time Shifts in *Ceremony*'s Prose

We might chart the time shifts in a variety of ways. Sometimes they do not break down clearly enough to lend themselves to a chart, especially when the poetry intervenes, but we can itemize the transitions in narrative time by listing the more or less opening words of each new time, at least for the prose part of the novel. Such a list oversimplifies things (for example, it leaves out shifts in perspective, which often have much to do with shifts in time), but it may still prove helpful as a rough series of landmarks for structure and pattern.

7	they had sat together
9	He had to keep busy
11	Jungle rain had no beginning or end
14	So he had prayed the rain away
14	For a long time he had been white smoke
15	The new doctor asked him
16	There was a cardboard name tag
18	He sat on the bed
20	that time in the eighth grade
21	Harley squatted down
22	The Montaño had not been
23	"It was too bad about the dog
27	she sitting in the corner
28	He started to cry

But unlike the first sections of *The Sound and the Fury*, *Ceremony* occasionally shifts outside its main focalizer's perspective, sometimes with striking results, as in the remarkable shift to Helen Jean's view (161–66). Suddenly, in a passage that seems to wake up the novel's usually latent feminism, we see the young *woman* with nothing to do, and instead of seeing her from the young men's leering perspective that turns up earlier in the novel, as in Emo's storytelling, we see her view of things, including her fear of Tayo, whose mother resembles Helen Jean but whose quiet way makes Helen Jean fear he might beat her up. Such turns of narrative angle, common in contemporary fiction, also began or at least famously accelerated with the high modernist experiments of Joyce, Woolf, and Faulkner. The result is not easy reading, for Silko is less concerned than many of her contemporaries to explain or regularize the transitions.

At the beginning, Tayo finds the multiple connections oppressively tangled, "like colored threads from old Grandma's wicker sewing basket. . . . He could feel it inside his skull—the tension of little threads being pulled and how it was with tangled things, things tied together, and as he tried to pull them apart and rewind them into their places, they snagged and tangled even more" (6–7). Rereaders of *Ceremony* can forget how new readers strain to work through the tangle, especially in the beginning as the narrative shifts back and forth between Tayo's present and his sprawling memories, shifting as well among the Laguna area, Los Angeles, where Tayo goes to the veterans' hospital, and the Philippine jungles of World War II, including the Bataan death march, unfamiliar territory to many readers. (Even some published critics think Tayo fought in the Korean war or the Vietnam war.) The narrative grows all the more difficult to follow because Tayo himself has trouble distinguishing between the different places. He hears Japanese Americans speaking Japanese in Los Angeles and thinks he is back with Japanese soldiers in the Philippines, and he sees or imagines that he sees his uncle Josiah and Willie Begay, Tayo's Navajo schoolmate, in the Philippine jungle, because each looks so much like a Japanese soldier. The various times overlay each other, like the distinctions between poetry and prose or oral and written story, not canceling but deepening each other as the book reimagines boundaries as transitions.

That reimagining shows especially in an often quoted passage: "He cried the relief he felt at finally seeing the pattern, the way all the stories fit together—the old stories, the war stories, their stories—to become the story that was still being told. . . . He had only seen and heard the world as it always was: no boundaries, only transitions through all distances and time" (246). While Silko makes no secret here of the way she uses Tayo's thoughts to explain the novel—the way she dispenses, we might say, with the boundary between plot and interpretation—it may still help to ask what is the difference (the boundary?) between a boundary and a transition? One separates, while still marking the wedge of separation as a point of contact; the other crosses or even merges, while still preserving a difference, a sense of a binary, since it hangs on to the notion that there are differences to merge. Such a comparison threatens to take the boundary between boundaries and transitions and convert it into a transition—and that is the point. Silko's transition to transitions is self-replicating and consuming; it absorbs other views and proliferates across other interpretations, trumping other interpretations that would see the world as a random spatter of separation and disconnection.

Thomas King's first novel, *Medicine River,* reinvents the restless young men of *Sundown, The Surrounded,* and *Ceremony.* While Louise Erdrich and Paula Gunn Allen reopened Indian novels to a focus on women not seen since *Cogewea,* King kept writing about restless men, though without separating them from women or from the community. Like many of his predecessors and contemporaries, King draws on oral literature and storytelling. He even wrote a dissertation called "Inventing the Indian: White Images, Native Oral Literature, and Contemporary Native Writers." Yet King differs from Mathews, McNickle, Momaday, Welch, and Silko in that his restless young men aren't all so young, and while they may not seem to do much by the business-centered, chamber-of-commerce standard of doing that haunts Chal Windzer in *Sundown,* still, gauged by King's relaxed way of narrating daily life and its pleasures, his young and middle-aged men do much that means a great deal to them. Even so, they worry about what to do. Harlen Bigbear worries mostly about everyone else's problems. Will—"Rose Horse Capture's boy" (139), the fortyish first-person narrator whose last name we never learn—worries with touching awkwardness about what role he should play as a man, a lover of the aptly named, independent-minded Louise Heavyman ("formidable," Harlen insists on calling her [217, 233]), and a potential stepfather to Louise's daughter. In this way, the novel is crowded with small but moving pleasures and worries, reaestheticizing the humdrum dramas of daily life that more melodramatic novels neglect, and exalting the extraordinary in the ordinary.

The men who populate *Medicine River* are no angels, but they aren't like Chal Windzer, Archilde Leon, Abel of *House Made of Dawn*, the haunted failures of Welch's *Winter in the Blood* or *The Death of Jim Loney*, or Tayo of *Ceremony*: they are not fraught with aimlessness, trouble, or disaffected angst. King doesn't concern himself much with aimless disaffection, lamenting the state of the Indian, or restoking Indian pride. *Medicine River* takes Indian pride not as something to be proved but as a given to work within. If anything, the alienated trouble bearers in *Medicine River* are whites, first Will's father (never identified by name) and later Will's Toronto girlfriend Susan Adamson, who carries her alienation happily like a luxury of the privileged. But King doesn't much concern himself with white people either.

Instead, King teases the expectation—even stereotype—of restless young men with nothing to do through a series of feints, comical and not so comical, hinting at an accent on restlessness that the novel never follows through on, from Harlen's restless meddling, Will's indecisiveness, the Friendship Centre's patched-together basketball team, and Floyd's gossipy, comical readiness to see Indian men's failure wherever he looks, to—more seriously—Jake Pretty Weasel's beating his wife January, and Clyde Whiteman's petty criminal, compulsive recidivism. But in *Medicine River*, woeful masculine restlessness is not the special province of Indian men, for its most immediate standard bearer is Will's white father. Much as Will wants to know more about his father, his father lingers as the model that Will does not want to live up to. When his mother sends him a photograph she draws an arrow pointing at his father's head, ostensibly picking him out from the group but also wishing revenge or punishment on his disloyalty and careless dishonesty, and underlining to Will his father's masculine failure: the father who deserts his family so that his son can't even recognize him. The challenges that she leaves Will come to a simplified but resonant point in his name, Will. Can he summon the will to a masculinity that he can respect, or will he lack that will and turn into another ne'er-do-well Will, not like other Indians necessarily, but like his white father and like what so many people expect from Indians?

With comical perseverance and assurance, Harlen tries to work Will into the local Blackfoot community, first by encouraging him to leave

Toronto to set up a photography studio in Medicine River and then by coaxing him to join the Medicine River Friendship Centre basketball team, little knowing or caring that Will's past efforts at basketball had bludgeoned his sense that he could earn other people's respect or fit in with a group. Will can live in town, but not on the reserve, because his father was white. Many readers (especially non-Canadians) miss the point, implicit in several episodes, that by Canadian law (until 1985) a Native woman like Will's mother who married a non-Native man lost her legal status as Native, and their children were not legally Native either, while a Native man who married a non-Native woman remained legally Native, as did their children. That keeps Will from growing up on the reserve after his father skips out (4, 9), and later it keeps him from getting a government loan to start his business (99). It leads his cousin Maxwell to tease him about not being Indian (9) and threatens to make it harder for Will to fit in as an adult. In the introduction to *All My Relations,* his edition of contemporary Canadian Native fiction (xiii–xvi), King describes the sense of community or group as a special preoccupation of Native writers, and comically but touchingly, in *Medicine River,* Will wants badly to fit in with other people. When he first asks Susan out, she says she's busy that night, but would he "like to go to an art opening with her on Thursday?" Too hard up to figure out what it means that she's least available on weekends (namely, she's married), he responds weakly but needily: "I love art" (108–9). Will's ability to tell the story and end the scene on that note whispers with the bemused mockery of self-recognition. It also suggests that Susan, or any one person in Toronto, far from Blackfoot country, cannot satisfy Will's unrecognized desire to be part of a larger group.

Harlen plays off Will's desire to fit in and spoofs his own sense of how everyone in the local Blackfoot world is connected to everyone else. He calls up Will in the "middle of the night": "Will, wake up. It's important. . . . Louise is pregnant. I'll be by in ten minutes." "Harlen . . ." protests Will (ellipsis in the original). "Okay, twenty" (30), Harlen answers. Louise is pregnant, so it's everybody's worry, and even an emergency, give or take ten minutes. The beginning of chapter 5 both epitomizes and makes fun of Harlen's sense of community connectedness and his desire to make Will rediscover his position in the skein of relations. I quote it at length, because its length makes the point and the joke:

> Big John Yellow Rabbit was Evelyn Firstrunner's blood nephew. Her father had married Rachael Weaselhead, which made Harley Weaselhead Big John's great-grandfather on his grandmother's side, which meant that Eddie Weaselhead, whose grandfather was Rachael's brother, was blood kin to Big John.
>
> Evelyn's sister, Doreen, had married Fred Yellow Rabbit just long enough to

produce Big John before Fred went off to a rodeo in Saskatoon and disappeared. Doreen married Moses Hardy from Hobbema, who wasn't related to
anyone at Standoff, but that doesn't have anything to do with the trouble.
    "You know John Yellow Rabbit, don't you, Will?"
    "Director of the Friendship Centre?"
    "Know Eddie Weaselhead?"
    "Charlie's cousin?" . . .
    "Martha Bruised Head came to see me yesterday. You know Martha?"
    I nodded. "Sure."
    "She's the secretary at the centre. Her mother's Rita Blackplume, Mike Big-
head's granddaughter. You know, she married with Buster Blackplume. . . ."
    (52–53)

When all this leads to the story about Big John and Eddie—"blood kin"—
hating each other, it marks how Harlen's sense of community is imagined
(in the sense of Benedict Anderson's famous term *imagined communities*)
and how, in a wobbly equilibrium of steps in opposite directions, the effort required to imagine it indexes the threshold of community as much
as it indexes the community's decline. As with Louise's pregnancy, Harlen
uses tears in the imaginary fabric as occasions to try (however feebly) to
sew people together. Perhaps the rip can't be mended. Perhaps Big John
and Eddie can't be reconciled, as Louise can't discover that she's not really pregnant. But for Harlen, recruiting Will and others into the effort to
fix things is a way to sustain the connections that are also always already
unraveling. King's sense of continuous process offers a gentler version of
Betonie's and *Ceremony*'s commitment to ongoing change, to transition
rather than boundary.
    In an episode that might cloy if it weren't so well paced, funny, and even
lyrical (indeed, it has attracted particular praise from reviewers and the
few critics who have written about the novel),[12] when Will takes the Blue
Horn family photo, the family and photo keep growing larger. Ever expanding and shifting, they even draw in Will, the photographer. "Then,
too, the group refused to stay in place. After every picture, the kids wan-
dered off among their parents and relatives and friends, and the adults
floated back and forth, no one holding their positions. I had to keep moving the camera as the group swayed from one side to the other. Only the
grandparents remained in place as the ocean of relations flowed around
them" (214–15). King's words allude to the widespread Indian expression
that he also draws on for the title of *All My Relations,* where he discusses
the expression in his introduction (ix). The Blue Horn family photo returns Will to the old portrait of himself with his now distant brother and
dead mother, tempering the cheery comedy of the extended Blue Horn

family with a wistful recollection of his lonely immediate family, setting Harlen's ideal against Will and Will's brother's restlessness, their father's restless desertion, and their mother's put-upon steadiness.

Coming at the same conflict from another direction, King's portrayal of the basketball team and Harlan's effort to recruit Will to play (Will is tall) repeatedly flirts with the expected role of restless young men with nothing to do. Harlen imagines the team as a refuge from that role for the "boys" and for Will. "All-Native team, Will," he says, "and we need a centre" (12). He tries to entice Will with a uniform: "Number four, Will. That's a sacred number" (13). "Friday nights," Will recalls, "we generally won. Floyd would put in those jump shots of his, and Elwood would muscle in on the boards. But after the game, the boys would go out to a bar and drink until closing. We generally lost our early game on Saturday, and the afternoon game wasn't much better. The championship game was played on the Sunday, and by then, most of the time, we were driving home" (14–15). After one such tournament, Harlen tries to take the boys out and center them, this time not via Will, who still can't play well, but by having them look at Ninastiko, Chief Mountain. If we had only Harlen's words, the effect might be ponderous:

"Come on, boys, hop out. I want you to see something."

. . . "Christ, Harlen," said Floyd. "It's cold and blowing like hell."

"You boys look around you," Harlen shouted, ignoring Floyd and the wind. "What do you see? Go on, look around. Where are you? What are you standing on?"

Elwood and Floyd looked down. "Looks like a road to me," said Floyd. "What about you, Elwood?"

"That's why you miss them jump shots. That's why you get drunk on Friday night and can hardly get your shoes tied on Saturday. That's why we lose those games when we should be winning . . . [ellipsis in the original] cause you don't know where you are."

"Couldn't we do this next week?" Floyd and Elwood and Leroy jammed their hands in their pockets and began to walk around to stay warm.

"You're standing on Mother Earth." Harlen looked at Floyd hard. "That's right, go ahead and smile." Harlen gestured with his chin. "You see what's over there?"

"Give us a hint," Floyd said, under his breath.

"Ninastiko." (15–16)

Here as in many other scenes with Harlen and even with Floyd (a minor character), King has it both ways. He makes fun of Harlen's chummy, good-citizen values while honoring those values at the same time. Similarly, King lets Floyd come across as a bit of a jerk yet also as a good guy who knows not to take things too seriously. Will notes that he can look past Floyd's faults because he likes Floyd (77). On Saturdays, the team may lose because of drinking the night before, but they have a team's camaraderie, they like each other (except for Ray Little Buffalo, but the point is that he's an exception), they hang out together, and they draw on and contribute to the community's and the Friendship Centre's sense of communal feeling. King doesn't ignore suffering, far from it, but rather than arguing for community he narrates a pleasure in community with a light sense of comedy and affectionate satire that keeps the healthy affirmation winsome rather than bathetic.[13]

Floyd trades on the expected stereotype of restless young men with nothing good to do, but King repeatedly turns Floyd's pessimistic gossip into a feint; one time after another Floyd's melodramas crumble before the mundane pleasures of ordinary life. Over a beer, Floyd paints Harlen's decision to play basketball as an effort to compensate for a humiliating slip in his youthful days of hoop-dancing. But soon Harlen tells Will that he never danced, that his cousin Billy was the dancer. In the same vein as his tale about Harlen, Floyd tells Will,

> "All you old guys are trying to recapture the past. You knew Pete Johnson, didn't you?"
> "Rodeo?"
> "Yeah. Got busted up by a bull in Calgary. Couldn't rodeo any more, so he took up stock-car driving."
> "So?"
> "So, he killed himself. Couldn't rodeo, wasn't much of a stock-car driver. One night he just drove his truck off Snake Coulee."
> "Floyd, I saw Pete last week."
> "What? . . . Oh, yeah . . . I remember now, it wasn't Pete, it was Jimmy Bruised Head."
> "Jimmy's in law school." (19; ellipses in the original)

Floyd takes glee in the gloom-and-doom gossip of stereotype, but for the most part the young men of *Medicine River* are enjoyably ordinary, not the angst-ridden ne'er-do-wells of earlier Indian novelists. Meanwhile, contrary to Floyd's sense of Harlen as a sad-sack on the court, when Harlen replaces Will at center he "didn't make a fool of himself. He played well" (20), though the chapter ends in deft enigma as the unreliable Floyd tells Will that Harlen, who can stretch a story as much as Floyd can, "doesn't have a cousin Billy" (24).

A couple of other guys on the team, Jake Pretty Weasel and Clyde Whiteman, each get a chapter in the spotlight, and they come closer to

Floyd's and the wider culture's gloomy expectations. But even they never settle into the fixity that Homi Bhabha posits as the burden of raw stereotype.[14] Talking about himself in an interview, King can brush off such stereotypes: "I don't want people to get the mistaken idea that I am an 'authentic Indian,' or that they're getting the kind of Indian that they'd like to have" (Weaver, "Thomas King," 56). In a related vein, Jake and Clyde have less to do with a portrait of restless young Indian men than with a broader critique of stereotypical, tough-guy masculinity across racial lines, so that even their stereotypical failures counter the impulse to pin their failures to an Indian pattern. Apart from his brilliance as an athlete, the compulsively recidivist Clyde seems representative of something more than himself but not of the community overall. Many of the guys have gone to jail, Will notes, trying to reassure Clyde. But we never get a hint that they've gotten in serious trouble. "'You ever been to jail?'" Clyde asks Will. "I was stuck. 'No, but I screw up all the time'" (125), Will responds, confirming Clyde's sense of Clyde's own extraordinariness and confirming the assertive ordinariness that drives *Medicine River*'s retake on Indian people and their daily lives, troubles, screw-ups, and pleasures. Clyde, who seems happier in jail, acts with something like the compulsive incapacity of Will's father. They both fit a traditional, cross-racial masculine image, the sports star (Will's father won a rodeo all-round title [169]), making more poignant Will's futile effort to offer Clyde fatherly comfort, as if Will's effort includes a desire to refather himself and get it right.

Jake beats his wife January, but he also holds a job and stays with his family, unlike Will's father. Like the Clyde Whiteman chapter, the Jake and January chapter implies a critique of tough-guy masculinity, not only in Jake's violence but also in the response of the other guys on the team. It looks as if January shoots Jake and stages it as suicide, but King (though he refers to it as suicide in an interview ["Interview with Tom King," 67]) leaves the possibility of suicide open, especially in the context of frequent suicide on the reserve that serves roughly as a model for the novel, including suicide connected to family violence.[15] In a show of post-facto masculine solidarity, Elwood and Leroy figure that Jake couldn't have shot himself, because he "'knew his way around guns and wouldn't have made a mistake like that. And besides, they said, he had everything—good-looking wife, nice kids, good job.'" With gun knowledge and a trophy wife, he is one of the guys, or even what the guys aspire to be. "'Only mistake Jake made,'" Elwood says,

> "was turning his back on January. That women's liberation's what's doing it. Fellow puts a woman in her place once in a while don't give her any call to shoot him. Hell, we'd all be dead."

Leroy's sister was married to one of January's brothers. "Sure, Jake pushed a little bit. That's what men do. But January should have said something. Jake would've stopped." (50)

King and his narrator Will let such remarks stand by themselves, implicitly confident that they critique their own claims more powerfully than if the novel or its characters did so directly. To Leroy, January is the agent of her own beating. King's implicit critique targets the complicity of tough-guy, masculine solidarity in such phrases as "we'd all" and "what men do," and in Leroy's failed identification with his sister and her other kin. Without commentary, Will recalls how January came to comfort Jake after a bad basketball game and Jake slowly twisted her arm, then punched her in the face, while "the rest of us just stood there, Harlen, and Floyd, and Leroy, and me" (45). Without the melodramatic vanity of chest-pounding self-ac-cusation, the simple "just stood there" and the chilling "me" at the end of the list point fingers of accusation at the silent solidarity that sanctions Jake's violence. They fill out the unspoken motives and the layers of irony in Will's words at the opening of the chapter: "I drove January Pretty Weasel out to the reserve for the funeral. Her arm was still in the sling, and Doc Calavano said the medication might make her drowsy. I didn't want to go, but January was kin, and it was her husband's funeral" (43).

King undercuts any impulse to read Jake's violence in racial or class terms by counterpointing it with Will's memory of Mrs. Oswald, the white woman hiding out from her wealthy, brutal husband. When young Lena Oswald tells Will and his brother about the violence, Will tells his mother Rose, who says he "should leave such things be, that it was best to let white people work out their own problems" (47), anticipating the way Will and his friends later stand by as Jake wallops January. But when Lena asks Rose for help and they find Mrs. Oswald severely beaten, Rose "looked at Mrs. Oswald for a long time, and then she called the ambulance" (48). With the brutality before her eyes, Rose hesitates and then forgoes a racial soli-darity of silence in favor of a female or human solidarity of action. Her son doesn't live up to the lesson when he and his friends see Jake beat Jan-uary, though his narrative critiques his own failure and, once he senses that failure, he does what little he can see to do in helping January.

Not that he does much. Will is not a character of forceful action, not with others and not on his own behalf. Traditionally, in culture at large as in fiction, many people define forcefulness and personal value in relation to heterosexuality. The traditional plot of novels, dramatic comedies, and many film comedies follows a search for marriage and concludes in mar-riage, as if marriages were necessarily happy, their beginnings were the end of the story, and everyone were heterosexual and eager to marry. By that measure, as we have seen, Chal Windzer and Archilde Leon come up looking like misfits, their masculinity and their commitment to boiler-plate heterosexuality subject to a skeptical scrutiny that *Sundown* and *The Surrounded* seem tempted to critique. *Ceremony* continues in that tradition. Erotically, Tayo is passive. He never shows any romantic or sexual interest except in a couple of spirit-women who practically swoop down on him, with Tayo taking no initiative of his own. Silko seems almost indifferent to the pressure to eroticize Tayo's imagination. With the Night Swan and Ts'eh she switches on his heterosexuality to advance the plot, but as soon as the needs of plot are fulfilled, she switches him back to asexual neutral-ity.[16] In *Medicine River*, King shows more interest in his characters' sexual-ity. Working in modes made possible by broad cultural shifts under way in ideas of gender, including the feminist-inspired rethinking of masculinity, King reinvents the critique of boilerplate heterosexual masculinity with relaxed confidence and clarity (and satirical good humor).

Will doesn't just ignore the possibility of marrying, like Chal, Archilde, or Tayo. He explicitly doesn't want to marry, and neither does the object of his timid affections, Louise Heavyman. King pokes fun at Harlen's med-dling efforts to get them to marry. It's typical enough to poke fun at med-dlers and matchmakers, but not so typical (especially outside of explicitly queer writing) is King's satire of the idea that someone would necessarily want to marry. Harlen suggests that Louise "think about getting married" and reports, "She said she'd consider it," but according to Elwood, that wasn't exactly Louise's response. "Should have heard her laugh," Elwood tells Will. "Big tears in her eyes. Had to blow her nose six or seven times" (26). Undeterred, Harlen urges Will on with comments like "A man's not complete until he has a woman by his side," "Nothing more important than the family," "Beats the hell out of eating your own cooking," "Seeing a man live alone is sad" (quotation may not bring out how, in context, the transparent but remorseless futility of Harlen's platitudes makes them enormously funny). He also appeals feebly to stereotypical masculine van-ity by suggesting, improbably, "A son of yours would probably be a sports star of some sort" (all on 27). Louise reports similar pressures from her friends: "Betty and Doreen and Shirley are convinced we're going to get married" (35). But Louise and Will persist in staying single by choice, even while their friends assume that because Louise gets pregnant (be-fore she starts seeing Will) and because she and Will stay together, they *naturally* will marry, as if everyone always wanted to marry.

In many other novels, vaguely including *Sundown*, the resistance to mar-riage carries suggestions about an interest in homosexual or queer possi-bilities, and it often leads to other characters' hounding the resisters, policing their sexuality by chastising them for evoking even the faintest whiff of models outside heterosexual marriage. The characters of *Medicine*

River are not free of homophobia. But even though Harlen tries to police Louise and Will into the marriage model, Louise and Will show little if any interest in homophobia and seem not the least susceptible to the panic that heterosexual policing tries to set off by casting aspersions on people's heterosexuality (Sedgwick, *Epistemology,* 19–21, 182–212; *Between Men,* 83–96). Elsewhere, though, such fears pepper the novel. Bertha tells Eddie, "You got more jewellery [*sic*] and stuff than that queer guy used to play piano on television. You maybe give us a bad name" (55). More gently, when he coaxes Will into buying a used canoe, Harlen decides they better paint it, because he might not "want to be seen in a pink canoe" (243). And more harshly, the brutal Ray taunts the novel's AIM sympathizer, David Plume, by saying "I hear that most of those AIM peckers are ex-cons and perverts" (253). When Floyd and Will go to the men's room while Harlen's brother Joe tells a lustily heterosexual story ("so there we were, ten gorgeous women just waiting for us down by the stream"), Joe taunts them on their return: "What'd you do, get married in there?" "Floyd proposed," Will responds. "But I said no" (152). We could read Will's retort as trifling with homophobia by trying to fasten the joke solely onto Floyd, but even more, I think, Will lampoons his own reluctance to pop the question to Louise.

Will echoes Chal, Archilde, and Tayo in the timidity of his heterosexuality. He has a tough time asking women for a date and fears that his stumbling makes him come across to them as pitiful. "Croak, croak" (108), he thinks as he first asks out Susan, and he fares no better with Louise, inviting her to see *Revenge of the Nerds* and "grab some burgers at Baggy's," just what she doesn't want to eat while she's pregnant (33–34). Yet, though both Susan and Louise take over the transaction quickly, Will does ask. His heterosexuality may be timid, but he seems more comfortable than Chal and perhaps than Archilde and Tayo with himself as heterosexual and, more broadly, as sexual. In short, King reinvents the "weak" young Indian man who doesn't fit the tough, expected masculine model, allowing him to stumble through life more or less happily without the looming failure of Chal, the catastrophe of Archilde, the wretchedness of Welch's protagonists, or the vague but grandly melodramatic heroism of Abel and Tayo. Indeed, King writes about ordinary happiness, one of the hardest things to write about. (Nor is it easy to write about writing about ordinary happiness.) As Tolstoy famously puts it in the opening words of *Anna Karenina,* "Happy families are all alike; every unhappy family is unhappy in its own way," as if we all know that happiness must be too dull to read about.

Harlen cannot imagine that Louise's or Will's independence could be happy. As already noted, before Will and Louise start to see each other,

Harlen—with a sense of crisis—wakes Will at 2 A.M. to tell him that Louise is pregnant:

> "Louise told Betty she had planned it this way. Said she wanted a baby, but didn't want to get married. That's Louise, isn't it?"
> "She's a strong woman."
> "No, I mean the front. You know, Will, lying like that, so everyone will think you're okay."
> "You think . . ." [ellipsis in the original]
> "Sure. She's all alone. Made a mistake. Scared to death. . . . Betty says you could never tell she was on the edge of a mental breakdown." (30–31)

Louise, it turns out, is just fine, but King continues the joke that no one can imagine that she or Will could happily remain unmarried. When her baby is born, the nurses address Will as "Mr. Heavyman," to the raucous delight of his friends (38–40). When Louise looks for a house and brings Will along, a real estate agent assumes that he is "Mr. Heavyman" and persists in misunderstanding even when Louise tells him there is no Mr. Heavyman (223). While King makes fun of the expectation that everyone is or wants to be married, he also mocks Will's reluctance to follow through on such desire to marry as, after all, Will nevertheless feels. The very name "Heavyman" comically underlines that Will is anything but the heavy and certainly no tough guy in his relations with women. Yet King also persists in allowing us to read Will's reluctance as something other than the weakness, oddity, or burden of heroism implicitly at stake for Chal, Archilde, or Tayo. Will wants to do better than his father, yet his father's failure burns into Will the difficulty and seriousness of marriage and fatherhood. When the father of Louise's child proposes romantically at the end of the novel, Louise is enchanted, but she turns him down, repeating that she does not want to get married and adding, to Will, that she likes Will because he understands her (259–60). All this puts Will in the line of Chal, Archilde, Abel, Welch's protagonists, and Tayo, but it also changes that line and helps release it from overbearing expectations about what men must do. Indian novels were already well engaged in resisting those expectations about masculine behavior and in constructing more flexible alternatives, as I have argued throughout this book. Writing in a later time that does more to encourage and respect a range of ways to perform gender, King can reinvent the possibilities for masculinity and, what's more, he can relax about and even tease the reinventions.

In a similar way, King sustains and yet reinvents earlier Indian novels' interest in oral storytelling. Instead of putting storytelling scenes in the plot, as in *The Surrounded, Medicine River* blends oral storytelling into the very conception of its formal structure. *Ceremony* does that too, but *Ceremony* and *Medicine River* build their form and its relation to oral story in different ways. *Ceremony* mixes storytelling into its narrative, but not usually through storytelling scenes in the plot. Instead, it turns back and forth between a main plot and poetic versions of analogous, mostly traditional oral stories. *Medicine River,* by contrast, takes much of its narrative structure from oral storytelling without putting traditional storytelling scenes into its narrative (though Will mentions that Lionel tells traditional stories to his family [172, 175]). The storytelling appears indirectly, in *Medicine River*'s narrative form, through repetition and a delightfully talky pacing and diction, as well as in casual stories about contemporaries and peers that run like gossip all through the dialogue.

In the novel's orally repetitive structure, King sets up each chapter almost like a separate story, or like an episode in a traditional oral story cycle such as a trickster cycle. Harlen as trickster meddles in everyone's business and reshapes the world around him while remaining paradoxically aloof from that world. As King puts it in an interview,

> Harlen is . . . the trickster figure, rearranged in some ways. . . . One of the roles of the trickster is to try to set the world right. . . . He's creator and destroyer. Harlen is always looking to do good—and sometimes he does good. Other times he gets things totally wrong. Or he creates a situation in which things don't go as well as they should. . . . He's a meddler, a constant meddler. He doesn't have a job, you know. I mean, nobody knows what Harlen does. He's got to do something for a living, but no one ever sees him working at a regular job. He just sort of appears. There's a certain surrealistic quality to Harlen. He's not like Will or Louise, who have reasonably normal lives. Harlen is just there. He's there all the time. He's like the land and the sky. ("Interview with Tom King," 67–68)

All this comes across more gently in the novel itself, where no one remarks that Harlen never works or that he suddenly pops up whenever he's most or least needed.

Nevertheless, Harlen's habit of barging in on things organizes the novel. Typically, a chapter begins with Will in his studio busy at some task of work or pleasure, when Harlen shows up and presses him to do something for one of Harlen's meddlesome schemes. Less often, someone else shows up or calls, again to wangle Will into doing something. Harlen circles conversationally around what he wants from Will, leading up to it gradually. "Whenever Harlen had something important he wanted to tell me, he'd sort of float around the subject for a while like those buzzards you see above Blindman's Coulee all the time. He'd start off cold and slow and have to warm up to whatever he had to say" (52–53). "Sometimes when he went around in circles, I'd wait and see how long it took him to ask the questions he wanted to ask" (126). "I was used to conversations with Harlen that didn't make much sense and didn't seem to go anywhere" (169). The pattern grows comical as we see it repeated in chapter after chapter. In the same way, later chapters often reintroduce characters from earlier chapters. In the interview, King confirms that he began by writing the chapters as separate pieces and that he liked the effect of reintroducing familiar characters, though his editors had him trim some of the reintroductions (63–64). Thus, a gathering set of patterns leads readers to approach each new chapter with pleasurably nostalgic recognition, like hearing a fondly familiar story or another in a continuing oral cycle of stories.

Thirteen of the seventeen chapters (all but chapters 3 and 10–12) also follow a striking pattern not dependent on oral models. They alternate between Will's stories of Harlen and their friends in Medicine River and his memories of something parallel from his past with his mother and brother or with Susan in Toronto. The poignant counterpoint makes the recent and the slightly distant past resonate through analogy to each other. In teaching *Medicine River,* I offer students the option of writing a new chapter for the novel, with a paper discussing what their new chapter can tell us about the novel itself. Just having the option, even if they don't take it, sharpens their eye for the novel's fractured, hopscotch syntax of dialogue and narrative, its alternating patterns of parallels and repetitions.

While the alternation multiplies the range of Will's storytelling, his stories remain about contemporary times, versus stories of old or ancient times like those in *The Surrounded* or *Ceremony.* Silko, as we have seen, attacks white writers who appropriate older stories in abusive ways, although Paula Gunn Allen attacks Silko for using them in *Ceremony* ("Special Problems"; Allen uses such stories, however, in her own novel, *The Woman Who Owned the Shadows.*)[17] King draws on older, traditional stories in high postmodern parodic mode in his second novel, *Green Grass, Running Water* (1993), but he doesn't get into details from the stories of particular peoples. In *Medicine River* and in the title piece of his collection of stories *One Good Story, That One* (1993) he mocks non-Indians' expectation that Indian stories must be about ancient times, stories of so-called myth rather than of contemporary people like the ones listening to the stories.

Chapter 12 takes up the contrast between old stories and new stories by introducing Lionel James, a respected elder just back from a storytelling trip to Ottawa, where a hotel clerk refused him a room, even though he had a reservation and cash. Having a "reservation" (figuratively, Indian land) isn't good enough in the national capital (figuratively, the national government and even the national ideology, which pay little heed to Indian land rights) without a credit card (without a national ideology ready to take seriously, to grant credit to, Indian beliefs and claims). Therefore—at Harlen's prompting, of course—Lionel wants Will's help getting a credit card. "You know," says Lionel,

> "in Germany I told the story about how Coyote went over to the west coast to get some fire because he was cold. Good thing he went travelling in the olden days before he needed a credit card."
> We all laughed.
> Lionel straightened his jacket and smiled. "Well, you know Coyote ran along until his feet hurt real bad, and pretty soon he was in the trees and the prairies were behind. 'Boy,' he said, 'I'm real sleepy. Maybe I'll just lie down here and sleep for a while.' But you know, Raven saw Coyote, and she flew down, and sat on a limb near where Coyote was trying to go to sleep, and she said, 'You can't sleep here unless you got a credit card.'"
> Harlen slapped his knee. "You're a good storyteller, Lionel." (172)

Lionel puts a contemporary twist on old stories, and Harlen and Will make a receptive audience, but when Lionel travels, his listeners disappoint him by wanting stories about olden, not contemporary times. Lionel fears they appreciate his storytelling not because he is a good storyteller but because he is Indian, and implicitly because he is an old Indian, someone they can fit into the Hollywood, TV-commercial stereotype of the wise old noble red man. "People want me to talk about what it's like to be an Indian. Crazy world. Lots of white people seem real interested in knowing about Indians. Crazy world" (170). Audiences respond so favorably, Harlen says, because Lionel is "such a good storyteller." "I don't know," Lionel replies. "Maybe cause I'm Indian. You know, I didn't see any white storytellers over there" (174). Non-Indians who presumably would not applaud a story about their own beliefs or religion puzzle him by giving him a standing ovation, matching his stories to their idea of entertainment.

> "I told them the story about Old Man and Old Woman, and when I was done, everybody stood up and clapped."
> "You're a good storyteller, Lionel," said Harlen.
> "You know, it was my wife who knew all the stories. She used to tell them to the kids. Crazy world. Everybody on the reserve knows that story." (173)

Lionel could just be modest, as he is modest about asking Will for cream and sugar in his coffee or jam with his bread (though he manages to ask for all those things nevertheless), or he could be sincere and even accurate in his belief that he is not so special a storyteller. Either Lionel is a quietly spectacular performer, or his audiences respond to something other than his performance. Perhaps many readers defer to Harlen's refrain that Lionel is a good storyteller, but the little we hear from him isn't unusual and even sounds flat next to Harlen's knee-slapping response. Harlen's enthusiasm can cast doubt on his sincerity, and he isn't usually a reliable witness anyway. As Lionel says, "everybody on the reserve knows that story." Lionel is suspicious of the outsider's impulse to convert Indian ordinariness into stagy extraordinariness, and in that way Lionel gets exactly, and reflexively, at the distinctive manner of *Medicine River,* a narrative style that evokes not formal storytelling but, instead, conversational storytelling.

Like Lionel, *Medicine River* takes particular pleasure in the contemporary and the unnovelistically ordinary. When Will realizes that Bertha left some not- so-fresh cream in his refrigerator, allowing him to offer Lionel cream for his coffee, Harlen rhapsodizes (satirically? with Harlen you can't tell) about how extraordinary it is to get real cream, concluding, "Boy, I'll bet you don't get real cream for your coffee every day," to which Lionel responds, tactfully but wittily, "That's right, . . . only at home" (167). He's no primitive, even if he lives on the reserve and doesn't have a credit card. In the same fashion, Young Bear jokes about non-Indian schoolchildren who ask where he hunts. He tells them that he hunts by walking down the aisles at the grocery store (Young Bear, Poetry reading, 1991, and "Journal," 1C). "You know," explains Lionel,

> "sometimes I tell stories about today, about some of the people on the reserve right now. I like to tell about Billy Frank and the Dead River Pig. All the people back home like to hear that story. When I was in Norway, I told the story about the time your father and mother went to one of those chicken restaurants after a rodeo. . . . But those people in Germany and Japan and France and Ottawa don't want to hear those stories. They want to hear stories about how Indians used to be. I got some real good stories, funny ones, about how things are now, but those people say, no, tell us about the olden days." (172–73)

As someone who can tell stories both of the old times and of Will's parents, especially the father that Will can't remember, Lionel offers two links to Will's past. He deftly tells Will about his father without heavy-handedly announcing to Will that he knew his father and trying to gain points by his privileged knowledge. "I'd like to hear some of your stories when you have time," Will says. "We could talk about other things, too" (174), he adds, in a gentle way of saying that he wants to hear about his parents. When he goes to Lionel's house, Lionel tells old stories and new stories both, but he and Will seem more interested in the new stories. After all, when Lionel first drops into his studio, Will thinks that he "didn't know Lionel James very well, but I had heard stories" (167).

Stories are part of Will's everyday air, the conversations that mark daily life. Harlen regales him with stories throughout the novel, mostly with stretchers, and Will grew up with stories. "Every so often," he recalls, his mother "would get in a story-telling mood. Most of the stories were about when we were little" (123). "Sometimes the stories were about when she was younger, before she had us" (127). "Each time my mother told her stories, they got larger and better" (128). Every story from his mother that Will mentions tells about family and friends, about contemporary times, never about the ancient or even the distant past. It's not necessarily an Indian thing, either. Rose's best friend Erleen is white, and "the two of them would laugh, tell stories, and sing songs" (55). Erleen "liked to tell stories" about fishing with her husband. "James and me liked Erleen's stories. She'd sit at the kitchen table and cut out coupons and tell stories" (57). Lionel tells a story about Rose throwing up at a chicken restaurant and another about Will's father at the laundromat hiding baby Will from Rose in a clothes basket. Later, Lionel and Floyd's granny help welcome Will into their familial and social world by remembering what funny stories Floyd's granny's son told and how Will reminds her of him. "She says maybe she should adopt you," Lionel says. "That boy of hers always had a good story" (211). In that context aflow with the pleasures of the contemporary, Lionel cannot understand the non-Indian reduction of Indians to the past and the accompanying desire to favor stories of the ancient past. "'It's a crazy world,' Lionel said, as he walked me out to my truck, 'them people living in the past like that.' He looked back at the kids, who were playing on the porch. 'They all got up and clapped, Will. Just stood there and clapped. Like they never heard that story before'" (175). What he takes for granted strikes them as deliciously exotic, and what seems most to delight him, the daily life of chicken restaurants, laundromats, trucks, jam on his bread, cream in his coffee, and children playing on the porch, things that Indians and non-Indians alike can find all around them, strikes them as too mundane for the aesthetics of story. In confining him to his traditions, supposing that he lives in the past, they misread both his present and his traditions, for no tradition faces only its past. A living tradition also looks at the children playing on the porch and Coyote's need for a credit card. Reflexively, Lionel's conversational aesthetic models the novel's aesthetic of the contemporary and the ordinary, its turn away from melodrama in favor of understatement and modesty as repositories of heroic humor and beauty.

In an essay King describes what he calls "associational" literature (also discussed in his dissertation [121–25], though he didn't yet use the term)—a mode he calls characteristically Native:

> Associational literature, most often, describes a Native community. While it may also describe a non-Native community, it avoids centering the story on the non-Native community or on a conflict between the two cultures, concentrating instead on the daily activities and intricacies of Native life and organizing the elements of plot along a rather flat narrative line that ignores the ubiquitous climaxes and resolutions that are so valued in non-Native literature. In addition to this flat narrative line, associational literature leans towards the group rather than the single, isolated character, creating a fiction that de-values heroes and villains in favour of the members of a community, a fiction which eschews judgements and conclusions. ("Godzilla," 14)

King's description of associational literature reads like a formula for *Medicine River*. He never provides a time, place, or reason for Will to tell the story or write it down. The story simply emanates from Will, as if it came not from his telling it but merely came the way it might come if he would tell it. Without any particular motive or plot lever for Will to tell the story, King flattens the melodrama and lets the novel concentrate on the routine of communal Blackfoot ordinariness. When a climax seems ready to rise, he changes the topic to a parallel event in the same chapter or a different event in another chapter. After Louise gives birth and Will catches himself reveling in a fantasy of being the father, we might look eagerly for the next episode in the gentle soap opera of Will and Louise, but the novel goes a long time without even mentioning Louise. The parallel plots within chapters thus suggest not so much cause and effect, with the earlier events and attitudes causing later events and attitudes, as they suggest a web of associations—a sense that we live with events and with our feel for them in association with a history and a future woven through with related events and feelings, in a continuous and more or less climax-less repetition of communal and personal association.

Though I haven't yet met a reader who doesn't get it, it seems reasonable to expect that some readers would be so conditioned to Gustav Freytag's pyramid of rising action ascending to a climax and a peripateia (a reversal of fortune) followed by a falling action that they would feel at a loss to fathom how the novel sets itself against those expectations and the cultural assumptions they embody. Indeed, one reader reviewing the book for Amazon seems utterly perplexed: "*Medicine River* had no exciting plot. Not that the book was a bore, it's just that it wasn't going anywhere. . . . What confuses me is why the author set out to right [*sic*] this novel—what was the point?" (reader from Canada). Drawing on the arguments Paula

Gunn Allen and Kimberly M. Blaeser make about the form of Indian literature, we could say that the point is a circular ethos rather than the linear ethos that the perplexed Amazon reader expects to find. But (as we saw in chapter 1), circularities blend with linearities. Will's father leaves and his mother dies, but they don't come back except as memories and photographs. Many events in the novel pass by, circularly gathering association with other events while also moving linearly onward. I would favor a metaphor of talk over one of linearity or circularity, for talk brings out the conversational mix of linear and circular and, by contrast to a metaphor like "the oral," talk suggests an ordinariness that includes storytelling but distinguishes the storytelling of ordinary life from formal storytelling about the ancient or sacred.

The characters of *Medicine River* are ordinary people, except perhaps for the mythic ordinariness in Harlen's tricksterism. They infuse the novel with the sound of voices speaking in conversation, storytelling, joking, but they do not speak in anything like what we usually call poetry, such as the poetry that Hymes, Tedlock, and their followers discover in Indian storytelling. They speak articulately, with a love for speech, and they read, but they are not elite or art readers. When Will goes in Susan's tow to a poetry reading in Toronto, the point is that he moves out of his element, trying needily to join hers. She reads Native literature, but there's no sign that he does, though the book seems to be written with a sense of a Native audience. As King remarked soon after the novel was published, in "*Medicine River* I'm really writing initially for a Native audience. . . . I think about that Native audience and how much I hope they'll enjoy the book and the kind of storytelling that goes on in the book."[18] King's dialogue spills over with the droll cross-purposes of everyday speech, as different characters talk about two different topics at the same time in the same way that most of the chapters tell two stories at once. The talky, sometimes incomplete sentences and broken-up stories don't need finishing, because they trade on a common history of assumptions between different participants in the dialogue, gradually shaping a conversational ethos that drives Will's narration.

King says:

it sustains my writing to keep that [Native] audience in mind. For instance, I try to keep away from poor language in the book . . . —obscenities, for example, that Native people would find offensive. I also try to stay away from dialect. Dialect creates centres, and so instead of creating dialects I try to reorder my syntax. People can argue with you and say, "Well, if you change the syntax around you create a dialect." But I am willing to say "No, that doesn't necessarily happen." Syntax is very difficult [different?] from "you seeum moon come upum over mountain," that kind of thing. I think of that as a responsibility not to show Native people as illiterate or stupid, because dialect has that tendency. ("Interview with Tom King," 73)

King's casual remarks won't settle any debates over the representational effects of "nonstandard" English, whether Black, Red, working-class, or any other English. My point, nevertheless, is that King sustains the commitment of Indian novelists to orally based representation while eschewing the poetical and reinventing the oral in an art and aesthetics of the prosaic.

In the process, King's work also has the effect of arguing that traditional, stereotypical representations and appropriations of Indians get Indian speech ridiculously wrong, not because they exclude the oral and the poetic but because they reduce Indian speech to a narrow, tilted sense of both. "You seeum moon come upum over mountain" spoofs the oral, faux-poetic lingo that so many nineteenth-century translators and twentieth-century screenplay writers felt obligated to confine themselves to for Indian speech, as if by clumsy contrast to express not only the white illusion of superiority in a naturalized standard English, but also white fears of distance from nature and of deficient poeticality. Hence the first chapter of *Medicine River*, where Harlen keeps mysteriously punctuating his conversation with the interjection "Hey-uh." At first, Will ignores it and changes the topic, figuring (rightly, it turns out) that Harlen, as usual, has something in mind beyond what he starts off mentioning:

> "Hey-uh," said Harlen, which is not the way Harlen normally says hello.
> "What?"
> "Hey-uh . . . what do you think, Will?"
> "Real busy, Harlen. Somebody in trouble?" (2; ellipsis in the original)

At the end of the chapter, as Harlen responds to Will's sadness about how badly Will's father treated Will's mother, Harlen says:

> "Hey-uh. Maybe he was just young. Hey-uh. What do you think, Will?"
> "About what?"
> "*Hey-uh*. Saw Will Sampson on television. It was a movie about him being a sheriff. That's what he said all the time. *Hey-uh*. He's a real Indian, too. What do you think?"
> I couldn't help it. I started to laugh. "Harlen," I said, "it sounds dumb as hell."

"Hey-uh," said Harlen, loud enough for the cooks in the kitchen to hear, and he began to laugh, too. The two of us sat there laughing. (10)

Harlen's lyricism comes not in flowery rhetoric about green grass and running water (the catch-phrase King mocks in the title of his second novel), but in his mockery of the garbled lyricism that popular ideas hold up as Indian eloquence. King is probably also thinking of W. P. Kinsella, a white writer who claims no knowledge of Indians but whose stories and novels set on a fictional Alberta reserve beg comparison to *Medicine River,* and whose stereotypes and fake dialect have provoked resentment from some readers, including King.[19]

But instead of concentrating on resenting or decrying garbled appropriations of Indian culture, King and his characters comically reappropriate the appropriations and laugh at how preposterous they sound. The strategy recalls Bhabha's discussion of the subversiveness of mimicry, but when Harlen mimics the moviemakers' mimicry of Indians, the spiral of mimicry gets funnier and more devastatingly playful than Bhabha anticipates. Will Sampson, the Creek actor who first made his name playing Chief Bromden in *One Flew Over the Cuckoo's Nest,* is a "real Indian," because the moviemakers dictate his position as representative Indian actor. As Jean Baudrillard explains in his famous essay on simulacra, for postmodernity the representation of the real has become the real. When the moviemakers write Sampson as real and write his script, they appropriate the public's sense of the agency—the filmic representation—that determines Indian identity. By reappropriating that appropriation, Harlen submits it to the comedy of its own presumption, not exactly recovering his own agency, which *Medicine River* suggests that Indian people have never really lost, but still taking pleasure in the comic contrast between Indians' continuing agency and the outer world's steamrollering obliviousness to it.

Ratcheting the joke yet another twist, for the basketball-preoccupied world of this novel and the community it represents, Will Sampson is also the name of a basketball player so tall—at 7'4"—that as a representative player he seems more real than the real, the comically exaggerated realization of the role at center that the Will of the novel cannot live up to. The hyper-representativeness of Will Sampson the basketball player and Will Sampson the Indian actor makes each seem yet more comical. In fact, in 1989, the year that *Medicine River* came out, Tim Sampson, son of Will the actor, appeared in *War Party,* a movie about Blackfeet that got a lot of press in the *Kainai News,* and the paper printed a cartoon that joked about the actor's and the basketball player's overlapping names (see figure 6). The *Kainai News,* the local newspaper that Harlen wants to send "a picture of us standing over Custer's grave" (110), is full of the stuff of *Med-*

icine River—basketball, battered wives, suicide, the Friendship Centre, humor, and so on—though its cooler journalistic tone highlights by contrast the craft that King brings to his novel.

What happens, not just to the real itself, but to the idea and criteria of the real when an impostor culture sets the real's conditions and dictates its content? That is the topic of Gerald Vizenor's trickstery speculations about what—drawing on Baudrillard—he calls "postindian" simulation of Indian identity amidst the postmodern evacuation of any real real (*Manifest Manners*). While I wouldn't in every respect call it postindian, King gets at something uproariously like what Vizenor describes when Will waits for Louise to give birth, surrounded by his friends who can't stop laughing at how the nurses mistake him for Louise's husband and the father of the baby. Without setting out to do so, he finds himself, willy nilly, in the position of husband and father that isn't real, but that, once it's attributed to him, seems as if it might just as well be real. As a nurse ushers him down the hospital's south wing into the maternity ward, he can't resist the pleasures of the position he finds himself appropriating.

> They made me put on a gown before they would let me hold her. She was wrapped up in a blanket, and all you could see was her face and eyes. . . . They were open, and she was looking at me.
> "I'll bet you have a name all picked out for her."
> All I could see was the big sign outside the maternity ward. "Yeah," I said, feeling really good with the baby in my arms, "we'll probably call her South Wing." I guess I expected the nurse to laugh, but she didn't.
> "Is that a traditional Indian name?"
> "I was just joking."
> "No, I think it's a beautiful name." (40)

Before Will knows what has happened, the nurse has written "South Wing Heavyman" on the bassinet, not knowing that Louise has made the baby represent Louise's own uncertainty by naming her Wilma, a name that partly asks a question about the baby's mother and partly joins her mother to Will. With trepidation, we expect Louise's proud family to cast off the name "South Wing" in anger. Next evening Will returns sheepishly, confessing that it was supposed to be a joke, but Louise says her father likes the name, and South Wing the girl is for the rest of the novel.

With "hey-uh," in a characteristically odd mix of biting and gentle satire, King and Harlen reappropriate the false appropriation and use its ridiculousness to mimic the colonizing mimicry, turning the foolishness back on itself. With the reappropriation of "South Wing," the cultural crossings compound in a labyrinth of reverberating suggestion. Too secure in their

Fig. 6. Cartoon by Lance Tailfeathers from the *Kainai News*, 1989. Reprinted by permission of Lance Tailfeathers.

Indianness to resent the nurse's generously meant mistake, Louise's family reappropriates her unwitting appropriation of Will's joke. The nurse, in assimilating Indians to the hokum clichés of humorless stoicism and nature metaphors, misses Will's playfully irreverent mimicry of both the colonizers and the colonized: of Indian names in themselves, of Indian naming narratives and non-Indian disrespect for them, of institutional (e.g., hospital) names and signs, and of non-Indian amusement at Indian names. Through Will's joke and its improbable persistence, King mimics the appropriations and misappropriations of language itself, the way that words and names quiver in and out of metaphoricity, and the way that cultural filters and differences play *fort* and *da* (the child's game of gone! and there again! that Freud describes [8–10]) with the incessant cycle of loss and recovery that the quivering of metaphor continually refigures.

King's dense but light-hearted knotting of parody and piety announces a threshold in the invention of Native American literature. With *Ceremony,* Silko brings into imaginative synthesis the history of oral and written Indian literature. King used *Ceremony* as the culminating text of his dissertation, which charts the whole history of Indians in American literature, from their reduction by white writers to inferiority and imminent disappearance (the last of the Mohicans routine), through transcribed oral literature, and on to the climactic rewriting of Indian representations and the merging of oral and written literature in *House Made of Dawn, Winter in the Blood,* and finally, *Ceremony*. In *Medicine River,* King draws on the vast canon represented in his dissertation and, in a lighter tone than Silko's but still a tone that Silko's conclusive synthesis helps make possible, he manages to keep a jocular distance on that canon. Like Sherman Alexie's hilarious yet sad send-up of Indians in white writing, "How to Write the Great American Indian Novel" (*Summer,* 94–95), King's novels and stories shine a light on the white writing that came before them and expose how ridiculous much of it looks next to the lives of ordinary Indians. For King, women can have the independence that traditional masculine heroes long for, without men's macho overcompensation. Men, even if they're alert to the history of macho posing, don't need to let it rule their lives. Indian prose can be infused with the rhythms of conversation and orality without pumping itself up by posing mystified claims about oral poetry, and Indian people can calmly reappropriate the appropriations of white culture, the buffoonery of *hey-uh* and the lyricism of South Wing, without swaggering claims for essentialized Native authority that calcify Native histories and imaginations. After the invention of Native American literature, Native writers at last have the liberty to make of Native literature what they will, and—from Silko to King to Alexie to countless others—they are at it with enthusiasm, writing their way into the age of the post-canon.

CHAPTER 7

Material Choices: American Fictions and the
Post-canon

Continuing to address Native American literature but now as one among many American literatures, in this final chapter I ask how the expanding range of materials that we study and teach changes not just what we interpret but also how we interpret. After the death of canonical confidence, in an age alert to the noisy inefficiency of language and representation, a text cannot bear a one-to-one relation to the social group its author belongs to, as if a Native American or African American text, for example, could represent all Native Americans or African Americans. Instead, our reading of Native American and other American literatures can respond to the promise of the new American literature by reinventing how and what American literature represents.

To take the challenge to concrete particulars, suppose that you are asked to teach an undergraduate course called "The American Novel." What novels will you teach? That is the usual question, but instead, I ask: What *principles* will you try to follow in choosing the novels you teach? The principles behind pedagogical choices matter for both teaching and scholarship, because just as scholarship can produce teaching, so also the crucible of teaching can test and produce scholarship. The number of novels unequivocally canonized and the number that most histories of the American novel discuss in detail are both about the same as the number that conveniently fits into a typical college course. Such a pattern seems more than raw coincidence, and indeed, in recent years the new self-consciousness about canonicity has led to the demise of selective histories of the American novel, like Richard Chase's once influential *The American Novel and Its Tradition*, in favor of big reference books that can (but shouldn't) suggest comprehensiveness, like the *Columbia History of the American Novel*.

168

Rather than repeat the now-routine arguments for changing the canon of American fiction, I reexamine some of the ways we think about and produce such change.[1] The goal is to bring together two discussions that have mostly carried on apart from each other: the theorizing of representation and the politics of rethinking which materials to study.

REPRESENTATION

Scholarship does not often directly ask what principles to follow in choosing novels to study, but the implied (and occasionally stated) answers are usually about the same as those I hear when colleagues explain their choices for teaching or when I ask students what principles they would follow. In one form or another, the most frequent answers call for the *best* or the *major* novels or say that the novels should *represent* some category or interest. To ask for the so-called best is another way of saying that we should *represent* the best. Some people say their choices are more pragmatic and depend on which books fit the issues they want to explore that semester, or on what they happen to have read or taught before, or read and not yet taught. But the issues we select and the novels we have read or taught are themselves selected through principles of representation, whether we purposefully endorse those principles and the themes, forms, and texts they select, or merely inherit them. Thus the various answers each depend on assumptions about representation itself. Most often, these days, critics and teachers address the need to represent the "range" or "diversity" of Americans or the need to represent particular groups, such as (to mention those named most often) men and women or blacks and whites.

In a critical discussion or syllabus with eight to twelve writers, a nationally representative proportion of black writers would add up to one black writer, at the most, if we represent the national population per se, and zero black writers if we represent the novels actually written or even the proportion of black readers of novels, especially over the two-century history of American novels. And if we represent the national population per se, we end up with zero Native American writers and zero writers from any number of other groups that have produced work we might want to study. Thus when we study black novelists—as most scholars and teachers of the American novel now do—we do not simply represent black people. We represent a construct of "America." Black writers, like white writers, portray a culture both distinct and polymorphously hybrid or multicolored, even those black writers, like Langston Hughes or Zora Neale Hurston, who portray black characters without making it seem as if black people's most pervasive concern is to worry about white people. The choice to study novels by black writers makes a statement about those particular novels and about the pivotal role black culture plays in American culture at large and often in the regional cultures where we teach. That pivotal role is thus not the automatic product of mere numbers. It is, on the contrary, the massively labored-over product of a particular cultural history that makes African Americans crucial to American culture for reasons that go far beyond their numbers. And we can say the same for Native Americans, though Native writing still receives little attention except from critics and teachers who make it their main interest.

Much can be gained and much lost by portioning people out into different social groups, as we can see from the now protracted clash between the urge to see identity as deconstructed and the urge to resent its deconstruction. It now seems, as many have argued, that we can hold onto the pleasure and the practical political value of group identity by choosing a socially, politically charged version of the anti-essentialist impulse, constructing identity out of a language of relatedness and positioning. There is no such thing, in this view, as a pure race. The rhetoric of purity is the rhetoric of exclusion—and, through exclusion, of privilege. But there are groupings, and though the groupings can separate and hurt people, they can also produce alliances, solidarity, and community. Thus we have a mixed blessing when we parse ourselves out into namable social groups; and to contemplate both sets of effect can help make the good effects outweigh the bad.

When critics address how our division into social groups bears on selecting materials to study, they usually discuss which *authors* to study and ignore that authors have otherwise become a suspect object of critical reflection in diverse quarters old and new, from the old "new" criticism to poststructuralism, historicism, and cultural studies. They also ignore that we can address these concerns not only through authors but also through characters and settings. Characters, like authors, have become a suspect focus of study in much theoretical criticism, but, at the same time, remain a routine topic of study, especially in the classroom. Thus across much of the profession, for scholarship and especially for teaching, people choose or at least claim to choose the novels they study according to the social groups that their authors belong to, yet in practice often dismiss talk of authors as vulgar biographism in favor of discussing characters. Meanwhile, depending on which novels we choose, those same characters can often "represent" different social groups from those their authors supposedly represent. And such representations, though dubious for both characters and authors, often remain useful and are probably inevitable. We may lament the way white writers can botch the representation of Indian characters, but it doesn't therefore follow that Indian writers necessarily get it right, or that we can always predict what it might mean to get it right, or that any writer can stick to portraying that writer's own race, gender, sexuality, class, region, cultural disposition, and so on through the curlicue of identities that mean so much to us. Thus the intense focus on choosing novels according to their authors' social groups does not play so large a role as is often claimed, nor does it offer criteria to choose *which* works to study by any given writers.

Rethinking the canon has provoked some reconsideration of which works to study by already familiar writers, but that has not figured much in the larger debate, perhaps because it can blur with the concern readers have always held for refreshing interest in lesser-known works by well-known writers. The difference is that the new attention to such works takes its impetus from broader motives for rethinking canonicity. Scholars have unearthed, for example, the many political poems that Langston Hughes published in periodicals but never reprinted in his books (Hughes; Nelson, 258, 313–15). Aristophanes' *Lysistrata* now turns up in courses instead of just *The Birds* or *The Frogs*. Feminist Shakespeare criticism calls more attention to the comedies and romances and proportionally less to the four "major" tragedies separated out by A. C. Bradley. Similarly, we might study Tennyson's *The Princess*, with its interest in feminism, as well as *In Memoriam*, with its interest in the friendship between two men, or study *The Awakening* but also Chopin's stories, which often give more serious attention to black and working-class people. Although we would not entrust the representation of black people, for example, entirely to white writers, still, if we want to study what Hughes, Tennyson, Chopin, and so on *can* represent, then we will need to accept that a writer can represent many different things in different works or in the same work, a truism that often slips away when polemical urgencies drive us to assert why we should teach writers who "belong" to this or that group.

Thus the confidence in representation that often forms the backbone of arguments about rethinking the canon twice assumes what in other contexts is now often recognized as unassumable: first, that there is a stable and coherent entity to be represented (e.g., black identity, white identity, any given writer's identity, the link between any given writer's identity and the identity of any given group); and second, that the process of representation itself is reliable and coherent, that there can be an equation or one-to-one relation between signifier and signified, and that the signified (e.g., identity) somehow rests independently of and underneath the process (e.g., a novel) of signifying it. Nor does such confidence consider how one text is never only "one" text, because it represents multiple and contradictory things, as in Bakhtin's "dialogic."

It would be hard to say, for example, in what sense Yellow Bird's *The Life and Adventures of Joaquín Murieta, the Celebrated California Bandit* (1854) can represent "Indian" literature. Yellow Bird did not sign his novel with the untranslated name he went by among Cherokees, Chees-quat-a-law-ny. Most accounts replace Yellow Bird's name with the Anglo name he used among whites, John Rollin Ridge. Moreover, this first known "Indian" novel is mostly about relations between Mexican Americans and Anglo Americans. It romanticizes Mexicans, at once sympathetically and condescendingly, and has probably had its largest effect as a spur to the derogatory stereotype of Mexicans as bandits. The novel's Mexicans, brutally treated by Anglos who run them off their land, much as whites had forced Yellow Bird and other Cherokees out of the American southeast, become at once Mexicans and metaphorical Cherokees. And though the novel skirts mention of it, many of the Mexicans, of course, are Indian or mestizo, which suggests Chees-quat-a-law-ny–Yellow Bird–Ridge's "half-breed" status and bicultural life.[2] Meanwhile, throughout the novel, Indians of diverse nations keep appearing in a remarkable variety of cameo roles, sometimes patronized and other times taken seriously or indifferently. And to extend the palimpsest, this novel, which some of my readers might think impossibly obscure, is currently in the tenth printing of its paperback reissue in a series called the Western Frontier Library, which would seem to connect it with the supposedly manifest destiny of westward-conquering Anglos rather than with its dispossessed Mexican hero or Indian author. Turning the screw yet more, it has taken on a landmark role in Chicana/Chicano studies, drawing on a long Chicana/Chicano history and a wider Latin American history that take Murieta as a folk hero.[3] Although its unfamiliarity (to some readers, at least) may make it seem unusual, the crowd of representations in Yellow Bird's novel is not a special case in our polymorphous culture where culturally multiple writers produce multiple, dialogic portraits for multiple, dialogic audiences.

There is always a conflict between a text's capacity to represent any group it belongs to or speaks for or about and the distinctiveness that makes us select that particular text. Few writers—regardless what they might claim—strive to be undifferentiable from the groups they nevertheless also and often eagerly represent. Instead, they strive for distinguishing difference. Readers produce difference by choosing certain texts and not others, and produce likeness by thinking of those texts as connected to more or less particular groups. In some senses Henry James can represent white people, though we are more likely to allow that to go on unwittingly than to seek it. And in some senses, Henry Miller can also represent white people, but few readers think of him as much like Henry James. Those difficulties suggest a corresponding caution about making, for example, Jessie Redmon Fauset represent black people, who might also be represented by, say, Ishmael Reed, or making Tomás Rivera represent Chicanos, who might also be represented by John Rechy. The representation will go on; we cannot escape it. But we can reconceive it in multiple and qualified terms or in terms keenly specific about exactly which black or Chicano or white people are at issue.

Anticanonical polemics and routine, anticanonical assumptions sometimes represent an author's identity so confidently that they assume it can predict the values in that author's writing. That leaves a troubling contradiction, because anticanonical arguments often note that there is no inherent meaning or value in a work of art—to the horror of conservatives who misconstrue that as denying *any* meaning or value. When conservatives argue for transmitting the values of "Western" civilization through "classics," they assume that a text transmits specific and consistent values to different readers and generations, but the now familiar anticanonical rethinking denies that assumption (e.g., Derek Longhurst, Alan Sinfield). Even so, anticanonical polemics frequently ask us to choose works that present alternatives to the values in canonical works. In key ways, that is to accept the conservatives' assumptions, even if not to accept their preference for canonical texts, because it accepts that we can isolate certain values as the indelible identity cards of canonical texts and other values as the identity cards of alternative texts. That argument twists the anticanonical view into endorsing what it sets out to oppose and misses that the revisionary values lie in the choice to study alternative texts and not necessarily inside the texts themselves. It allows no room for reading canonical texts in ways that contest canonical values, and it deludes us into neglecting that noncanonical texts will sometimes be read in ways that reconstitute the canonical values they supposedly break down. In American literature in particular, much of the canon has often been read as an oppositional canon that speaks not in the complacent or reactionary voice of Ronald Reagan, Alexander Hamilton, or Stephen Douglas so much as in the anguished and protesting voice of Emerson's "Hamatreya," Thoreau's "Civil Disobedience," or Melville's "Benito Cereno." In the same light, any of those three canonical but oppositional texts, along with any anticanonical alternatives, can be read—to a degree that varies only with the ingenuity of readers—as unwittingly if not outrightly complacent and reactionary.

It is not enough, then, to say we should teach works by, for example, black writers. The choice of books depends also on how we teach them and on how students receive them. With their portraits of violence against women, *Native Son* and *The Color Purple* make dramatic examples of novels that can partly undermine their own supposedly high principles by reinforcing racist ideas about African Americans.[4] Related issues come up with any works that depict members of a group beset by offensive stereotypes. For example, some anthologies (especially older ones) or reading lists highlight Dickinson poems that can be read to produce a portrait of quaintness and cheery triviality, and give less weight to poems of feminist, intellectual, or theological protest, anguish, rumination, and struggle. It does not necessarily matter if we ourselves do not interpret as trivial such poems as "Bring me the sunset in a cup" or "I taste a liquor never brewed" (which ends with "the little Tippler / Leaning against the—Sun—"). We may read them as records of a patriarchal ghettoizing of women's imagination, or ironic protests against such ghettoizing, or celebrations of an imaginative world women have appropriated for themselves or as a refuge from men. Such readings will help in scholarship and *can* help in the classroom, but especially in the classroom they cannot be counted on utterly to remove more disturbing and often unconscious readings. The debate over which texts to assign is therefore only a beginning. Sometimes, with less canonical or recently canonical writers (e.g., Dickinson, Chopin, Larsen), to teach against trivializing and similar derogatory readings can mean to discuss readings that disturb us, like a reading of *Native Son* as racist or readings of *Sundown, The Surrounded,* or *Ceremony* as complicit with internalized stereotypes of young Indian men with nothing to do. Moreover, such discussion will not always make much difference if the attitudes it confronts are deeply supported by the surrounding culture.

It is not only that texts cannot be tied to particular values. Texts are also reversible: any novel that we call misogynist we can also read as serving feminist purposes by exposing misogyny, which unsettles some of the principles many people follow in selecting what to study. That reversibility is no license to assign *anything*, however, for each text still receives different responses from other texts. We still read from within material conditions that carve particular—though not fully predictable—grooves into which our readings slide, and so we need to choose texts according to how they might relate to those grooves. There are many ways to do that: we can aim to reinforce the grooves, to subvert them, or to do both at once or something in between. Put another way, we cannot select texts apart from selecting ways to read them; and we cannot select ways to read them apart from selecting texts. But it does not end there, for we cannot fully anticipate the unconscious ideological investments of our own readings or of our readers' and students' readings. Let us step aside, then, from the trust in representation that might allow us to *predict* the transmission of values with confidence. Nevertheless, one way or another, values are transmitted, and we influence which values are transmitted whether we intend to or not.

Which still leaves the much ballyhooed issue of representing the "best," of what criteria to follow in choosing among works that accomplish related goals of social and aesthetic representation. Those who privilege a canon supposedly selected through universally truthful criteria that noncanonical writings fail to meet almost never address the arguments for the "contingency of value" developed by, among others, Barbara Herrnstein Smith and Pierre Bourdieu. Even revisionist arguments often need to take more account of the reconsiderations of aesthetic value they partly derive from, because otherwise they sooner or later loop back to the conservative aesthetics they mean to reject. There are at least two arguments against the conservative plea for loyalty to a time-tested tradition of studying the "best." First, there is no such tradition; the long ages nostalgically reconstructed as celebrating some pristine best selected apart from social and historical conditions have, it turns out, a short history that mostly dates, in the study of American literature, from the 1920s and '30s. Over the decades and centuries the choice of works to study has shifted according to conscious and unconscious criteria having to do with gender, class, imperialism, nationalism, race, religion, networks among writers, critics, and publishers, publishers' marketing, and so on.[5] And second, as Smith argues, there is no such thing as the best per se. Bestness is not absolute, inherent, or timeless. Instead, we must ask, the best *for what?*

And yet the same revisionist arguments that rely on dismissing the standard of the "best" often reinvoke it when, with no sense of contingency in what the "best" might mean, they call for teaching and studying the "best" works by groups that have been more or less excluded. To be sure, we can never escape aesthetic criteria, nor would I want to;[6] but since we can never justify aesthetic criteria in pure, inherent, or absolute terms, we must find impure, contingent terms for directing our choice of texts.

Perhaps the most common revisionist argument that loops suddenly back to reactionary criteria has to do with ideas about literary complexity. The argument either defends the choice of particular noncanonical texts on the grounds that those texts are really as complex as canonical texts, or it dismisses the criterion of complexity as too exclusive and instead celebrates the noncanonical texts' simplicity. Any text, however, can be read as complex in one way or another, and we do not admire all things that we see as complex. Nor do we admire all things that we see as simple. Paul Lauter, perhaps the most influential proponent of rethinking the canon, says that "while formalist *explication de texte* was effective both as a classroom tactic and for exploring a great many powerful texts, it provided no useful basis for approaching that great body of literature that placed a premium on simplicity, transparency, and emotional directness—from American Indian chants and spirituals to Langston Hughes and Gwendolyn Brooks, from *Uncle Tom's Cabin* to *Daughter of Earth*" ("Introduction," xviii).[7] The reigning critical bias, he says elsewhere, "sets at a discount art which strives for simplicity, transparency and unity in its effects. Obviously, it leads to the preference of 'A Valediction: Forbidding Mourning' over 'Roll, Jordan.' No doubt the spiritual lacks the complex language and ambiguity of John Donne's poem; but then 'A Valediction' has never inspired many thousands to survive tyranny" ("Race and Gender," 450). Remarks like these misplace the epistemological site of complexity, and the result is an unintended condescension to noncanonized writers and texts. Whether or not complexity and simplicity reside *inside* texts in a way that allows them to reside in some texts and not in others, they can each reside in the *reading* of *any* text, and like the proverbial tree falling in the forest, they cannot meaningfully reside at all except when they reside in the reading. How you read depends on the tools of reading you bring. There is no shortage of tools for complex readings of Indian "chants" or African American spirituals, even if until recently we have rationed out such tools, as if they were scarce, for certain texts and not for others.

Since that plenty derives not from the specific characteristics of chants or spirituals but rather from the relation of reading itself to any text, we need not look at chants or spirituals to prove the point. *Anything* can be read in a way that attributes complexity to it, as critics of popular culture and theorists of reader-response and reception have shown. Still, because Native American chants and African American spirituals remain rarely studied, and because this book tries to raise our expectations for the study of oral literature, we might find practical value and a useful reinforcement of the point if we look briefly at examples.

Consider this Navajo prayer from the Nightway, one of the best known Indian "chants":

> Owl!
> I have made your sacrifice.
> I have prepared a smoke for you.
> My feet restore for me.
> My legs restore for me.
> My body restore for me.
> My mind restore for me.
> My voice restore for me.
> To-day take out your spell for me.
> To-day your spell for me is removed.
> Away from me you have taken it.
> Far off from me it is taken.

Far off you have done it.
To-day I shall recover.
To-day for me it is taken off.
To-day my interior shall become cool.
My interior feeling cold, I shall go forth.
My interior feeling cold, may I walk.
No longer sore, may I walk.
Impervious to pain, may I walk.
Feeling light within, may I walk.
With lively feelings, may I walk.
Happily may I walk.
Happily abundant dark clouds I desire.
Happily abundant showers I desire.
Happily abundant vegetation I desire.
Happily abundant pollen I desire.
Happily abundant dew I desire.
Happily (in earthly beauty) may I walk.
(Not translated). [*sic*]
May it be happy before me.
May it be happy behind me.
May it be happy below me.
May it be happy above me.
With it happy all around me, may I walk.
It is finished in beauty (or happily restored).
It is finished in beauty.
                    (Matthews, *Night Chant,* 73)

Or, while I do not suggest that two such different works from diverse cultures are much alike, consider this spiritual:

I know moon-rise, I know star-rise,
  I lay dis body down.
I walk in de moonlight, I walk in de starlight,
  To lay dis body down.
I walk in de graveyard, I walk troo de graveyard,
  To lay dis body down.
I lie in de grave an' stretch out my arms,
  I lay dis body down.
I go to de jedgment in de evenin' of de day
  When I lay dis body down,
An' my soul an' your soul will meet in de day
  When I lay dis body down.[8]

Next to the complexity that can be read in such works, some readers might find Donne's poetry simple and its supposed complexity merely superficial and clever (some readers always have seen Donne that way), but that would impose on Donne the same mistake that celebrators of simplicity impose on chants and spirituals.

The patterns of repetition in these two extremely different works depend on suggestive parallelisms and an immense breadth of allusion. The Navajo "chant" is here given in Washington Matthews's classic, often quoted rendition, which is nevertheless a white mediator's composite of different versions that Navajo singers conceive as unvarying and yet also as never the same twice (James C. Faris, 21–22, 106); and this itself is only one of three renditions set up to be read together—the composite Navajo text, a literal translation, and this free translation.[9] Matthews's text removes the repetition from this precisely ordered moment in the second day of a nine-night, eight-day healing ceremonial, where a "patient" repeats a singer's words sentence by sentence. Such repetition mystifies the referent of the first-person singular pronouns, which thus refer not only to the one sung over but also, more obscurely, to the singer and to a larger plural that the ceremonial—a public event with many participants and witnesses—condenses into the personal. As the words pass between singer and person sung over, they evoke an encompassing system of cosmic exchange: a narrative of anticipated recovery provoked partly by the prayer itself—addressed to the lore-laden owl, a creature of ill omen—and by the sacrifice that the prayer testifies to. The same and variant "lines," phrases, and patterns of "incremental parallelism" (Walton and Waterman, 37–42) reappear systematically through this particular ceremonial and through the larger repertoire of Navajo prayer (see Sam D. Gill), with each prayer, song, and ritual alluding to every other in a network so vast and saturated with allusion that it takes many years of arduous study for a singer to learn just this one ceremonial. This particular variant progresses incrementally, rising from static feet up to legs and the larger realm of body, then from body up and in to mind, and from mind both in and out to the profounder metonymy of body and mind in voice, eventually transforming the static to a going forth and walking in happiness and beauty, the much pondered Navajo concept of *hozho* that Matthews strains to translate by approaching it from multiple directions: "happy," "happily," "happily restored," "in earthly beauty," and "finished in beauty." At the same time, the linear narrative of recovery crosses with a multidirectional, cyclical plane of ritual reference that envelops the progression in a full surround of sacred universe into which each repetition fits: from dark clouds to showers to vegetation to pollen to their collective metonymy in dew, which cycles back again into dark clouds, and all before, behind, below, and above.

In the spiritual, right from its first words the mystery of unadorned assertion that the mere self knows what would seem to escape knowledge lofts us into a haunting economy of figurative reverberation betwixt and amongst the corporeal self and its many diaphanous objects: moon and star, moon-rise and star-rise, moonlight and starlight, "dis body" and death itself, the grave, the judgment, and "my soul an' your soul." We move, as if suspended, through a temporally cross-directional narrative of future (When I lay dis body down), past or present (I walk in de moonlight), and continuous present (I know moon-rise), all rendered in a present tense that slowly, amidst the dialectical breathing in and out of lines sung alternately by the leader and by the group or congregation, converges to climax within a particular present in the part surrender and part defiance of an achingly tactile rehearsal for death: "I lie in de grave an' stretch out my arms." At the last, death breaks the proudly anguished isolation of the repeated first-person singular, of I, I, I and this body, this body, this body, as if the stretching out of "my arms" can reach to the grandly anticipated meeting of "my soul" with "yours," where the second-person reference, in the social setting of a group or congregation, reaches toward the plural as well as the singular. W. E. B. Du Bois, keenly observing both formal and social inflections, notes how spirituals speak in "eloquent omissions and silences. Mother and child are sung, but seldom father; fugitive and weary wanderer call for pity and affection, but there is little of wooing and wedding; the rocks and the mountains are well known, but home is unknown" (*Souls of Black Folk*, 187). The saying of so much about the conditions and emotions of slavery while saying it so indirectly can seem complex indeed. Like the Navajo prayer, the spiritual's performance also comes blended with music and bodily movement (though not as keyed to particular movements or ceremonies as the prayer). For many years, the verbal and musical complexity of spirituals kept literate listeners from writing them down, and the first to try transcribing the lyrics or the music found the difficulties almost insurmountable (see Dena J. Polacheck Epstein).

Such discussion of the spiritual or the Navajo prayer could continue for potentially as large a commentary as critics have directed to Donne's "Valediction." Thus it will not hold to suggest that "formalist *explication de texte*" provides "no useful basis for approaching" such materials, though it provides no more sufficient an approach to chants and spirituals than to metaphysical poems.

If we are to represent the "best," the standards for what is best will be formalist and political, aesthetic and cultural all at once and in overlapping and ever-shifting combinations. They will vary from reader to reader, era to era, occasion to occasion, culture to culture, and subculture to subculture, and in any given instance many different and sometimes competing standards will come together more or less loosely and more or less consciously. Ideas of the "best" are inseparable from ideas of change.

MATERIAL CONDITIONS OF TEACHING

Recent changes in technology, markets, and means of distribution have reshaped the material conditions of teaching. New papers and glues make it possible to bind more pages in a volume, which helps anthologies include vastly more diverse selections. Along with the many reprintings of forgotten or repressed novels and the increasing access to out-of-copyright materials on the web, the new anthologies are changing what we teach. But no one has *had* to wait for new anthologies, reprints, or the world wide web, for the technological threshold was crossed at an earlier point: namely, with the rise of photocopying. The lament that materials cannot be taught because they are out of print continues. But photocopying long ago made it possible to reproduce out-of-print materials (obtaining permission, if copyrights apply)—and even to do so for fewer dollars than it costs to buy reprints. That is not to decry reprints, but only to say that there often remains a gap between the material possibilities and our more cautious conception of them.

Even now, with the canon a target of suspicion, such cautions often protect habits rooted in taking the canon for granted and thus allow us to underestimate the material possibilities for teaching. Hints of such caution can show up even in an excellent argument for rethinking the canon, such as when Lauter notes that classroom teaching might "lift" a Native American

> tale from the tribal context in which it takes its living shape. The actual audience for the tale would have received its ritualized clues as to the kind of tale about to be told and would thus have its expectations defined. Further, such an audience would generally be familiar with the central characters and thus need not be introduced to them. Often, beyond all that, the tale fulfills definable, perhaps sacred, functions within the life of a tribe. All these elements are missing or badly distorted in the classroom, where the tale becomes an artifact of study. The instructor's task thus begins to shift from interpretation of the text itself to recreation of the cultural, social, and performance contexts that shape it. ("Introduction," xxi; *Canons,* 108)

This makes a fine description of what can be at stake in the teaching and scholarly study of Indian oral literature. Someone might suppose that Lauter's comments about how "these elements are missing or badly distorted in the classroom" overlook Indian classrooms, but Greg Sarris has

searchingly reminded us that to study Indian literature in an Indian classroom—as many teachers and students have discovered—is not necessarily
to find a haven of comfy traditionalism (169–99).

But just as it won't do to call Indian chants simple, so it won't do to discuss Indian oral stories or noncanonical literatures in general as if their
complexity requires a breadth of cultural address that canonized literature does not call for. Lauter himself, in this piece and elsewhere, argues
powerfully for studying the cultural embeddedness of all writing, and his
remarks here about Indian oral stories can also fit the teaching and scholarly study of written, non-Indian stories, even such chestnuts as, say,
Hawthorne's "Young Goodman Brown" or Hemingway's "Hills Like White
Elephants." Readers of such tales also receive "ritualized clues"—an infi-
nite number of them—"as to the kind of tale about to be told," in the
form of classroom syllabi, writing assignments, and a heritage of canonical
saintliness surrounding such terms as *Hawthorne, Hemingway, author, literature, great work, masterpiece, classic, close reading,* or *university.* Those clues are
culturally specific and ethnographically thick, so that those who respond
to them usually take them for granted, without even noticing. In their cultural specificity, however, such clues might not draw the same response
from producers of traditionally handed down Indian stories. Contemporary Indian storytellers, by contrast, who might well be or have been college students, might respond to the clues like other students, but often
with more awareness of their cultural specificity.

The typical audience for the usually studied sort of tale is "generally familiar with the central characters and thus need not be introduced to
them," much as for Lauter's Indian tale. We know already, in Hawthorne's
story, what the "devil" is; and we recognize a Goodman, a Goody (as in
"Goody Cloyse"), a minister, a deacon, a "pretty young" "wife" named
"Faith," and so on, so that the story becomes a critique of that assumed
knowledge and also, more searchingly, a critique of too much anxious
readiness to critique it. Or in "Hills Like White Elephants," Hemingway,
much like Henry James, Stephen Crane, Gertrude Stein, and others, can
introduce characters as "the American girl," "the man," "the woman,"
with confidence that such general designations will serve. Like most stories, as Vladimir Propp argued for Russian fairy tales, these play intensely
in and off familiar rituals of plot and character, a *langue* (or broader system) out of which each story constructs its *parole* (its particular instance).
"Hills Like White Elephants" follows an argument over whether "the
American girl" should get an abortion, without ever needing to speak the
word *abortion* for us to recognize what is at issue, much as Hawthorne
never uses the word *adultery* in *The Scarlet Letter.*

Such tales fulfill what for the Indian tale Lauter calls "definable, perhaps sacred functions within the life of a tribe," though the tribe in this case is adolescence, college, or readers or scholars of literature, profane rather than sacred tribes, albeit still highly ritualized. As with the Indian tale in a traditionally organized course, "all these elements are missing or badly distorted in the classroom where the tale becomes an artifact of study" abstracted from the cultural world that seems so much more obvious with the Indian tale only because most readers who are not part of Indian culture take their own culture for granted, as if it were the norm and not cultural at all. If we insist on a broad address to culture when we study noncanonical works like oral Indian tales, then let us not imply that they need any broader address than canonical, non-Indian tales. The familiar might turn as strange as what most academics find distant, if we construct a distance to look from.

The non-Indian culture that can seem natural to people with experience in college and university humanities courses is on the contrary ideology, which is why the project of canon rethinking is so crucial and yet so difficult. Curricular change, however, tends to be seen from the perspective of curricular control, as if by mere force of will or hot air we could float out of the Kansas of ideology and land softly in some happy Oz where the texts and the ways to read them were all a different color. If only it were so easy, but there is much in ourselves, our cultures, and our students to resist that force of will. The resistance is one of the material conditions of teaching, and in pondering over changes in what we study and teach we need to consider the resistance more patiently. If it is at least possible to teach *Native Son* or *Ceremony* with an intent to undermine racism and yet end up reinforcing it more than undermining it, end up with students who—perhaps without realizing it—believe that African American men want to murder women and that Native American men are unemployable drunks, then the possibilities for curricular change would seem depressingly constrained.

Thus the conditions that shape the reception of assigned reading include the students' ideologies and the teachers' reinforcing or undermining of those ideologies. The teachers' work can include contrasting implicit and explicit messages, as in the case when someone's decision to teach *Native Son, Ceremony,* or any unwittingly condescended-to text backfires. Therefore, although teachers might want to assign texts conducive—in the cultural worlds their students read from—to provoking particular aesthetic and political responses, no one can reliably predict those responses. That is much better than if students were predictable, but it is a problem when we must decide what and how to teach. We might ask, then, as we consider whether to teach a text, how it might be read differently from the way we read or would like to read it. If we can expect students to read it, even unconsciously, in a way that troubles us, then whether we accept that troubling reading or not we are left to conjecture how much will be gained from teaching through or against that reading. In the classroom, teachers can provoke debates for and against the troubling reading. To confront a disturbing reading is to try to teach against ideology, just as we teach more deeply within ideology if we approach *Native Son* as a novel that protests racism and do not at least consider the possibility that it also succumbs to the racism it protests.

Our own ideological entanglement as teachers extends far beyond the choice of individual texts, or even strategies for teaching them, to include the very concept of novel and literature courses in the first place. Next to the huge number of published novels, the typically short list of assigned novels promotes the bourgeois or consumer-culture interest in turning study to a small number of "personalities"—in this case, some eight or ten—ballooned up into culture heroes, the "greats" or "major writers" of "masterpieces" (a term that suggests a class as well as a gendered exclusiveness). The "survey" course that lifts eight or ten from over half a million American novels is, statistically, hardly more a survey than a course that chooses two or three; it offers some .002 percent of what was published rather than .0004 percent—nothing to crow about. Perhaps, then, instead of focusing only on what our list of assigned novels represents, we might also address what it does not represent and what no literature course, no short list of novels, poems, stories, plays, or essays, ever could represent. That is another reason for seeing Native American literature as an invention rather than a natural category, for even in a subcanon of the larger canon, no body of works can represent what most readers ask it to represent.

From Canon to Post-canon: Representing Unrepresentativeness

The proliferating use of the term *canon*, although led by revisionists, can have the ironic effect of reinforcing the faith in canons that revisionists protest. Among the most frequently heard terms for rethinking the canon are such expressions as *revising, opening, adding to,* and *expanding*, which reinvigorate the canon by renewing it rather than challenging the concept of canonicity itself. Such terms, by clamoring for a piece of the action, can strengthen the concept of canonicity that they might seem to criticize. To the extent that we distrust canonicity, let us speak then not of opening or expanding the canon, but of dissolving or destabilizing it. When we speak of it critically, let us try to use the term and concept of *the canon* in ways that undermine rather than enforce canonicity, which—

some people apparently need to be reminded—is not in the least to suggest dissolving the individual works in the canon.

Even so, we cannot help contributing and perhaps, in some degree, wanting to contribute at least to a limited canonicity every time we recommend or assign or even mention a work; and when we mention lesser known works, then we take up more strenuously a polemic of canon formation. To reconceive how we select what to read in light of a dissolving, destabilized canon, we might set out to represent not, as has usually been said or implied, the representative, but instead to represent unrepresentativeness itself. That paradox can stage the impossibility of any comprehensive representation. A group of novels cannot finally "re-present" a culture or subculture. Yet it will represent—in the sense of "stand for"—cultures and subcultures, however partially and distortedly, in the sense that no theoretical provisos can keep us from landing sooner or later on one kind of representation or another. If the inevitability of at least partial consensus keeps us from eliminating canonicity altogether, then striving to represent unrepresentativeness might at least move us toward a *post-canon*, a canon whose very canonicity, though inescapable, is ironic, strategic, multiple, and self-contradictory.

It may help to reemphasize that this is not another argument for teaching multiculturalism. Rather, I take multiculturalism as given. By the early or mid-1980s, arguments for an anticanonical multiculturalism had become so canonical a genre unto themselves that, even this many years later, the theorizing of *how* to teach or write about literature within multiculturalism has remained underdeveloped and often even unrecognized as a need. In the 1980s and early 1990s it was crowded out by the endless debate—the newspaper and magazine articles, the TV panel discussions, the university forums, seminars, and committees—about *whether* to teach multiculturalism. More recently, the critical rethinking within multiculturalism has faded before the quiet triumph of an often merely superficial multiculturalism that takes itself too easily for granted. My work here is part of a movement from within multiculturalist advocacy to critique such bogus, cheery multiculturalism, a movement that David Palumbo-Liu calls "critical multiculturalism." A complacency has woven itself into the advocacy of multiculturalism, along with a self-congratulatory quietism that dulls the critical wedge and disruptiveness. Avery F. Gordon and Christopher Newfield, like Palumbo-Liu and others, offer incisive accounts of how multiculturalism can blend difference into sameness, insidiously leading to a surreptitious assimilation that suppresses conflict. In Native American studies, Elizabeth Cook-Lynn (*Why I Can't Read Wallace Stegner,* 78–96), M. Annette Jaimes Guerrero, and Arnold Krupat (*Turn,* 24–29) have mounted similar critiques. Indeed, multiculturalism carries special dangers for Native Americans and Native American studies that multiculturalist advocates typically overlook, because as indigenous peoples, Native Americans often seek a special status, including political sovereignty, much like what Charles Taylor defends in his widely remarked essay on multiculturalism, "The Politics of Recognition." But many advocates of multiculturalism seem to call for the same status for every group. Even so skeptical a canon reviser and advocate of critical multiculturalism as Henry Louis Gates Jr. can miss this distinctive difference in Native multiculturalism. He says that "pluralism," which he is defending, "sees culture as porous, dynamic, and interactive, rather than as the fixed property of particular ethnic groups" (*Loose Canons,* xvi). That is well and good in many multiculturalist contexts, but it can lead to overlooking the concerns about land, sovereignty, treaty obligations, and intellectual and cultural property that mean so much to most indigenous peoples—and it may underestimate concerns about cultural appropriation that resonate deeply for many African Americans.[10]

While I have qualms about parts of her argument, Jaimes Guerrero gets at the key issue when she writes: "To the extent that multiculturalism fosters the assimilation of American Indian Studies into the academic mainstream as a polite pseudo-intellectual vehicle maintained for the purposes of providing the appearance of 'ethnic diversity' on campus and for providing 'Indian validation' to the supposed insights and conclusions of Euro-American academia, it hinders the crucial task of American Indian Studies. That task is to build an autonomous Indian tradition of scholarship and intellectualism that carries a viable conceptual alternative to Eurocentrism and its institutions" (56). The helpful point here comes in the observation that feel-good multiculturalism threatens to turn into the same old assimilation sugared over with a sweeter name. Given the seriousness of that danger, I can understand why, if not endorse how, it leads Jaimes Guerrero to a question-begging caricature, for surely no advocates of multiculturalism understand themselves as polite pseudo-intellectuals out to assimilate Indians, not even those who fit that description exactly. On the other hand, not everything Jaimes Guerrero says begs the question: we have probably all heard college and university administrators (as well as politicians and CEOs) drone on about "diversity" as if they were inviting in those people they call diverse for the sake of those they think of as nondiverse, making dominated peoples yet once more shoulder extra work, and once more asking certain students in the classroom, dorm, or dining hall to serve as representatives of their race and as teachers for white students. Powerful as Jaimes Guerrero's argument may be, though, I must echo Krupat (*Turn,* 16–18) in professing not to understand how one could achieve what she calls "an autonomous Indian tradition of

scholarship and intellectualism." Of course, Jaimes Guerrero could reply
that my inability to understand is part of her point, but one does not have
to be a glib multiculturalist or closet assimilationist to recognize that however much we call for land rights, treaty rights, sovereignty, and intellectual and cultural property rights, isolation—for better or worse—is long
past impossible. Nor was it notably a characteristic of Indian cultures before the European invasion.

In short, the superficial multiculturalism that Jaimes Guerrero, Krupat,
Palumbo-Liu, Gordon, Newfield, Gates, John Guillory, and many of the
rest of us lament is dangerously prolific. Even the term *multiculturalism*
has acquired, by now, a ring of glib insincerity. Like any gathering of
ideas, multiculturalism has its self-undermining advocates who never got
it and who would slip it back into what it sets out to oppose. But that does-
n't mean we can become monocultural or autonomous. Multiculturalism
in some form is here to stay, the proverbial toothpaste that no one can
cram back into the tube.

Superficially or not, then, it remains impossible *not* to teach multiculturalism. Culture and literature are always already multi-. They are never
singular; they are always plural, always changing. Yet the public and scholarly discussion often proceeds as if the culture divided into its various
multiples only between literary texts and not within them, so that the only
issue is whether to choose these books or those books. A supposedly multicultural pedagogy thus often continues to act as if individual novels,
poems, plays, and stories were monocultural, and thus it subtly reinvigo-
rates the principles of exclusion it sets out to oppose. The argument here,
by contrast, fits Gerald Graff's insistence that we "teach the conflicts" but
underlines that each side of those conflicts is itself already conflicted. We
cannot draw a line between texts or methods and assume that beyond that
line the pluralizing of culture drifts to sleep or screeches to a halt. And
once we take account of how that pluralizing keeps spiraling through individual texts, then that in turn can influence how we choose an array of
texts in the first place.

The point is not to prescribe a set of principles for selecting texts, but
exactly the opposite: to argue against the adequacy, the representative suf-
ficiency, of any principle of selecting texts, and thus to argue only for
making each system—for we will still have our systems, and a great many
of them—not only represent what it systematizes but also advertise the
limits of its own systematicity.

Readers and students will not likely recognize a strategy so paradoxical
and so antithetical to the confidences of our cultural and economic oli-
gopoly unless we make it explicit. Many students, after looking at my syllabus, say "How come no Steinbeck?" as if I'd run out of advertised mer-

chandise. Teachers might assign historical or theoretical essays about how critics and teachers have selected literature for study, or set up classroom discussions about competing models of selection. At the beginning of a course—whether a course in the American novel or in any particular literature, including Native American literature—we might distribute a long and heterogeneous list of fictions or writers, including a written explanation that it is not only to provide a reading list but also to suggest that such a huge mass of material cannot be represented and to point to the inevitable contingency of any selection. To be sure, some students might take such a list as little more than pedantic bibliography and learned modesty. Still, if we cannot teach hundreds of novels, we might at least spotlight hundreds of possibilities, perhaps divided into groupings that allow the same fictions or writers to appear in more than one grouping. People often take history as simply a process of memory, which is to forget that historical study—of literature or anything else—can teach us that history itself is also an act of forgetting. From the great mass of materials history selects a tiny proportion to memorialize, and the act of memorializing that small proportion condemns the vast remainder to oblivion.

To represent unrepresentativeness, then, we might choose materials that undermine each other's aspirations to being socially representative, texts that our students might not expect to see next to each other. Like the novels and poems I've written about in this book, we can reconceive representation so that we at once undermine it and make it enliven the contingent "best" in us. A post-canon must think through the constraints of representation that drive us to a post-canon in the first place. Then our reading of Native American and other literatures can live up to the promises of post-canonicity by reinventing both the reading of representation and the representation of what we read.

APPENDIX

Legs, Sex, Orgies, Speed, and Alcohol, After Strange Gods: John Joseph Mathews's Lost Generation Letter

In 1930, deep in a bout of depression, John Joseph Mathews wrote his friends W. S. and Isabel Campbell a long, passionate letter, first chastising his own "lost" generation for its aimless dissipation, then experimenting with the possibility of deserting his generation's restlessness by rededicating himself to Osage tradition, and finally, embarrassed at his passionate dithyramb to Osage ways, defensively backing away from his own attraction to tradition. I reproduce that letter below.

The Western History Collections at the University of Oklahoma Library holds this letter and additional correspondence to and from Mathews that his biographers and critics have not previously drawn on. Mathews was close friends with W. S. Campbell, an English professor at the University of Oklahoma at Norman who wrote many books—some of them about Indian people—mostly under the name Stanley Vestal. Campbell's papers in the Western History Collections include an extensive correspondence with Mathews, and many of those letters add to what has thus far been published about Mathews's personal and professional life. In a letter of 5 March 1929, Mathews refers to some short stories he has drafted, and perhaps to some other writing, explaining that many people have encouraged him to write but that he took no interest in writing until Campbell encouraged him. In a later letter, Mathews announces: "I am now a columnist in the local paper; a column appearing three time [*sic*] a week, and devoted to the wild life of the Osage, sponsored by the Izaak Walton League. It is really great sport" (24 March 1930). (Here "the Osage" seems to refer to the place, not to the people.) To the best of my knowledge, no such column has been mentioned by scholars of Mathews's work. I have not succeeded in finding it, but we can look forward to some luckier or more diligent scholar's turning it up some day. The Western History Collections also includes correspondence with the University of Oklahoma Press about *Wah'Kon-Tah* and other matters and a letter of appreciation for *Sundown* from Frank F. Finney, a white who grew up among Osages (9 December 1934).

Mathews's "lost generation" letter refers to a book he is trying to write. As the date is too early for *Wah'Kon-Tah,* which he wrote in 1931 (Logsdon, 73), perhaps the book is a novel based on his time at Oxford that he tells Campbell he plans to write (4 March 1930) and that Campbell encouraged (28 March 1930). (An earlier Campbell letter [19 March 1929] refers to Mathews's plans to write a biography, but of whom it doesn't say.) The letter also refers to Joseph Brandt, Mathews's friend, the founding editor of the University of Oklahoma Press, and to Independence, Kansas, which is not far from Pawhuska, Oklahoma, Mathews's birthplace, the political center of Osage County, and the original for the town of Kihekah in *Sundown.*

As Stanley Vestal, Campbell went on to write about Mathews's great-grandfather, the famous frontiersman "Old Bill Williams," in *Mountain Men* (1937), and without his pseudonym he annotated Mathews's books in *The Book Lover's Southwest: A Guide to Good Reading* (1955).

The typescript of Mathews's letter includes words crossed out on the typewriter and in longhand. Since the revisions are not of substance, I give the text as Mathews revised it. Definite typos I have silently corrected; possible typos I have left intact. I have also left intact idiosyncrasies of punctuation, except for Mathews's tendency not to skip a space after a punctuation mark.

> Pawhuska, Oklahoma.
> December 3, 1930.

Dear W. S. and Isabel,

Every time I go to Norman I have to suppress a feeling that you have in some way tricked me; that you have been thoughtless of my pleasure by leaving. I am afraid that I take my disappointment out on poor old Joe Brandt, by talking "cabbages and kings" to him when he is busy.

I need you tonight. I have just come from town, and the fog aided by the tinsel and cheap decoration in the windows has depressed me. I have been depressed for two weeks; every thing has gone wrong. I have been attempting to write a chapter of my book for the last two weeks, but on reading what I have written, I find it as flat and uninspiring as stale beer.

I have just spent the week end in Independence, Kansas, among a few flaming youths of my acquaintance, thinking that the diversion would help me. They have lost their charm, those posing darlings of the post-war decade. All the daring has gone out of their favorite subjects and passtimes. Naked swimming parties have lost their thrill; thighs, and the erstwhile secret hills and valleys of feminine anatomy have become too familiar to arouse interest, even when dainty pink underthings create suggestions for the imaginative, and reveal so much by concealment. Conversations about female anatomy and tales of human frailty, illegal babies, and daring stories of half-conscious activities during drunken orgies, have become insipid to them through repetition. Even suggestive epigrams are wearing out. They have led their elders into broader views of life perhaps, but they themselves are lost, poor little illusioned nit-wits. They cling to silly catch-words, and senseless swearing in frantic effort to appear abandoned and sans morals. They bluff; bluff tenaciously, and this bluffing and apparent disregard for all pre war hypocritical decency, have been misunderstood by many of their elders, who in consequence have gone much farther than the youths. Graceless and clumbsy, without the charm of youth, they are often bestial in their drinking and sordidly carnal in their new found relationships; completely without the beauty of youth and romance.

They are a charming [these last four words are only partially legible, so here the transcript represents an editor's guess] lot, these smouldering youths, but how they have ne[here there is a page break between pp. 1 and 2, leaving something garbled—perhaps "neglected"]ed the beauty of life; their minds; their personalities, as they wildly followed Liberty in alcoholic fervor, through the barriers of pre war conventions. How this has all palled on them; they are lost. They are attempting pitiably to find Romance, and some of them are talking wistfully of home and babies. Legs, sex, orgies, speed, alcohol, abnormalities, exaggerated frankness, and flitting around the candle of lust, have lost their thrill; they have become flat and stingless and the devotees are stupified and listless, like children tired of their toys.

I must say I came back from Independence more dejected than ever. On my way back I thought of the night before when all of us were sitting stupidly around the room. The party was over and everyone had sobered up. There was no conversation; some were idly turning the leaves of magazines and others just sat. There was nothing to talk about; the jokes about someone sleeping with someone else had been exhausted; they had been spiritless in the first place, and amazingly unoriginal and without point. Alcoholic inspiration was the usual state with this company of youth; soberness was the unusual state and every one was at a loss. I sat on the divan and watched them. A girl of about eighteen came over and sat beside me. I think she was from K.U. She fondled me for a few minutes like some half hearted kitten, then she laid her highly scented head on my stomach, pulled her dress up to about half way between her sky blue garters and her pink shorts, cocked her feet upon the card table, and called God to witness that she "sure was bored".

With only a few days remaining until "peace on earth and good will to men", I have never felt so much like the personification of "What's The Use". If these statements of mine have any effect on your morale, I am too far gone to care, and would probably take a fiendish delight in the knowledge that I have company in my misery. If things become worse I shall resort to amulets and charms; I shall paint the spread-fingered hand of the Arabic Fatima on my door to ward off the evil eye, and pray fervently to strange gods.

Perhaps the gods of my red ancestors are jealous of my Europeanization, and think to win back my homage by causing disorder in my life. It may be that I shall turn to them; to Wahkanda, the Great Spirit, since the Greek gods have been of little aid. In fact turning from me. The goddess Vesta hath driven me from California. Diana hath sent an epidemic among the quail of the [illegible word] and thereby taken from me the pleasures of the chase. To Mercury I have never paid homage, so from him I can find no relief. And Pan, the beloved, is very likely piping among the reeds of the Tropics. I find no pleasure in the flickering goddess, Cinema, and I have never sold my soul to Mammon. I still sacrifice to Minerva, but this cold goddess cannot understand the muddling weaknesses of humanity. In the springing strength of vital manhood, I might find happiness at the altar of Aphrodite; I am sure she would smile upon my supplications. Or I might even confide in laughing Bacchus, but I have worshipped at their altars before and I have found them inconstant and whimsical; nor do I like their association with the ugly mortal, Remorse.

To Wahkanda, I think I shall turn as soon as I learn more Osage. I shall place before him the list of my wrongs, and assure him of my utter dejection because of them. I shall address him thus:

"Oh Wahkanda, Intatsa, it is I John, son of the Lame One, who comes to you with distressed heart and bleeding soul like the wounded bird in the grass. It is I, John who has looked upon the ways of the white man and thought them good. I, John, Oh

Wahkanda, the wanderer in many lands far from home; far from the blackjacks and the whispering prairie, am come back to you. Know you him who is the son of the Lame One, and the great, great grandson of Hard Rope, the teacher of his people.

Know, Oh Wahkanda, that he has loved in awe the blinding lightning of your temper, revealing the trees like ghosts when nights are black; that he has loved in fear the thunder of your anger echoing over the prairie, and has known in admiration the howling winds of your disfavor, when trees cried in frenzy and bent in homage to your majesty. Oh, Wahkanda, also has he loved you when your hot breath rattled the leaves of summer, and dried the water in the streams; when you sent the heat devils to dance over the prairie and dazzle the eyes of your children. He has revered you when you have painted the leaves of autumn with whimsical abandon; when the sumac becomes a bleeding wound in the hillside, and your hand guides the honking V's of geese across the sky. His lips, Oh Wahkanda, have moved in the prayer of a strange tongue, when you with generous strokes splash the west with crimson and gold, and tint the twilight hills with purple. He has dreamed of you Oh Wahkanda, when Noon, the mother has frightened the stags, her children, and covers the earth with silver and silence, and the insects, your children of the grass roots, sing your praise[nine spaces too faint to read]us, and the owl complains quaveringly.

Oh Wahkanda, drive into my soul the spirit of the prairie, which gave birth to mine own people, that in my creations I might glorify them, and thereby glorify you Oh Wahkanda, by speaking a language that is a true one. Turn mine eyes into mine own heart that I might see what is written there by your hand, and lift from my shoulder the tinsel mantle of deception and remove the sackcloth of convention, that my limbs may be free for action. Purge my heart and mind Oh Wahkanda of the phantasies of civilization, and fill the void with the things of earth; the truths that lie unheeded, and the true philosophy, that I may not spend my brief stay in trivial worry; one with the millions of fretful worried souls, who are but an incident in life; who strut for a brief hour and then pass on. Oh Wahkanda, like the Thanksgiving gobbler of the white man, who for one day struts and vociferates, and turns his burnished feathers to the sun, only to pass on, leaving but one wind tossed feather caught in the grasses to evidence his existence.

Oh, Wahkanda, Intatsa, the wanderer is returned; the seeker after strange gods is meek before you."

Writing such drivel has relieved the pressure, and I feel better. It is gratifying to be able to give vent to crazy thoughts sometimes.

Love to the Campbellettes and I hope you find time to write a note occasionally.

Sincerely,
Joe [signed]

Notes

Preface

¹ For example, Craig S. Womack, 6–7. By contrast, for outrage at white scholars for saying that "Native American literature is not part of American literature," see Wendy Rose, "Just What's All This Fuss," 16. David Palumbo-Liu reviews the issue in light of "ethnic" literature more generally.

Chapter 1. Tradition, Invention, and Aesthetics in Native American Literature and Literary Criticism

¹ The term comes from Kenneth Lincoln. A. LaVonne Brown Ruoff's foreword and other essays in the volume edited by Helen Jaskoski point out that earlier Indian writing has received less attention, and with Cheryl Walker and others they seek to remedy that imbalance. Craig S. Womack also argues for more attention to precontemporary Indian writing (2–4). Those beginning to study Indian writing would do well to start with two invaluable volumes: Paula Gunn Allen, ed., *Studies in American Indian Literature,* and Ruoff, *American Indian Literatures;* Ruoff also provides the fullest bibliography.

² Arnold Krupat provocatively begins to describe that process for 1990s Indian novelists (*Turn,* esp. 30–55), a discussion continued by Sidner Larson, 44–47.

³ For critiques of Clifton's volume, see Vine Deloria and the harsher account in Ward Churchill.

⁴ Adell, 131–32. I find Adell's challenging discussion of Houston Baker and Henry Louis Gates's efforts to establish a specifically African American criticism thought-provoking both in itself and for its potential analogies in Indian studies. See Adell, 118–37.

⁵ King, "Introduction," x–xi. For King's related comments in interviews, see "Interview with Thomas King" by Jeffrey Canton, 2, and interview by Hartmut Lutz, 108.

⁶ See Victor Shklovsky, Boris Eichenbaum, Boris Tomashevsky, and Victor Erlich, 239–46.

⁷ For thought-provoking examples of such contemplations, see bell hooks, *Talking Back,* 42–48, Diana Fuss, 113–19, hooks, *Teaching,* 77–92, and Judith Roof and Robyn Wiegman. For related discussions in Indian studies, see Devon A. Mihesuah, ed., *Natives and Academics.*

⁸ On white critics writing about literature by nonwhites as speaking *for* nonwhites, when I would see them as speaking *about* nonwhites, or, still more narrowly, as speaking about literature by particular nonwhites, see Linda Alcoff, Elizabeth Abel, Margaret Homans, and Pamela L. Caughie.

[9] Here I echo Gayatri Chakravorty Spivak's response (*Outside*, 60; *Critique*, 190–91) to Benita Parry regarding Parry's not-really-understanding critique of Spivak's famous essay "Can the Subaltern Speak?" ("Can the Subaltern Speak?" has appeared in two article versions, both listed in the Works Cited; the shorter version is more user-friendly. A third, long version appears in chap. 3 of Spivak's *Critique of Postcolonial Reason*, esp. 244–311.)

[10] Book-length studies of Indian autobiography include Gretchen M. Bataille and Kathleen Mullen Sands, H. David Brumble III, Arnold Krupat, and Hertha Dawn Wong. On Native theater, see the *Native Playwrights Newsletter*.

[11] Weaver, *That the People*, 22. For an effort to build a pro-essentialist argument, see Womack. Womack bases his portrayal of contemporary critical theory on ideas that had a brief vogue in the high deconstructionist moment of the late seventies and that virtually no one has advocated since then, although the rumor of their dominance has persisted, especially among right-wing pundits who would be anathema to Womack's anticapitalism. Just as I don't find Womack's arguments for essentialism convincing or well informed about the critical debates around essentialism, so I can't abide his implication that non-Native critics cannot contribute helpfully to the discussion of Native American literature. On the other hand, the often ugly history of white-produced writing about Indian peoples gives us reason to take Womack's point of view seriously. I also applaud his encouragement for the study of particular tribal literatures and the example he offers for a study of tribal literature that joins—as a work of writing—in the literature that it studies.

Chapter 2. Nothing to Do

[1] Allen, *The Sacred Hoop*, 202–3. See also Nancy Bonvillain, whose summary histories of diverse Indian peoples each fit Allen's model, and the bibliographical overview in Rayna Green, *Native American Women*, 10.

[2] Genovese, 285–324. See Du Bois, *Gift*, 52–79, esp. 53–54. Du Bois's ideas here offer an abbreviated, more lyrical version of a suggestive account by Sydney Olivier (72–85), which Du Bois cites. Olivier (who was, among other things, a socialist governor of Jamaica and uncle of the famous actor) anticipates much that Genovese says, without Genovese's vast fund of United States particulars. Thompson's thought-provoking article draws on, among other sources, a suggestive article by Keith Thomas.

[3] A review in the University of Oklahoma's *Sooner Magazine* found the campus episodes convincing: "Scenes about the campus and Norman [site of the University of Oklahoma] are penned with a keen sense for detail. The difficult task of attempting to picture phases of fraternity and student life is handled carefully enough to escape most of the pitfalls writers of campus life are beset by. The well nigh impossible task of showing campus life in full detail is not attempted. . . . Mr. Mathews shows only the highlights and they are done with feeling."

[4] See the broader discussions of these cultural patterns by Philip J. Deloria and Shari M. Huhndorf.

[5] Much has been written about Indian thinking as less concerned than European or Euro-American thinking with individuality, especially in the scholarship on Indian autobiography. For a helpful and concise example from an Osage writer, see Carter Revard's "History, Myth, and Identity among Osages and Other Peoples" (Revard, 126–41). Carol Hunter, an Osage critic, sees the novel as "essentially focusing on Chal's character development" ("Protagonist as a Mixed-Blood," 330), yet elsewhere she provides the fullest review of *Sundown*'s social and historical setting ("Historical Context"). My reading joins with that of Robert Allen Warrior, an Osage intellectual historian, in seeing the character focus as pointed much more in social and political directions, but one can still see Mathews's

focus on a single character as tied to the tradition of individuality that his work neverthe-less critiques. Chickasaw novelist Linda Hogan's *Mean Spirit* (1990), also set among Osages during the oil boom, allows an illuminating comparison. "Hogan's novel pays more atten-tion to the tribal community than does Mathews's," Louis Owens notes aptly, yet it "is con-siderably more romantic in its methods and conclusions" (*Other Destinies*, 261n1). For an-other comparison, see Edna Ferber's 1930 number one best-seller, *Cimarron*, more impressive for its feminism than for its treatment of Osages. The hoopla about Oklahoma Indian oil wealth was a familiar trope of the times, turning up, for example, in passing al-lusions in Fitzgerald's 1934 *Tender Is the Night* (79) and Faulkner's 1946 "Appendix" to *The Sound and the Fury*. Oliver La Farge's review of *Sundown* notes: "Since the writer is skilful, observant, and knows his material well, it is also an excellent literary document on Okla-homa, something to be taken, and enjoyed, as a little salt on Miss Ferber's too gorgeous 'Cimarron.' "

⁶ Warrior, 58. See Mathews, *The Osages*, 740–70; Garrick Bailey, *Changes*, 85–89; Terry P. Wilson, *Underground Reservation*, 197–200; Bailey, *The Osage and the Invisible World*, 5, 18–19; see also Mathews, *Wah'Kon-Tah*, 322–23, 336, and *Talking to the Moon*, 84–85, 132, 227, 238–39. In a valuable article, Hunter ("Historical Context") identifies the models and so-cial setting for many characters and events in the novel, but she does not address the change from traditional Osage religion to peyotism, perhaps because the novel steers clear of references to the change (except obliquely on 81–83).

⁷ Granted, Mathews tells more about traditional ways in his last book, *The Osages* (1961), but even when it describes religion, that work focuses more on history. *The Osages* was pub-lished a generation after *Sundown,* and by that time the older ways were more distant and hence less threatened by exposure. Moreover, one could argue that the audience for the 823-page *The Osages* is predominantly Osage, whereas *Sundown* assumes and has found a wider audience.

⁸ A 1934 census counted 83 percent of Osages as mixed-bloods (Ruth Boutwell, 2), and every cultural history of the Osages—e.g., Mathews, *The Osages;* Bailey, *Changes;* and Wil-son, *Underground Reservation*—labors over relations between full-bloods and mixed-bloods and their often competing attitudes to assimilation. In the last chapter of *Wah'Kon-Tah*, Mathews anticipates *Sundown* with a portrait of pressures to assimilate and young people's restless rebellion during the oil boom. Both books' portraits match the descriptions by so-cial workers Ruth Boutwell and Lucy Boutwell Gayler. Reviewers, however, predictably dis-agreed over whether Chal is a representative figure. At one extreme, a reviewer for the *Daily Oklahoman* saw *Sundown* as "the story of what must be actually happening to thou-sands of young Indian boys all over the west, who are trying in vain to adjust themselves to white civilization" (K.). At the other extreme, a reviewer for the *Tulsa World* takes pains to describe the novel as "the story of an Osage youth who felt himself different from the oth-ers of his race, somehow feeling that he was superior but by his actions always seeming in-ferior," adding that "Mathews, himself a member of the Osage tribe, has drawn a splendid picture of an Indian youth, but it is not autobiographical," as if to say that Osage youths are not really like Chal.

⁹ Garrick Bailey notes that Mathews's family "did not participate in traditional Osage ceremonial or social life. The Osage clan system was patrilineal, and the Osage ancestry of the Mathews family had passed through a matrilineal line; thus they were not part of the clan system" (Bailey, "John Joseph Mathews," 207; see also *Changes*, 93).

¹⁰ For such matters in traditional Osage culture, see the work of Francis La Flesche, in-troduced in Bailey, *The Osage and the Invisible World*. Revard's "History, Myth, and Identity among Osages and Other Peoples" draws on La Flesche's descriptions of Osage traditions and likens them to a larger American Indian context (Revard, 126–41).

¹¹ By contrast, the even more pervasive contemplation of birds in Mathews's *Talking to*

the Moon comes weighted with none of Chal's romantic associations between birds and freedom. In *Talking to the Moon,* Mathews writes as a naturalist determined to observe birds' behavior rather than to translate that behavior into metaphors of human dreams.

[12] Compare King-Kok Cheung's and Traise Yamamoto's thought-provoking discussions of agencies and demeaning stereotypes linked to Asian American silence.

[13] Wiget uses this phrase in quotation marks to paraphrase a reductive perspective that he objects to (*Native American Literature,* 77). Warrior also finds it objectionable, although he misattributes the perspective to Wiget. Regardless, I join with Warrior and Wiget to argue against readings that would confine Chal to what Warrior calls "identity struggle as strictly biological-cultural rather than political-ideological" (54).

[14] Boutwell (71) notes that such problems were common for Osages in white-dominated schools. Gayler offers a representative example: white students provoking fights by calling an Indian student a "black Injun" (95).

[15] Patricia C. Albers discusses ideological assumptions that have limited whites' and sometimes Indians' views of Indians as workers, steering Indians away from jobs not traditionally associated with Indians (e.g., crafts, tourism, seasonal labor). For a statistical review of low Indian employment rates in the first decades of the twentieth century, see Cardell K. Jacobson, 163–64.

[16] For the lack of employment, see Gayler, 87 (see also 96). Gayler oversaw a survey of 100 full-blood families out of "less than one-hundred and fifty such families" (5). Even if her survey is less than entirely reliable and distorts the wider pattern by leaving out mixed-bloods, it offers a revealing rough gauge. She cites oil income statistics "from the records of the tribe's income from oil and gas at the Indian Agency in Pawhuska" (92). Revard recalls that during that time his " 'fullblood' " (5) "Osage stepfather worked when he could, but" even combined with the Osage payment check, the money he earned didn't cover the "grocery bills and gas bills and cow-feed bills. And in the winter time there just was not any of the work that put food on the table in summer or fall—no corn to hoe, no hay to pitch or haul, no wheat to shock or shovel" (58). Revard's way of putting it underlines that his stepfather worked hard when work was available, unlike Mathews's or at least Chal's implication that Osages didn't work at all. (For Revard's nonpessimistic view of Osage work during his depression childhood, at least compared to Mathews's view, see also 103.)

[17] Knack and Littlefield note the changing gender patterns in relation to Indians' role in the labor economy. For a popular review of the breadwinner's role expected from white American men, see Barbara Ehrenreich, 1–28, although she does not note the partly race- and class-specific character of the pattern she describes.

[18] In the 100 families in Gayler's survey, only five people had extensive vocational training (4 to 24 months), and only one of those had ever "used their training for the purposes of making money," working seventeen days in 1933 (39).

[19] Wilson notes that Mathews was an ardent supporter of the New Deal ("John Joseph Mathews," 160). "Collier met with the [Osage] council in October, 1934, and it was Mathews who shouldered the primary burden of espousing Osage support for the IRA and defending the tribal position in an open debate with Oklahoma Senator Elmer Thomas" (Wilson, "Osage Oxonian," 280, citing the *Osage County News,* 19 October 1934). The telegraphic, sometimes obscure council-meeting minutes record Mathews's political fervor as he tried—successfully—to convince the council to support the IRA:

> You have seen in the Osage for years the interest of that group that have always lived
> off the Indian, they don't want the rich gold mine to get away from them and natu-
> rally they form the majority opinion in this State and naturally Senator Thomas as a
> politician is falling in with them. . . . Those opposed are those who have lived off the

Indian for years. I didn't think I would find [the] press so prejudiced and unfair, personally I am quite ready to take a stand. . . . These rumors forcing Indians on Reservations, forcing them back to the times of forefathers, perpetuation of the Indian Bureau, inherited lands in the colony finally dwindling away. . . . I believe as I see it today as at Miami and Muskogee, will be direct insult to our intelligence. We are capable of thinking, the only reason we haven't got what we wanted, political control. Now we have opportunity with backing of Commissioner, Secretary and President. One thing I can not tolerate is unfairness and having my intelligence insulted. I am not going to be this intense, I am going to pat this man [Collier] on his back as important to our affairs in Washington but that is situation that Council ought to know and that is what I have been trying to tell them. ("Proceedings," 17 October 1934, 1–2)

Sundown also pokes fun at Herbert Hoover, Roosevelt's Republican predecessor, in its scathing portrait of Miss Hoover, the white liberal teacher who—inspired by James Fenimore Cooper—wants to help Indian students but ends up despising them.

[20] In a long, apparently extemporaneous speech before the Osage Council explaining his case to an OIA representative, Mathews put the political history and argument from *Sundown* into more direct and compacted form.

We have got to do something with these young Osages. I suppose that before we can do anything, before any plans or dreams come to fruition they will probably be assimilated and that will be the end of it. Many of the young men my age and younger, full blood Osages, can't even speak their own language now. Many of them don't care to speak it. Of course I think they are assuming what they believe to be a civilization, which isn't. I can't see it as civilization, this thing. . . . I think this thing with which they have come in contact is probably a manifestation of the Anglo-Saxon's worst characteristics, his greed, his—there is nothing beautiful in this. This is all grabbing. There is nothing beautiful there. There is nothing for the young man to imitate. He can't go out and buy beans for ten cents a pound and sell them for fifteen. It isn't in his blood, it isn't in his tradition. And he knows now that the only interest that people have in him is the money he has. . . . [W]e can't get rid of these hangers—you can't get rid of buzzards where there is carrion, you can't get rid of the dope peddler, you can't get rid of liquor, you can't get rid of taxi drivers coming in and marrying girls, giving them social diseases and what now. You can't do it. It is a problem.

I should like to suggest to you a picture. You have got a territory here represented as about a million four hundred acres. . . . That was Indian land. That was the Osage Reservation. Now they were allotted in 1906, homesteads, then surplus, and about that time the first oil well was drilled and then the development grew, grew and grew until it reached the apex about 1926. All right, you have got then a country where there is not a pin factory, not a mattress factory. They make no spoons, no stockings, no shoes, no hats, they make nothing. There are a few refineries within the limits. . . . Otherwise there is nothing. The only thing there is in this country to produce wealth outside of cattle . . . is the . . . exploitation of hydro-carbon, the oil and gas. Now the big companies came in and . . . sent the oil and gas out of the country. . . . But there you had wealth created, didn't you? Now the Osages held those hydro-carbons in community. They got a certain percentage of it as royalties, a fifth and a sixth. They lived here. That was the money that stayed. Therefore the Osage people with their royalties became the industry, and flocking to them from all ends of the earth came every type of person, rats as well as fairly decent citizens. They all came and now the Osage is the industry and that is your picture. That is the only industry in this country. If the Osage payments were stopped tomorrow there would be nothing here in six months, there would be coyotes howling in the streets down there. There is nothing. ("Proceedings," 18 December 1935, 12–13)

[21] On *Talking to the Moon* in relation to *Walden* and the writing of John Muir, see Ruoff, "John Joseph Mathews's."

[22] Wiget also notes the "lost generation" mood later in *Sundown* (*Native American Literature,* 75). In a stunning letter of 1930, printed as an appendix at the end of this book, Mathews describes his lost generation in terms that strikingly anticipate and may well have helped lead to the portrait in *Sundown.* This letter gives the impression that Mathews's disgust with his generation's aimless dissipation also contributed to his renewed interest, after years away from home, in returning to and dedicating himself to Osage lands, culture, and history.

[23] Warrior complements Owens with a rather less strained effort to read the ending as more hopeful than other critics suggest (52–53, 56, 82–83). For the other critics, see the *New York Times* review ("Educated Indian," 20), Larson (61), Hunter ("Historical Context," 63–64, 71; "Protagonist as a Mixed-Blood," 333–35), Wilson ("Osage Oxonian," 278), and Wiget (*Native American Literature,* 76). Without insisting that realist assumptions necessarily underlie *Sundown* or its final episodes, I think it of interest to note that according to admissions procedures for Harvard Law School in 1933: "The following men will be admitted without examinations . . . :—1. Graduates of colleges of high grade presenting approved college records. 2. Graduates of other colleges of approved standing who ranked in the first quarter of the class during the Senior year." Chal quits school to enlist, so he never graduates, let alone graduates from what Harvard Law in 1933 would have considered a college of "high grade." His university grades are low, presumably nowhere near the top quarter of his class. Nor is he ready to gain entrance through examination, though over a decade earlier, before his alcoholism, he shows considerable academic ability when he applies himself. University of Oklahoma graduates were not unheard of at Harvard Law, but in 1933 only two of 1,514 Harvard Law students had Oklahoma BAs. Tuition was $400, not clearly out of the question for Chal, with oil income at $712 in 1932, but still an obstacle (*Law School of Harvard University,* 5–6, 26, 96). Mathews wouldn't have known these details, but he didn't need to, for the general picture bolsters the already firm impression that we should not take Chal's plans for Harvard any more seriously than he ends up taking most of his plans throughout the novel, especially after he returns from the Army.

[24] For another fictional account of an Osage peyote ceremony, published just before *Sundown*'s, see Ferber, 310–15.

[25] In 1972, Mathews told an interviewer that after *Wah'Kon-Tah* publishers pressured him "for another book. He was persuaded to write a novel. 'So, I sat down and wrote it. I've never read it since it was published' " (Guy Logsdon, 73). Similarly, in a 1976 letter he explains that "after the success of Wah'Kon-Tah . . . publishers hounded me to write a novel and somehow in the confusion I did promise to write one. I am a hunter by nature and once home in the Blackjacks the Quail season was open and I found myself wanting to hunt instead of wanting to write. I finally sat down to write the book without any inspiration" (Larson, 13). See also Bailey, "John Joseph Mathews," 211. The photograph appears in Wilson, "Osage Oxonian," 265.

Chapter 3. Who Shot the Sheriff

[1] So far as I know, the only novel by a Native American and about Native Americans published between *The Surrounded* and *House Made of Dawn* is McNickle's young adult novel,

Runner in the Sun (1954), set in pre-contact times, unless you count Natachee Scott Momaday's (the mother of N. Scott Momaday) *Owl in the Cedar Tree* (1965), a children's novel about the length of a long short story. Admittedly, the "by and about" formula is tricky, both in use and in value, and Native Americans wrote more than a few other novels during those years, published and unpublished. On common patterns for novels of the American Indian renaissance, see William Bevis, "Native American Novels."

² As on many reservations, a diverse group of Indian peoples live on the Flathead Reservation, where McNickle grew up and where he sets *The Surrounded,* including people whose ancestors lived there before it was a reservation and others whose ancestors were pressured to move there by the federal government. The best summary I have seen, by Ronald Lloyd Trosper, an economist and member of the Confederated Salish and Kootenai Tribes of the Flathead Reservation, puts it this way: "Most of the Indians on the reservation were and are Salish. The 'Flathead' band and the Pend d'Oreille band both spoke the Salish language. They intermarried with each other and with other groups, such as the Nez Percé who are not identified as Salish people. The Kootenai is an entirely different grouping of Indians. . . . Because of this heterogeneity of origin, when the Indians of the Flathead Reservation formed a tribal government under the Indian Reorganization Act, they designated themselves as the 'Confederated Salish and Kootenai Tribes.' It is incorrect to refer to the Indians as a single tribe, although it is certainly easier to say 'the Flathead Indians' than 'the members of the Confederated Salish and Kootenai Tribes' " (14–15).

³ On anthologies, see Jane Tompkins, 190–91; on salvage anthropology, see Clifford, *Predicament of Culture,* 189–214. Purdy has edited a collection of essays on McNickle in which William Brown, Phillip E. Doss, and Robert Evans elaborate his focus on *The Surrounded*'s relation to oral storytelling (see also Bill Brown). My own perspective differs from Doss's or Evans's, as Doss seems to me to romanticize the oral, discussing what he calls its "purity" (54–57), and Evans reifies difference as a thing in itself rather than a comparative term that depends on points of reference. He thus sees mediation between or mixing of Indian and white cultures, including Indians' use of English, as forfeits of true Indianness.

⁴ The biographical details come from McNickle's correspondence and diaries in the Edward E. Ayer Collection of the Newberry Library and from the biography by Dorothy R. Parker.

⁵ For a local history of Indian horse stealing, see James William Carroll, 143–48.

⁶ Since Spivak raised the notion of "strategic essentialism" (*In Other Worlds,* 202–15; *Outside,* 3–10), it has become a reference point and lightning rod for many cultural critics. Because Spivak's provocative discussions are forbiddingly dense, I try to define the concept as I bring it up.

⁷ For a searching contemplation of traditional northwest storytelling, ecology, and hunting, see Ramsey, 60–75; see Laird Christensen for an eco-critical reading of *The Surrounded.*

⁸ In a manuscript version in the Newberry Library, perhaps a first draft and probably one of the drafts that McNickle called *The Hungry Generations,* Archilde's decision not to shoot the buck is less deliberate, more a failure of masculinity than a redefinition of it: "He became aware of how intensely excited he was when he found perspiration on his forehead. He was breathing quickly and his chest felt hot. Once more he brought his gun to his shoulder and deliberately took aim but his hands were quivering. He couldn't hold the gun steady. He had never experienced such a thing before and he couldn't understand it. . . . Never had such a thing happened to him and as he started back to camp he felt silly" (*Hungry,* 66). For similar variations on the theme of hunting, see McNickle's story "Meat for God" in the September 1935 *Esquire,* where the magazine dubbed him its "Discovery of the Month." Robert F. Gish ("Irony and Consent") discusses hunting as a broader metaphor in *The Surrounded;* my own reading matches Gish's suggestions that Archilde

goes hunting to connect with his Native heritage, and that McNickle relates hunting to gender (107, 108). On *The Hungry Generations*, see Owens, *Other Destinies*, 74–77, and "Red Road"; Birgit Hans, "Because" and "Re-Visions"; and Purdy, *Word Ways*, 14–18, 34–38.

[9] On this point it can help to compare Ruppert's notion that the novel suggests a revealing gap between its implied author and McNickle himself ("Textual Perspectives").

[10] For a parallel response to Purdy, see Owens's review of Purdy's book.

[11] Barre Toelken argues resourcefully against reading Euro-American expectations of didacticism onto traditional Native oral storytelling, and Greg Sarris describes the multiplying ways that oral stories can teach over time rather than hardening into an immediate moral (194).

[12] McNickle's letters in the Newberry Library include a longer version of his "Note" to the novel, with more cultural history, referring to "the establishment of trade resulting, on the trader's part, in profitable enterprise and on the Indians', in growing dependence on the new tools and weapons and an accompanying decline of the old arts and ways of life" (letter to Ruth Rae).

[13] On the anti-Catholic and anti-Christian dimension of *The Surrounded*, see Christensen. According to Dusenberry's letter to McNickle describing the novel's enthusiastic local reception, "It is reported that Father Taelman read your book and has stated that he thinks you have gone completely mad. That [is] the one dissenting voice amid the cheers 'The Surrounded' has received." For another local response from a little farther away, see the review by McNickle's undergraduate teacher at the University of Montana, Harold G. Merriam.

[14] See Ruppert's discussion of the novel's parallel structure (*D'Arcy McNickle*, 20–21). Alas, I am not the first critic to compare *The Surrounded* to contemporary African American novels. While *The Surrounded* was generally very favorably received, one dissenter compared it to black writing in the most derogatory terms. I quote in full a review from the *Washington Star*:

> The recent slow but sure encroachment of the American Indian on the pages of sentimental fiction has caused reviewers to wonder hopefully whether they might not look for a corresponding decrease in Negro novels of the popular consumption type. For, while there would seem to be little or nothing to choose between in the two types of books, the Negro novel is getting thin just from use.
>
> But the hope, even if realized, seems likely to prove barren, for the burning-browed literary boys who set up as interpreters of the long-suffering red man have to date no more to offer and that is of a less meaty quality. The utmost they have demonstrated yet is that to be an Indian is to be unhappy and, in some mysterious but very lofty sense, superior to everybody else. It makes slightly attenuated fare.
>
> The present novel follows along this pattern. For the technically minded the information is offered that the tribe and hero are Flatheads, the latter a half-breed, or, as the publisher terms him, a "half-caste." For the less expert reader, however, it is to be feared that one fiction Indian will seem very like another, or even, in the words of Sancho Panza, "oftentimes a good deal worse."

The scornful, threatened vulnerability in these comments, propping up a desire to take prejudice for granted, leads to complaints that may misread *The Surrounded* but that land roughly on target for the publisher's publicity and for much other fiction portraying Indian people.

[15] For a history of punishment by whipping and how such punishment changed in the early reservation years, see Carroll, 149–55.

[16] Womack has recently made much the same argument (15–16, 65), and I take our converging views as mutually reinforcing. Rainwater pays particular attention to contemporary Indian fiction as *writing*, even when it works with oral traditions.

¹⁷ Nancy Oestreich Lurie offers a speculative, anecdotal effort to begin describing patterns in Indian attitudes toward money, roughly corroborating the reading in this chapter.

¹⁸ On the IECW, see chapter 2. In September 1935, the IECW employed 410 men on the Flathead Reservation out of a "working population" of 624 and a total population under 3,000, as reported by Mary Heaton Vorse in *Indians at Work,* the IECW magazine. Collier appointed the socialist, feminist Vorse, a prominent labor journalist and novelist, to edit *Indians at Work,* which reported on IECW activity at the Flathead Reservation in almost every issue. In 1936 it published McNickle's "Train Time," a fine story about the superintendent of a Flathead-like reservation sending unwilling children off to boarding school. Eventually, Vorse left *Indians at Work* under pressure from the House UnAmerican Activities Committee, but McNickle continued to write for the magazine (Dee Garrison, 267–69; D. R. Parker, "D'Arcy McNickle," 7–11, and *Singing,* 71–72). For a broader history of federal efforts to take lands from Flathead Reservation Indians, see Kickingbird and Ducheneaux, 90–103; and for a broader study of the devastation that allotment wreaked on Indian economics on the Flathead Reservation, see Trosper. An earlier version of this chapter puts together more statistics about the irrigation project (R. D. Parker, "Who Shot," 919–20), but at that point I had not seen Trosper's excellent and much fuller account (48–62, 183–96).

¹⁹ In *The Hungry Generations,* Archilde goes to Paris à la *The Sun Also Rises.* Purdy reads McNickle's early title as alluding to Gertrude Stein's crack about the "lost generation," made famous in the epigraph to Hemingway's novel. Reviews in the *Buffalo Times* and the *Camden Post* (see below) supposed Hemingway among McNickle's influences. Perhaps the sharpest comments on gender in *The Surrounded* come in a brief summary from Owens: "Indian men in *The Surrounded* have been rendered impotent, incapable of 'making' something of themselves in the priest's words. In the resulting role reversal, those who act forcefully and attempt with disastrous results to control events are the Indian women" ("Red Road," 243). Perhaps the women's position is no more—and no less—a reaction to the men's than the men's is to the women's.

²⁰ I regret to say that I see such prescriptive realism in an article by Roseanne Hoefel. While I applaud her refreshing attention to gender and to the women characters of *The Surrounded,* especially to the understudied Agnes and Elise, and I am intrigued by her analogies between *The Surrounded* and moments in Mourning Dove's autobiography, Hoefel strains to see the female characters in romantically favorable terms. According to Hoefel, when Catharine kills the warden, "She becomes in an instant the decisive, instinctively avenging mother . . . , operating on the code of Indian justice" (47). *The* mother, *the* code—such generalizing terms might give us pause. It seems rash to call Catharine's act "Indian justice" when the novel offers a picture of much more deliberative and communal Indian justice—settling scores, smoking the pipe, making restitution, and wielding the lash (205–6). We could at least as easily tie impulsive vigilante killing to "white justice," but just as there is more variety than that in white behavior, including more systems of justice, however imperfect they are, so there is more variety and—usually—more deliberation than that in Indian justice. Catharine's equivocal act hardly seems ripe for such unequivocal endorsement. Similarly, though Hoefel's work joins mine in appreciation of Elise, Elise's role is at least as equivocal as Catharine's. Hoefel, though, says that "Archilde has a gold-mine" in Elise (59). At the end, Hoefel thinks, "Elise is reasoned. . . . She becomes Archilde's shadow. . . . Her attentiveness and practicality make possible their escape" (60). But Elise leads and Archilde follows, so she is not his shadow. Moreover, they do *not* escape. Their attempt to escape fails because Elise's reasoning, which Hoefel calls "decisive, almost instinctive," extends only a moment's length into the future. She leads Archilde to where there is no escape. With Archilde, she lets their love distract them from keeping watch, so that they do not see

their pursuers moving in on them (291). Then she overlooks the oddity of Quigley's walking up in full view, gun undrawn (291), which should tell her that he is not alone, and she overlooks his surprising mildness and his remark that he has already caught their horses, even while Archilde wonders how Quigley could catch the horses by himself (292–93). Not least, she overlooks the risk of killing Quigley, perhaps an ethical as well as a pragmatic risk. She reasons out how to shoot him but no further, and McNickle drops in tellingly that she shoots "from the hip" (294). "How in hell you figured killing a man would keep us together—you're just a damn fool!" yells Archilde, surrounding his rebuke with an embrace and a kiss (295). Quigley is a thug, but killing him is still less than a reasoned act, and it is easy to imagine arguments that killing him is far worse than unreasonable, whether we accept those arguments or not. In short, it does not advance feminist criticism or our views of female characters (or characters of any social group) to see them as more or less all wise, just, and good.

Chapter 4. Text, Lines, and Videotape

[1] On definitions and criteria for oral poetry, see Ruth Finnegan, *Oral Poetry*, 24–28. For a good introduction to comparisons between oral and literate cultures, see Walter J. Ong. Ong's description of oral cultures, however, takes little account of Native Americans, and he sometimes privileges written accounts from colonizers over oral accounts from the colonized (e.g., 48). For a wider survey of the study of traditional oral literature, see Finnegan, *Oral Traditions*. On the history of textualizing Native American orality, see especially David Murray, and on textualizing orality more broadly, see Elizabeth C. Fine.

[2] Quoted in Brian Swann, ed., *On the Translation of Native American Literatures*, xv–xvi. For a historical study of Timberlake's work, see William M. Clements (*Native American Verbal Art*, chap. 4). For a broader history, see Krupat, "On the Translation of Native American Song."

[3] Curtis prints a facsimile of Roosevelt's letter, of which I quote the entire text (p. xx). Zolbrod's *Reading the Voice* works from the same assumption, bringing much sensitive discussion to the Native oral expression that he classifies as poetry while defining *poetry* as an honorific, a term for language that he finds aesthetically fulfilling.

[4] Clements, " 'Tokens,' " 43. In 1823, Schoolcraft responded to a similar, widely distributed questionnaire from Lewis Cass; see *Schoolcraft's Indian Legends*, 288–93.

[5] Momaday, *House Made of Dawn*, 146–47. The prayer comes from the Navajo Nightway, which Matthews describes in his famous *The Night Chant, a Navaho Ceremony*, 1902. For his translation of another prayer from *The Night Chant*, see chapter 7. For wider discussions of the Nightway in relation to American literature, see chapter 7 and Kenneth Roemer. I quote Matthews from *Navaho Legends*, 60; for a further example of his comments on poetry, see *Navaho Legends*, 22–29.

[6] On Austin and the vogue for comparing Indian song and modernist poetry, see Ruppert, "Discovering America"; Michael Castro; and Krupat, *Voice*, 110–12.

[7] The best known and most widely distributed anthologies include *The Path on the Rainbow*, 1918; rpt. 1934, 1970, 1991, 1997; *The Winged Serpent*, 1946; rpt. 1962, 1973, 1992; *The Sky Clears: Poetry of the American Indians*, 1951; rpt. 1964, 1983, which includes much more commentary; and *In the Trail of the Wind*, 1971; rpt. 1987, 1993, 1999. In all these, the only poems actually written by a Native American as poetry are two poems in *The Path on the Rainbow* by the Canadian Mohawk Pauline Johnson. When Louis Untermyer attacked Johnson's poems, the volume's editor, George W. Cronyn, gave way, agreeing that they were poor stuff and explaining that his publisher asked him to include them; see Castro, 31–32, 43–44. Neither Nellie Barnes (1921) nor Eda Lou Walton and T. T. Waterman

(1925), in their substantial studies of what they call "American Indian verse" or "American Indian poetry," address any poems written by American Indians.

8 For more of the controversy, see Bevis, "American Indian Verse Translations"; Clements, "Faking the Pumpkin"; Castro; Rothenberg, " 'We Explain Nothing' "; Krupat, *Voice,* 118–22, and *Ethnocriticism,* 194–200; and Clements, *Native,* 43–50, 129–53.

9 Hymes, "*In Vain,*" 309. "Discovering" first appeared in *New Literary History* in 1977. Hymes elaborates his argument in many articles; I have only chosen representative and influential examples. See especially, in addition to "Discovering," "Louis Simpson's 'The Deserted Boy' " ("*In Vain*"). Even apart from the claim for "discovery," the title of Hymes's landmark article is grandiose: his topic is not "American Indian narrative," which would include written short stories, novels, autobiographies, and a good deal of poetry as well as nontraditional oral narrative (like other people, Indians continue to tell stories every day). Much more specifically, his topic is traditional Indian oral narrative.

10 Besides Hymes's article in *New Literary History,* see, for example, Ramsey, "Wife," published influentially in *PMLA* and later included in Ramsey's *Reading the Fire,* 96–114; and Karl Kroeber, "Deconstructionist Criticism." Ramsey has returned to another story from Howard in the 1999 edition of *Reading the Fire,* 139–55. For a broader, pathbreaking address to Howard's stories, see Siobhan Senier, *Voices.*

11 Hymes's categories may fit the sonnet analogy more closely than the analogy to Greek and Slavic epic. Albert B. Lord, for example, hedges questions of intent in *The Singer of Tales,* his classic study of Serbo-Croatian and Homeric oral narrative poetry. The Serbo-Croatian singer, he writes, "obtains a sense of ten syllables followed by a syntactic pause, although he never counts out ten syllables, and if asked, *might* not be able to tell how many syllables there are between pauses. . . . [T]he singer's concept of the formula is shaped though not explicit. He is *aware* of the successive beats and the varying lengths of repeated thoughts" (32; emphasis added). Lord stresses both the singers' habitual usage, which can suggest less conscious intent, and their deliberate training, which can suggest more conscious intent. My own, far from specialist's sense is that more recent Homeric scholarship continues Lord's hedge. See also note 20.

12 After reading Kinkade's work-in-progress, Hymes—ever ready to retranslate other people's translations—proposed an alternative set of divisions, which Kinkade describes in the finished article (286–88).

13 Sarris throws additional doubt on Hymes's assumptions about authoritative texts by studying how Indian oral stories take varying forms in varying contexts (22, 45).

14 More recently, Tedlock has translated (in prose) the Mayan *Popol Vuh* (1985), which won the PEN Translation Prize. *Finding the Center* has also influenced transcriptions and translations of oral stories from outside Native America, especially African stories. See, for example, Isadore Okpewho, chs. 7 and 11, and Tedlock, *Finding the Center,* 2d ed., xix. Outside of book reviews and discussions of translation theory, there has been little direct discussion of the Zuni narratives that Tedlock published. The major exception is the excellent article by Senier, "Zuni Raconteur."

15 See the preface and introduction to both editions of *Finding the Center* and Tedlock, "On the Translation of Style." For an example of how Tedlock's later work continues to highlight process and mediation by advocating what he calls "dialogue," see his "Questions Concerning Dialogical Anthropology."

16 On verbal performance, see especially Richard Bauman.

17 In Tedlock's transcriptions of Zuni narrative in *The Spoken Word,* he adds boldface and italics, but leaves them out of his explanations, including his new "Guide to Reading Aloud." His latest work, *Breath on the Mirror,* takes advantage of word processing to add still more variations.

18 For an objection of much this sort, see Mattina, 143.

[19] Tedlock, "Learning to Listen," 123. In an earlier version of this chapter (R. D. Parker, "Texts, Lines, and Videotape," 153–56), I also critique Tedlock's tendency to confuse runover lines with line breaks. Since then he has mostly corrected that problem in the new edition of *Finding the Center* (see p. xviii), and so I have not retained that critique here.

[20] A possible exception would come in the so-called lines of metered oral narrative, such as the poetry of Homer or Serbo-Croatian singers. Neither Hymes nor Tedlock makes any claim for a system of metrics, however, and we might do well to recall Lord's description of Serbo-Croatian singers: "When the singer is pressed then to say what a line is, he, whose chief claim to fame is that he traffics in lines of poetry, will be entirely baffled by the question; or he will say that since he has been dictating and has seen his utterances being written down, he has discovered what a line is, although he did not know it as such before, because he had never gone to school" (25). Still, it might beg the question to say that the singer's claim to fame comes from trafficking in lines of poetry, since the question is whether, to the singer, the poetry comes in lines or not.

[21] Jakobson's "Concluding Statement" offers the most famous instance of his argument. For additional examples, see Jakobson's work as discussed in Culler. Much of Culler's critique of Jakobson parallels my critique of Hymes, as when Culler argues that "linguistic categories are so numerous and flexible that one can use them to find evidence for practically any form of organization" (62). See also Roger Fowler, 162–79, and Terence Hawkes, 80–82; Hawkes concludes that "Jakobson is talking about our response, as members of a community, to poetry and to prose, rather than about poetry and prose *per se*," in part because "poetry and prose do not exist *per se*. Their nature is determined by the conventional role society gives to the particular uses of language in which they engage" (82). Kroeber, "The Wolf Comes" (esp. 103–4), also criticizes Jakobson's and Tedlock's distinctions between poetry and prose, and Murray (144–49) criticizes Tedlock's reification of form.

[22] Bhabha, "Of Mimicry and Man," 86, 89. On translation and American internal colonization, see Silko, "Old-Time Indian Attack"; Hobson; Eric Cheyfitz; and Krupat, *Ethnocriticism*, 173–200.

[23] Although Mattina's arguments against Tedlock and, more so, against Hymes are mostly congruent with my own, I have not repeated them except where noted. I recommend Rice's astute discussion and, since I first came upon it after drafting this chapter, I take it as corroboration. For a milder dispute with Tedlock and Hymes, see Hegeman, who criticizes them for asking other translators to follow their methods.

[24] For a detailed linguistic study of Indian English, see William L. Leap.

[25] On the ideological technology of the reality effect, see, for example, the classic essay by Jean-Louis Comolli, "Machines of the Visible," as well as Steve Neale, 8, 13–22, 50–52. On the psychic structure of the "impression of reality," see Jean-Louis Baudry, although his argument fits cinema more than video. On the more general convention of realism, I have found John Ellis especially helpful (6–10 and passim).

[26] See Bhabha, "The Other Question," where he argues: "The stereotype is not a simplification because it is a false representation of a given reality. It is a simplification because it is an arrested, fixated form of representation that, in denying the play of difference . . . , constitutes a problem for the *representation* of the subject" (75).

Chapter 5. The Existential Surfboard and the Dream of Balance, or "To be there, no authority to anything"

[1] On the difference between poetry, short story, and novel, Young Bear says in an interview that he is a "believer that the various forms of writing are not that far apart. It all de-

pends on the length of the sentence, the tone, and the message-intent. I operate in many different levels." Regarding *Remnants,* which he was writing at the time, he notes that "my NYC editor and I have differences as to what makes a novel. . . . I'm hoping there's enough experimentation, enough of the real me, to make critics and scholars wonder for many, many years what I was doing" ("An Interview," 39, 40). For still more of the (moderately) explanatory turn in Young Bear's work, in the form of lyrical prose autobiography, see his "In the First Place of My Life" (which is partly incorporated into *Remnants*). Robert Gish ("Mesquakie Singer") and especially Ruppert's review of *Winter of the Salamander* ("Outside the Arc") comment astutely on the difficulties in Young Bear's poetry.

² The Meskwaki (formerly spelled Mesquakie), which means Red Earth People, live on the Meskwaki Tribal Settlement near Tama in central Iowa. The French mistook a clan name for a tribal name and thus dubbed the Meskwaki the Fox, a name that stuck to them against their preference. There is a great deal of anthropological writing on the Meskwaki, most of it dated but none of it yet considered in relation to Young Bear's poetry. For overviews, see Frederick O. Gearing, Robert McC. Netting, and Lisa R. Peattie; Fred McTaggart; and Charles Callender. For useful discussions of Young Bear's distinctive style, see David L. Moore, "Myth, History, and Identity" (378), and "Ray A. Young Bear" (323).

³ Bataille, 17; and Young Bear, "Connected," 348, "Reaching Out," 26, and *Remnants,* 115, 119–30. The balance between what to say and what not to say can get delicate. Young Bear notes that his grandmother warned him against revealing what should not be revealed (*Black,* 255–56), though in an interview, immediately after saying that he had better not explain the salamander ("It symbolizes something that can be discussed, but for safety reasons, I refrain"), he also says that his grandmother encouraged him to "please let the greater world know what is going on here—of who we are and where we come from" ("Staying Afloat," 209).

⁴ Kallet. On Stella Young Bear's beadwork, see Young Bear, "Sun's Glint."

⁵ *Winter of the Salamander,* which is four times as long as most books of contemporary poetry, is out of print. Young Bear usually receives brief mention in surveys of American Indian literature, and his poems are often anthologized, especially the shorter and more accessible ones. Aside from book reviews, I know of only a few, mostly brief articles about his poetry (Gish, "Memory and Dream" and "Mesquakie Singer"; Ruppert, "Poetic Languages"; Moore's two articles) and a few discussions in works devoted to larger topics (Ruppert, "The Uses of Oral Tradition"; Wiget, *Native,* 114–16; Peters, 240–41; and Fast, 78–83, 136–50). McTaggart's *Wolf That I Am* gives an extensive portrait of him. As an undergraduate, Young Bear—already an accomplished poet and musician—played something like an informant's role for McTaggart, and he gradually becomes one of the most intriguing figures in McTaggart's book. I note his role there with reluctance, given that McTaggart disguises the Meskwaki with fictional names, but the portrait is so obviously Young Bear that it can hardly stay unrecognized, and McTaggart himself says that it may have been unnecessary to use fictional names (xvi). Gish has noted McTaggart's portrait ("Memory and Dream"), and in *Remnants,* Young Bear has the fictional Edgar Bearchild meet with an unnamed graduate student who sounds like McTaggart (124). Later, Edgar spoofs McTaggart's account as "commendable but unsuccessful efforts in a book entitled *Wolf That I Iz*" (125).

⁶ Here I am thinking of the re-theorizing of race, ethnicity, and cultural identity by such people as Stuart Hall ("Cultural Identity," "Minimal Selves"), Clifford, and many others. See also Krupat's response to Clifford (*Ethnocriticism,* 101–26).

⁷ See also the liner notes to the Woodland Singers, *Traditional Mesquakie Songs:* "Under the leadership of Ray Young Bear . . . , Woodland has gradually become an important vehicle for the retention of traditional Mesquakie music. While artistic self-expression is the sole motivation, the members also feel their endeavor is a testament to the wishes of the Settlement's early founders—to be Mesquakie."

[8] In the Meskwaki Settlement's most storied squabble of local, interracial identity politics, the Meskwaki, after initially trying to keep their children out of school, have tried to keep them in a school on the settlement. See Gearing, Netting, and Peattie; Gearing; McTaggart; and United States, *Race Relations,* 39–46. *Remnants of the First Earth* often recounts the perplexities of Meskwaki children in predominantly white schools.

[9] While the particulars here may be Meskwaki, the outlines, especially the focus on transformation, fit witchcraft in many Native cultures. In his classic yet oddly cursory ethnography of the Meskwaki, William Jones, a Meskwaki anthropologist who studied with Franz Boas, reviews witches, evil spirits, and ghosts, referring to ghosts who "take on various forms," including the form of a turkey (26–30; see also Jones, "Notes," 216–17). Young Bear quotes Jones in *Black Eagle Child* (163), and in *Remnants of the First Earth* he revises a tale that Jones recorded (68–70). For his familiarity with Jones's work, see also McTaggart, 83–90, 98, 103–4, and Young Bear, "Connected," 348. But Young Bear surely knows much more about the topic than Jones, for he grew up and has lived in Meskwaki culture much more, and witches are an ordinary part of the Meskwaki universe. Young Bear repeatedly refers to witchery (often called "sorcery") in *Remnants.* For an anthropologist's account of Meskwaki views of witchcraft—probably more reliable for its information (which closely matches *Remnants*) than its interpretation—see Eugene Fugle.

[10] For more on Young Bear's frustration with poetry editors, see Young Bear, "Connected," 341–42, and "Interview," 40.

[11] Ruppert ("Poetic Languages") also addresses the performative in Young Bear's poems, although we use the concept in different (though not clashing) ways. Moore's view of Young Bear's poetry as focusing on "relationality" and "agency without mastery" matches my reading of Young Bear's attitude to authority ("Myth, History, and Identity").

[12] Young Bear, "Reaching," 22–24. It may help place Young Bear's humor to add that he has spoken enthusiastically about his love for opera (Young Bear, Poetry reading, 1991).

[13] Early post-contact Meskwaki history is too widely documented to cite here in detail (though many non-Meskwaki historians rely too trustingly on white-produced documents and neglect oral history), but see Margaret Welpley Fisher; Natalie F. Joffe, 259–62, 279–99; Bertha Waseskuk; Callender, 643–44; Richard White; and R. David Edmunds and Joseph L. Peyser. Fisher concludes that, even by 1900, "it would be remarkable if many specifically Fox traits survived" (1), though she may conflate Meskwaki (Fox) culture in general with pre-contact Meskwaki culture in particular, which itself was presumably in continuous change. Lisa Peattie provides a wide-ranging review of Meskwaki cultural change from about 1900 to the mid-1950s. On the French genocide, see Young Bear's poem "The Reptile Decree from Paris" (*Rock,* 13–16).

[14] On Meskwaki biculturalism, see Steven Polgar. Most discussions of the modern Meskwaki social and political world address factionalism. See especially Miller, "Authority"; Gearing, Netting, and Peattie; Donald Wanatee; and Young Bear's *Remnants of the First Earth.*

[15] Snodgrass's "Powwow" recounts his visit to the annual Meskwaki tribal celebration. "They all see the same movies," it begins. "They shuffle on one leg, / . . . / Shuffle on the other. / They are all the same." Among this melting pot of the Indian "same" Snodgrass names the Sioux, the Chippewa, and the Dakota. "Even tricked out in the various braveries," he continues,

> They all dance with their eyes turned
> Inward—like a woman nursing
> A sick child she already knows
> Will die. . . .

He and his family leave the bleachers to look for hot dogs but find the celebration closing and the Indians changing into "dungarees and khaki— / Castoff combat issues of World

War II." Ready to go home, he asks directions from Indians who, he imagines, "have to drive all night / To jobs in truck stops and all-night filling stations," but "They scuttle away from us like moths." At last he stumbles on an old drummer. To Snodgrass's ears, the drummer is

> Howling his tribe's song for the restless young
> Who wander in and out.
> Words of such great age,
> Not even he remembers what they mean.
> We tramp back to our car,
> Then nearly miss the highway, squinting
> Through red and yellow splatterings on the windshield—
> The garish and beautiful remains
> Of grasshoppers and dragonflies
> That go with us; that do not live again.
>
> (*After Experience*, 51–52)

Wright's "I Am a Sioux Brave, He Said in Minneapolis" begins with the following stanza, roughly matching Snodgrass's description of the Meskwaki drummer's supposed ignorance of his own song:

> He is just plain drunk.
> He knows no more than I do
> What true waters to mourn for
> Or what kind of words to sing
> When he dies.
>
> (*Above the River*, 152)

"Powwow" first appeared in the *New Yorker* in 1962 as "Powwow (Tama Reservation, Iowa, 1949)" and was reprinted in *The New Yorker Book of Poems*, indicating the high esteem it won from editors. At least when the poem was first published, Snodgrass apparently did not know that the Meskwaki Settlement, founded by the Meskwaki on land they purchased, is not a reservation, a point of great pride to the Meskwaki. In the only remarks I have found on "Powwow" by a critic or reviewer, Robert Phillips accepts the poem's inaccuracies, calling it "magnificently reverberant . . . , a trenchant comment on the destruction of the culture of the American Indian." He concludes, in defiance of the U.S. Census, that "the bright guts of insects [on the windshield] resemble the bright war paint of the Indians, who also flung themselves against the oncoming force and shall not live again" (65–66).

[16] For a review of the concept of false consciousness and the problems with it, see Terry Eagleton. The term describes people's supposedly passive absorption of ideologies from the larger culture (through movies, for example) even when those ideologies work against (are false to) people's own interest.

[17] Snodgrass's remarks appear in a 1975 anthology that sandwiches "Powwow"—"appropriately or inappropriately," as Young Bear has said—between two poems by Young Bear, who first saw it there ("Connected," 346). Despite Young Bear's concern that editors of prestigious journals are not receptive to his work, "in disgust and in response" appeared in *Poetry Northwest* in 1976, and "for the rain in march: the blackened hearts of herons" came out in the *American Poetry Review* in 1978.

[18] Young Bear, Poetry reading, 1992. Note also the two veterans' songs on the Woodland Singers, *Traditional Mesquakie Songs*.

[19] For example, one otherwise insightful review goes astray, I would argue, by submitting Young Bear's poems to the ordinary standards of mainstream belle lettrism, lamenting that the poems are often "concerned with dreams, or contain dream passages; and while

everyone is fascinated by his own dreams, it is awfully tedious having to listen to someone else's" (Sheridan, 428). Gish ("Memory and Dream") and Fast also note the reliance on dream in Young Bear's poetry. In an interview, Young Bear recounts how he often builds poems out of dreams: "I depend greatly on dreams for my inspiration. I have a very diverse method of looking at dreams, because some people view dreams as being non-essential to reality and so forth. But I am mesmerized by my dreams and continually write images in my journals. And eventually, when I collect ten or twelve dreams, I piece them together like a jigsaw puzzle and try to form some sort of statement" ("Staying Afloat," 206).

Chapter 6. The Reinvention of Restless Young Men

[1] This list leaves out Vizenor's fascinating first novel, *Bearheart* (1977). Highly iconoclastic and lacking the resources of a commercial publisher, *Bearheart* has never achieved the same degree of canonicity as the other books I name here, although Vizenor has certainly become a major figure to scholars. Moreover, he has gone on to publish so much that he partly becomes his own competition, so that while *Bearheart* remains his most widely noted work, teachers who want to assign a Vizenor novel have many others to choose from.

I will note that there is a great deal more criticism on *Ceremony* than I cite here. I have done my best to read it all (probably missing some more recent work), but given the quantity of material and the availability of bibliographies (William Dinome, Connie C. Thorson), there is not the same need for extensive citation that I try to live up to in discussing other works. Moreover, so much criticism has come out so quickly, often produced by critics who do not read each other's work, that redundancy is the norm. Thus I have confined myself to citing the criticism that most pertains to my arguments.

[2] *Winter in the Blood* came out so soon before *Ceremony* that Silko may have had little chance to take it into account, though *Ceremony* seems to echo Welch's novel pervasively.

[3] Any discussion of the agency of ceremony owes a debt to Paula Gunn Allen's famous title essay in *The Sacred Hoop*. Allen may overstate the distinctiveness of ceremony as a specifically Indian category, but her alertness to its role in Indian culture remains invaluably illuminating.

[4] On English as an Indian language for storytelling and political resistance, see especially Simon Ortiz, and Vizenor, *Manifest*, 105–6.

[5] Ruppert helpfully insists on the value of studying form in *Ceremony* ("Reader's Lessons," *Mediation*).

[6] See Ramsey, 231; several articles by Swan; Groß, 92, 98; Peter Freese, 637; and Lawrence Buell, 518–19.

[7] Curiously, Tedlock revises all these phrases in the 1999 second edition of *Finding the Center*. See also Toelken, 92–93, and Wiget, "Telling the Tale," 329, for discussions of phrases translated from Navajo and Hopi as "it is said."

[8] On Jakobson and on technological determinism, see chapter 4, as well as chapter 1's discussion of the relation between literary form and cultural content.

[9] For a description of pattern-poems, see John Hollander, *Rhyme's Reason*. Hollander also provides an unusually full-scale example with an entire book of pattern-poems, *Types of Shape*. In an argument that I find strained but that others may find more convincing, David E. Hailey Jr. sets out to prove that Silko's poems visually represent Ka't'sinas and other figures throughout the novel.

[10] For earlier discussions of the relation between poetry and prose in *Ceremony*, see especially Groß, 92–94; Mary Slowik; Ruppert, *Mediation*, 80–82; and Rainwater, 13–16, 95–96.

[11] For a chart of the Benjy section of *The Sound and the Fury* analogous to table 2 here, see R. D. Parker, " '*Where you want . . .*' " Silko's spotted cattle also echo Faulkner's spotted horses.

[12] For example, Bencivenga, Brody, Koch (B90), Simard (75), and Steven Smith, as well as Percy Walton, Mary M. Mackie, and Stuart Christie. Christie also offers a thoughtful discussion of photography in the novel more generally. On the other hand, King shapes *Medicine River* through unusually distinct episodes, and almost every episode attracted particular praise from reviewers. I turn to reviews for critical context, because, despite reviewers' enthusiasm and a trio of awards (the P.E.N./Josephine Miles Award, a best novel award from the Writer's Guild of Alberta, and a runner-up citation for the Commonwealth Writer's Prize), *Medicine River* has received little critical attention. When I drafted this chapter, there was only one extended critical discussion of the novel (Walton); at last revision there are two more (Mackie, Christie; see also Camille R. La Bossiere's extended encomium to Harlen via—improbably—King's metaphors of food [49–53]). By contrast, *Green Grass, Running Water*, which playfully appeals to university critics by tweaking the English lit curriculum and was much more heavily marketed by its publisher (Weaver, "Thomas King," 57), has received a great deal of critical attention. King has even joked that *Green Grass* "is the one to work with" in university courses, "because it has everything an academic can possibly want stuffed in there" and, compared to *Medicine River*, "it gives you more to talk about than simply good characters and nice scenery" ("Border Trickery," 177).

[13] In a sampling of words from reviewers, the novel is "warm and satisfying" with "humor, gentleness, and insight without sentimentality" (Candace Smith), "funny, unsentimental" (Brody), "sweet, unsentimental" (Koch, B90), "joyfully offbeat" (James B. Hemesath), "good natured and relaxed" with a "charming and companionable" narrator (*Books in Canada*), "economical, precise and elegant," "most satisfying" (Jack Butler), with "humor in a mix of warmth and poignancy" (Calvin Ahlgren). Among the reviews I've found but had no occasion to cite, I would single out one by M. T. Kelly, author of the novel *A Dream Like Mine* (1987), which was made into the movie *Clearcut* (1991), starring Graham Greene and Tom Jackson, who also star in the movie of *Medicine River* (1992). In writing strangely committed to stereotype, Kelly praises King for defying stereotype. Asked about Kelly's work in an interview, King indicates his skepticism ("Interview with Tom King," 70).

[14] See chapter 4, n. 26. Percy Walton focuses on the way that *Medicine River* offers stereotypes only to undermine them.

[15] For statistics and a sad commentary about suicide on the Blood Reserve in the 1980s, a model for *Medicine River*, see Ron Good Striker, and for the same about "battered wives" in the area's Indian population, see Scott Ross.

[16] For another approach, see Edith Swan, "Laguna Prototypes of Manhood in *Ceremony*," which matches Tayo to ethnological accounts of historical Laguna masculinity under an implicit anthropological present, whereas my approach addresses contemporary conflicts.

[17] For a sympathetic view of Allen's critique, see Jana Sequoyah. For Silko's dismissal of Allen's criticism, see Silko, "Listening," 178.

[18] "Interview with Tom King," 73. A few years later, when *Green Grass, Running Water* came out, King went further: "I really don't care about the white audience," he said. "They don't have an understanding of the intricacies of Native life, and I don't think they're much interested in it" (Weaver, "Thomas King," 57). For a different perspective, see Rainwater, who argues that in a variety of ways Native writers programmatically adapt to non-Native audiences.

[19] For King's response to Kinsella, see "Interview with Tom King," 70, and H. J. Kirchhoff. Widely known in the United States for his baseball fiction, including *Shoeless Joe*

(1982), made into the film *Field of Dreams* (1989), Kinsella is famous in Canada for stories and novels set on a fictional Blackfoot reserve, more or less the same territory as *Medicine River,* if much less convincing, although even King concedes that a few of Kinsella's stories are impressive. Kinsella's first Indian book, *Dance Me Outside* (1977), is loosely the model for the more appealing film of the same name (1994), which in turn spawned a short-lived CBC television show, *The Rez* (1996). King also expresses skepticism about another white-written Indian novel famous in Canada and more or less unknown in the United States, Rudy Wiebe's *The Temptations of Big Bear* (1973), though he curiously alludes to it in the name of Harlen Bigbear. For King it is not a matter of race per se, for he says that Tony Hillerman and William Eastlake, also white writers, "do a pretty good job" ("Interview with Tom King," 70).

Chapter 7. Material Choices: American Fictions and the Post-canon

¹ The arguments for changing what until recently scholars and teachers routinely studied have already been put extraordinarily well and aired innumerable times. See—to give a brief list that can only begin to suggest the range of materials—Ernece B. Kelly; Baym, "Melodramas"; Paul Lauter, "Introduction," "Race and Gender," and *Canons*; Joanna Russ; Jane Tompkins; Russell Reising; Krupat, *Voice*; and Cary Nelson. I also recommend John Guillory's *Cultural Capital: The Problem of Literary Canon Formation,* which appeared the same year as an earlier version of this chapter and offers arguments that dovetail with my arguments here. While I could fill many pages discussing and debating fine points in response to Guillory, it is more to the point to see the broad sweeps of his work and mine as mutual corroborations of similar critical projects.

² On Yellow Bird, see the autobiography in the preface to Ridge, *Poems;* Ridge, *Trumpet;* and James W. Parins. I use the term *novel* for Yellow Bird's prose fiction posing as biography, in the same way no one hesitates to bestow the term on Poe's *The Narrative of Arthur Gordon Pym of Nantucket.*

³ For alerting me to the point about Chicana/Chicano studies, I thank Rolando Romero. A number of other critics have thoughtfully addressed the novel. Alone among them, Peter G. Christensen denies Murieta's role as a metaphorical Cherokee, whereas Louis Owens (*Other Destinies,* 32–40) gives the earliest account of the novel's hybridity, an idea particularly dwelled on by Timothy B. Powell.

⁴ For the reading of *Native Son* as racist, see, e.g., Nathan A. Scott Jr.'s comparatively succinct and diplomatic remarks: "the novel is controlled by precisely those assumptions about Negro life which elicited its rage, and its protagonist's sense of his own identity is formed by just that image of himself which, as it lives in the larger culture, has caused his despair. So, in its entirety, the novel moves wholly within the envenomed abstractions of racial myth" (151). For a fuller and more forthright expression of similar views, see Cecil M. Brown. On *The Color Purple,* see Trudier Harris, who argues that for many readers "the book reinforces racist stereotypes they may have been heir to and others of which they may have only dreamed" (155).

⁵ For American literature, see H. Bruce Franklin, xvi–xxi; Lauter, "Race and Gender"; Tompkins, esp. 3–39, 186–201; Richard H. Brodhead, esp. 3–16, 48–66; Nelson; and Baym, "Early Histories."

⁶ See Gates, *Loose Canons,* 178 for a similar reminder and a similar argument.

⁷ In a later version of these comments, Lauter—to his credit—has changed the key phrase "simplicity, transparency, and emotional directness" to "*apparent* simplicity, transparency, and emotional directness" (*Canons,* 105; italics in the original). I cite the earlier

phrasing because it appeared in an influential essay and voices a widespread way of thinking.

[8] I use the transcription from James Weldon Johnson (42), modifying "throo" to "troo," because the phonetic spelling of standard pronunciation is pointless at best and is inconsistent with Johnson's usual practice, and because "troo" appears in William Francis Allen et al. (19), one of the two earliest transcriptions.

[9] Matthews, *Night Chant,* 297–98. For more on Matthews's translations, see chapter 4. See Zolbrod, 60–63, for a reading of another prayer from the Nightway (the prayer that Momaday draws on in the title of *House Made of Dawn*), John Bierhorst, 281–87, for a reading of the Nightway's larger structure, and James C. Faris for a fascinating history.

[10] On the consequences of more critical and less critical multiculturalism for differing cultural groups, see the bracingly instructive collection of essays *Is Multiculturalism Bad for Women?* ed. Joshua Cohen, Matthew Howard, and Martha C. Nussbaum.

Works Cited

Abel, Elizabeth. "Black Writing, White Reading: Race and the Politics of Feminist Interpretation." *Critical Inquiry* 19 (spring 1993): 470–98.

Adell, Sandra. *Double-Consciousness/Double-Bind: Theoretical Issues in Twentieth-Century Black Literature.* Urbana: University of Illinois Press, 1994.

Ahlgren, Calvin. "Tales of Exploited Peoples." Review of *Medicine River,* by Thomas King. *San Francisco Chronicle,* 9 December 1990, 8.

Albers, Patricia C. "From Legend to Land to Labor: Changing Perspectives on Native American Work." In Littlefield and Knack, eds., *Native Americans and Wage Labor.* 245–73.

Alcoff, Linda. "The Problem of Speaking for Others." *Cultural Critique* 20 (1991–92): 5–32.

Alexie, Sherman. *One Stick Song.* Brooklyn: Hanging Loose Press, 2000.

———. *The Summer of Black Widows.* Brooklyn: Hanging Loose Press, 1996.

Allen, Paula Gunn. "The Feminine Landscape of Leslie Marmon Silko's *Ceremony.*" In Allen, *The Sacred Hoop: Recovering the Feminine in American Indian Traditions.* Boston: Beacon, 1986. 118–26.

———. "The Sacred Hoop: A Contemporary Perspective." In Allen, *The Sacred Hoop: Recovering the Feminine in American Indian Traditions.* Boston: Beacon, 1986. 54–75.

———. "Special Problems in Teaching Leslie Marmon Silko's *Ceremony.*" *American Indian Quarterly* 14, no. 4 (1990): 379–86.

———. *The Woman Who Owned the Shadows.* San Francisco: Spinsters/Aunt Lute, 1983.

———, ed. *Studies in American Indian Literature: Critical Essays and Course Designs.* New York: Modern Language Association, 1983.

Allen, William Francis, et al., eds. *Slave Songs of the United States.* New York: A. Simpson, 1867.

Anderson, Benedict. *Imagined Communities: Reflections on the Origin and Spread of Nationalism.* Rev. ed. London: Verso, 1991.

215

Bailey, Garrick Alan. *Changes in Osage Social Organization: 1673–1906.* University of Oregon Anthropological Papers, no. 5. Eugene: University of Oregon Press, 1973.

———. "John Joseph Mathews, Osage, 1894." In *American Indian Intellectuals,* ed. Margot Liberty. 1976 Proceedings of the American Ethnological Society, ed. Robert F. Spencer. St. Paul, Minn.: West Publishing, 1978. 205–14.

———, ed. *The Osage and the Invisible World: From the Works of Francis La Flesche.* Norman: University of Oklahoma Press, 1995.

Barnes, Nellie. "American Indian Verse: Characteristics of Style." *Bulletin of the University of Kansas: Humanities Studies* 2, no. 4 (1 December 1921).

Barrus, Maxine. "Osage Novel by Mathews Wins Praise." Review of *Sundown,* by John Joseph Mathews. *Tulsa Tribune,* 7 November 1934.

Bataille, Gretchen M. "Ray Young Bear: Tribal History and Personal Vision." Review of *Winter of the Salamander,* by Ray Young Bear. *Studies in American Indian Literatures,* o.s., 6, no. 3 (1982): 1–6. Reprinted in *Studies in American Indian Literatures,* n.s., 5, no. 2 (1993): 17–20.

Bataille, Gretchen M., and Kathleen Mullen Sands. *American Indian Women: Telling Their Lives.* Lincoln: University of Nebraska Press, 1984.

Baudrillard, Jean. *Simulations.* Translated by Paul Foss, Paul Patton, and Philip Beitchman. New York: Semiotext(e), 1983.

Baudry, Jean-Louis. "The Apparatus: Metapsychological Approaches to the Impression of Reality in the Cinema." *Camera Obscura* 1 (1976): 104–26.

Bauman, Richard. *Verbal Art as Performance.* Rowley, Mass.: Newbury, 1977.

Baym, Nina. "Early Histories of American Literature: A Chapter in the Institution of New England." *American Literary History* 1 (1989): 459–88.

———. "Melodramas of Beset Manhood: How Theories of American Fiction Exclude Women Authors." *American Quarterly* 33 (1981): 123–39.

Bencivenga, Jim. "Searching for Home in High-Plains Canada." *Christian Science Monitor,* 3 October 1990, 13.

Benjamin, Walter. "The Storyteller: Reflections on the Work of Nikolai Leskov." 1936. In *Illuminations,* ed. Hannah Arendt, trans. Harry Zohn. New York: Schocken, 1969.

Benveniste, Emile. *Problems in General Linguistics.* Translated by Mary Elizabeth Meek. 1966. Reprint, Coral Gables: University of Miami Press, 1971.

Berkhofer, Robert E., Jr. *The White Man's Indian: Images of the American Indian from Columbus to the Present.* New York: Knopf, 1978.

Bevis, William. "American Indian Verse Translations." *College English* 35 (1974): 693–703.

———. "Native American Novels: Homing In." In Swann and Krupat, eds., *Recovering the Word,* 580–620.

Bhabha, Homi K. "Of Mimicry and Man: The Ambivalence of Colonial Discourse." In Bhabha, *The Location of Culture.* London: Routledge, 1994. 85–92.

———. "The Other Question: Stereotype, Discrimination, and the Discourse of Colonialism." In Bhabha, *The Location of Culture.* London: Routledge, 1994. 66–84.

Bierhorst, John, ed. *Four Masterworks of American Indian Literature.* New York: Farrar, 1974.

Blaeser, Kimberly M. "Like 'Reeds through the Ribs of a Basket.'" In *Other Sisterhoods: Literary Theory and U.S. Women of Color,* ed. Sandra Kumamoto Stanley. Urbana: University of Illinois Press, 1998. 265–76. Reprint of *American Indian Quarterly* 21, no. 4 (1997): 555–65.

———. *Trailing You.* Greenfield Center, N.Y.: Greenfield Review Press, 1994.

Bonvillain, Nancy. "Gender Relations in Native North America." *American Indian Culture and Research Journal* 13, no. 2 (1989): 1–28.

Bourdieu, Pierre. *Distinction: A Social Critique of the Judgment of Taste.* Translated by Richard Nice. 1979. Cambridge: Harvard University Press, 1984.

Boutwell, Ruth. "Adjustment of Osage Indian Youth to Contemporary Civilization." Master's thesis, University of Oklahoma, 1936.

Brodhead, Richard H. *The School of Hawthorne.* New York: Oxford University Press, 1986.

Brody, Leslie. "Jamboree on the River." Review of *Medicine River,* by Thomas King. *Hungry Mind Review* (winter 1990–91): 39.

Brown, Bill. "Trusting Story and Reading *The Surrounded.*" *Studies in American Indian Literature* 3, no. 2 (1991): 22–27.

Brown, Cecil M. "Richard Wright: Complexes and Black Writing Today." In *Richard Wright's "Native Son": A Critical Handbook,* ed. Richard Abcarian. Belmont, Calif.: Wadsworth, 1970. 167–77.

Brown, William. "*The Surrounded:* Listening between the Lines of Inherited Stories." In Purdy, ed., *Legacy,* 69–84.

Brumble, H. David, III. *American Indian Autobiography.* Berkeley: University of California Press, 1988.

Buell, Lawrence. *The Environmental Imagination: Thoreau, Nature Writing, and the Formation of American Culture.* Cambridge: Harvard University Press, 1995.

Butler, Jack. "Dad Was with the Rodeo." Review of *Medicine River,* by Thomas King. *New York Times Book Review,* 23 September 1990, 29.

Callahan, S. Alice. *Wynema: A Child of the Forest.* 1891. Reprint, edited and with an introduction by A. LaVonne Brown Ruoff, Lincoln: University of Nebraska Press, 1997.

Callender, Charles. "Fox." In *Northeast,* ed. Bruce G. Trigger. Vol. 15, *Handbook of North American Indians,* ed. William C. Sturtevant. Washington, D.C.: Smithsonian, 1978. 636–47.

Campbell, Walter S. (Stanley Vestal). *The Book Lover's Southwest: A Guide to Good Reading.* Norman: University of Oklahoma Press, 1955.

———. Letter to John Joseph Mathews, ts. 19 March 1929. W. S. Campbell Collection, box 32, folder 27. Western History Collections, University Libraries, University of Oklahoma, Norman.

———. Letter to John Joseph Mathews, ts. 28 March 1930. W. S. Campbell Collection, box 32, folder 27. Western History Collections, University Libraries, University of Oklahoma, Norman.

Carlson, Leonard A. *Indians, Bureaucrats, and Land: The Dawes Act and the Decline of Indian Farming.* Westport, Conn.: Greenwood, 1981.

Carroll, James William. "Flatheads and Whites: A Study of Conflict." Ph.D. diss., University of California, 1959.

Castro, Michael. *Interpreting the Indian: Twentieth-Century Poets and the Native American.* Norman: University of Oklahoma Press, 1983.

Caughie, Pamela L. *Passing and Pedagogy: The Dynamics of Responsibility.* Urbana: University of Illinois Press, 1999.

Chase, Richard. *The American Novel and Its Tradition.* Garden City, N.Y.: Doubleday, 1957.

Chatman, Seymour. *Story and Discourse: Narrative Structure in Fiction and Film.* Ithaca: Cornell University Press, 1978.

Cheung, King-Kok. *Articulate Silences: Hisaye Yamamoto, Maxine Hong Kingston, Joy Kogawa.* Ithaca: Cornell University Press, 1993.

Cheyfitz, Eric. *The Poetics of Imperialism: Translation and Colonization from "The Tempest" to "Tarzan."* New York: Oxford University Press, 1991.

Chinweizu, Onwuchekwa Jemie, and Ihechukwu Madubuike. *African Fiction and Poetry and Their Critics.* Vol. 1 of *Toward the Decolonization of African Literature.* Enugu, Nigeria: Fourth Dimension, 1980.

Christensen, Laird. "'Not Exactly Like Heaven': Spiritual and Ecological Imperialism in *The Surrounded.*" *Northwest Review* 35, no. 3 (1997): 57–66.

Christie, Stuart. "Time-Out: (Slam)Dunking Photographic Realism in Thomas King's *Medicine River.*" *Studies in American Indian Literature* 11, no. 2 (summer 1999): 51–65.

Chrystos. *Fire Power.* Vancouver, B.C.: Press Gang, 1995.

Churchill, Ward. "The New Racism: A Critique of James A. Clifton's *The Invented Indian.*" In *Fantasies of the Master Race: Literature, Cinema, and the Colonization of American Indians,* ed. M. Annette Jaimes. Monroe, Maine: Common Courage, 1992. 163–84.

Cixous, Hélène. "The Laugh of the Medusa." Translated by Keith Cohen and Paula Cohen. 1976. In *New French Feminisms,* ed. Elaine Marks and Isabelle de Courtivron. New York: Schocken, 1981. 245–64.

Clements, William M. "Faking the Pumpkin: On Jerome Rothenberg's Literary Offenses." *Western American Literature* 16 (1981): 193–204.

——. *Native American Verbal Art: Texts and Contexts.* Tucson: University of Arizona Press, 1996.

——. "'Tokens of Literary Faculty': Native American Literature and Euroamerican Translation in the Early Nineteenth Century." In Swann, ed., *On the Translation of Native American Literatures,* 33–50.

Clifford, James. *The Predicament of Culture: Twentieth-Century Ethnography, Literature, and Art.* Cambridge: Harvard University Press, 1988.

Clifton, James A. *The Invented Indian: Cultural Fictions and Government Policies.* New Brunswick, N.J.: Transaction, 1990.

Cohen, Joshua, Matthew Howard, and Martha C. Nussbaum, eds. *Is Multiculturalism Bad for Women?* Princeton: Princeton University Press, 1999.

The Columbia History of the American Novel. Edited by Emory Elliott. New York: Columbia University Press, 1991.

Comolli, Jean-Louis. "Machines of the Visible." In *The Cinematic Apparatus,* ed.

Teresa de Lauretis and Stephen Heath. New York: St. Martin's, 1980. 121–42.

Cook-Lynn, Elizabeth. *Why I Can't Read Wallace Stegner and Other Essays: A Tribal Voice*. Madison: University of Wisconsin Press, 1996.

——. "'You May Consider Speaking about Your Art . . . '" In *I Tell You Now: Autobiographical Essays by Native American Writers*, ed. Brian Swann and Arnold Krupat. Lincoln: University of Nebraska Press, 1987. 55–63.

Culler, Jonathan. *Structuralist Poetics: Structuralism, Linguistics, and the Study of Literature*. Ithaca: Cornell University Press, 1975.

Curtis, Natalie. *The Indians' Book*. 1907, 1923. Reprint, New York: Dover, 1968.

Deloria, Philip J. *Playing Indian*. New Haven: Yale University Press, 1998.

Deloria, Vine, Jr. "Comfortable Fictions and the Struggle for Turf: An Essay Review of *The Invented Indian: Cultural Fictions and Government Policies*." In Mihesuah, ed., *American Indians*, 65–83.

Derrida, Jacques. *Of Grammatology*. Translated by Gayatri Chakravorty Spivak. Baltimore: Johns Hopkins University Press, 1976.

Devens, Carol. *Countering Colonization: Native American Women and Great Lakes Missions, 1630–1900*. Berkeley: University of California Press, 1992.

Dickinson, Emily. *The Complete Poems of Emily Dickinson*. Edited by Thomas H. Johnson. Boston: Little, Brown, 1955.

Diné Bahane': The Navajo Creation Story. Translated by Paul G. Zolbrod. Albuquerque: University of New Mexico Press, 1984.

Dinome, William. "Laguna Woman: An Annotated Leslie Silko Bibliography." *American Indian Culture and Research Journal* 21, no. 1 (1997): 207–80.

Doss, Phillip E. "Elements of Traditional Oral Narrative in *The Surrounded*." In Purdy, ed., *Legacy*, 53–68.

Du Bois, W. E. B. *The Gift of Black Folk: The Negroes in the Making of America*. 1924. Reprint, New York: AMS, 1971.

——. *The Souls of Black Folk*. 1903. Reprint, New York: Fawcett, 1961.

Dusenberry, J. Verne. Letter to D'Arcy McNickle, ts. 3 June 1936. Edmund E. Ayer Collection, Newberry Library, Chicago.

Eagleton, Terry. *Ideology: An Introduction*. London: Verso, 1991.

Edmunds, R. David, and Joseph L. Peyser. *The Fox Wars: The Mesquakie Challenge to New France*. Norman: University of Oklahoma Press, 1993.

"An Educated Indian." Review of *Sundown*, by John Joseph Mathews. *New York Times Book Review*, 25 November 1934, 19–20.

Ehrenreich, Barbara. *The Hearts of Men: American Dreams and the Flight from Commitment*. Garden City, N.Y.: Doubleday, 1983.

Eichenbaum, Boris. "The Theory of the 'Formal Method.'" In Lemon and Reis, eds., *Russian Formalist Criticism*, 99–139.

Ellis, John. *Visible Fictions: Cinema, Television, Video*. 2d ed. London: Routledge, 1992.

Ellis, Vivienne Rae. *Trucanini: Queen or Traitor?* Rev. ed. Canberra: Australian Institute of Aboriginal Studies, 1981.

Epstein, Dena J. Polacheck. *Sinful Tunes and Spirituals: Black Folk Music to the Civil War*. Urbana: University of Illinois Press, 1977.

Erlich, Victor. *Russian Formalism: History, Doctrine.* 3d ed. New Haven: Yale University Press, 1981.

Evans, Robert. "Lost in Translation: McNickle's Tragic Speaking." In Purdy, ed., *Legacy,* 85–101.

Evers, Larry, and Felipe S. Molina. *Yaqui Deer Songs/Maso Bwikam: A Native American Poetry.* Tucson: University of Arizona Press, 1987.

Fabian, Johannes. *Time and the Other: How Anthropology Makes Its Object.* New York: Columbia University Press, 1983.

Fahey, John. *The Flathead Indians.* Norman: University of Oklahoma Press, 1974.

Faris, James C. *The Nightway: A History and a History of Documentation of a Navajo Ceremonial.* Albuquerque: University of New Mexico Press, 1990.

Fast, Robin Riley. *The Heart as a Drum: Continuance and Resistance in American Indian Poetry.* Ann Arbor: University of Michigan Press, 1999.

Faulkner, William. "Appendix: Compson, 1699–1945." *The Sound and the Fury.* New York: Vintage, n.d.

———. *Light in August.* 1932. New York: Vintage, 1990.

Ferber, Edna. *Cimarron.* Garden City, N.Y.: Doubleday, 1930.

Fine, Elizabeth C. *The Folklore Text: From Performance to Print.* Bloomington: Indiana University Press, 1984.

Finley, Mary Stousee. *Story of the Shooting of Four Flathead Indians in Swan River Area, Western Montana, 1908.* Translated by Louis J. Tellier. N.p., 1958.

Finnegan, Ruth. *Oral Poetry: Its Nature, Significance and Social Context.* Cambridge: Cambridge University Press, 1977.

———. *Oral Traditions and the Verbal Arts: A Guide to Research Practices.* London: Routledge, 1992.

Finney, Frank P. Letter to John Joseph Mathews, ts. 9 December 1934. Finney Collection, box 4, folder 28. Western History Collections, University Libraries, University of Oklahoma, Norman.

Fisher, Margaret Welpley. Introduction. In Jones, "Ethnography," 1–7.

Fitzgerald, F. Scott. *Tender Is the Night.* New York: Scribner's, 1934.

Flathead Culture Committee. *A Brief History of the Flathead Tribes.* Rev. ed. St. Ignatius, Mont.: Flathead Culture Committee of the Confederated Salish and Kootenai Tribes, 1993.

Fowler, Roger. *Literature as Social Discourse: The Practice of Linguistic Criticism.* Bloomington: Indiana University Press, 1981.

Franklin, H. Bruce. *The Victim as Criminal and Artist: Literature from the American Prison.* New York: Oxford University Press, 1978.

Freese, Peter. "Marmon Silko's *Ceremony:* Universality versus Ethnocentrism." *Amerikastudien/American Studies* 37, no. 4 (1992): 613–45.

Freud, Sigmund. *Beyond the Pleasure Principle.* Translated and edited by James Strachey. New York: Norton, 1961.

Fugle, Eugene. "Mesquakie Witchcraft Lore." *Plains Anthropologist* 6, no. 11 (February 1961): 31–39.

Fuller, Hoyt W. "The New Black Literature: Protest or Affirmation." 1970. Reprinted in Gayle, ed., *Black Aesthetic,* 346–69.

——. "Towards a Black Aesthetic." 1968. Reprinted in Gayle, ed., *Black Aesthetic*, 3–17.

Fuss, Diana. *Essentially Speaking: Feminism, Nature, and Difference.* New York: Routledge, 1989.

"Game Warden Killed by Flathead Indians." *Daily Missoulian,* 20 October 1908, 1.

Garrison, Dee. *Mary Heaton Vorse: The Life of an American Insurgent.* Philadelphia: Temple University Press, 1989.

Gates, Henry Louis, Jr. "'Ethnic and Minority' Studies." In *Introduction to Scholarship in Modern Languages and Literatures,* ed. Joseph Gibaldi. 2d ed. New York: Modern Language Association, 1992. 288–302.

——. *Figures in Black: Words, Signs, and the "Racial" Self.* New York: Oxford University Press, 1987.

——. *Loose Canons: Notes on the Culture Wars.* New York: Oxford University Press, 1992.

——. *The Signifying Monkey: A Theory of Afro-American Literary Criticism.* New York: Oxford University Press, 1988.

Gayle, Addison, Jr., ed. *The Black Aesthetic.* Garden City, N.Y.: Doubleday, 1971.

Gayler, Lucy Boutwell. "A Case Study in Social Adjustment of One Hundred Osage Families." Master's thesis, University of Oklahoma, 1936.

Gearing, Frederick O. *The Face of the Fox.* Chicago: Aldine, 1970.

Gearing, Frederick O., Robert McC. Netting, and Lisa R. Peattie, eds. *Documentary History of the Fox Project, 1949–1959: A Program in Action Anthropology Directed by Sol Tax.* Chicago: University of Chicago, 1960.

Genette, Gérard. *Narrative Discourse: An Essay in Method.* 1972. Translated by Jane E. Lewin. Ithaca: Cornell University Press, 1980.

Genovese, Eugene D. *Roll, Jordan, Roll: The World the Slaves Made.* New York: Random House, 1974.

Gildner, Gary, and Judith Gildner. *Out of This World: Poems from the Hawkeye State.* Ames: Iowa State University Press, 1975.

Gill, Sam D. *Sacred Words: A Study of Navajo Religion and Prayer.* Westport, Conn.: Greenwood, 1981.

Gish, Robert F. "Irony and Consent: Hunting and Heroism in D'Arcy McNickle's *The Surrounded.*" In Purdy, ed., *Legacy,* 102–14.

——. "Memory and Dream in the Poetry of Ray A. Young Bear." *Minority Voices* 2, no. 1 (spring 1978): 21–29.

——. "Mesquakie Singer: Listening to Ray A. Young Bear." *A Publications* 4, no. 22 (1979): 24–28.

——. "On First Reading Young Bear's *Winter of the Salamander.*" *Studies in American Indian Literature,* o.s., 6, no. 3 (1982): 10–15.

——. "Retrieving the Melodies of the Heart." Review of *The Invisible Musician,* by Ray Young Bear. *Bloomsbury Review* 10, no. 3 (May/June 1990): 9.

"Going Back to the Soil. Osage Chief Hails End of Oil Riches for His People." *New York Times,* 6 June 1931, sec. 3, 6E.

Good Striker, Ron. "Native Suicide a Growing Concern among Natives." *Kainai News* (Stand Off, Alberta), 22 February 1990, 3.

Gordon, Avery F., and Christopher Newfield. "Introduction." In *Mapping Multi-culturalism*, ed. Gordon and Newfield. Minneapolis: University of Minnesota Press, 1996. 1–16.

Gower, Calvin W. "The CCC Indian Division: Aid for Depressed Americans, 1933–1942." *Minnesota History* 43, no. 1 (spring 1972): 3–13.

Graff, Gerald. *Beyond the Culture Wars: How Teaching the Conflicts Can Revitalize American Education*. New York: Norton, 1992.

Green, Rayna. *Native American Women: A Contextual Bibliography*. Bloomington: Indiana University Press, 1983.

——, ed. *That's What She Said: Contemporary Poetry and Fiction by Native American Women*. Bloomington, Indiana University Press, 1984.

Groß, Konrad. "Survival of Orality in a Literate Culture: Leslie Silko's Novel *Ceremony*." In *Modes of Narrative: Approaches to American, Canadian, and British Fiction, Presented to Helmut Bonheim*, ed. Reingard M. Nischik and Barbara Korte. Würzburg, W. Germany: Königshausen and Neumann, 1990, 88–99.

Guillory, John. *Cultural Capital: The Problem of Literary Canon Formation*. Chicago: University of Chicago Press, 1993.

Hailey, David E., Jr. "The Visual Elegance of Ts'its'tsi'nako and the Other Invisible Characters in *Ceremony*." *Wicazo Sa Review* 6 (1990): 1–6.

Hall, Stuart. "Cultural Identity and Cinematic Representation." *Frameworks* 36 (1989): 68–81.

——. "Minimal Selves." In *Black British Cultural Studies: A Reader*, ed. Houston A. Baker, Manthia Diawara, and Ruth H. Lindeborg. Chicago: University of Chicago Press, 1996. 114–19.

Hans, Birgit. "Because I Understand the Storytelling Art": The Evolution of D'Arcy McNickle's *The Surrounded*." In Jaskoski, ed., *Early Native American Writing*, 223–38.

——. "Re-Visions: An Early Version of *The Surrounded*." *Studies in American Indian Literature* 4, nos. 2 and 3 (1992): 181–95.

Harjo, Joy. *What Moon Drove Me to This?* New York: I. Reed Books, 1979.

Harris, Trudier. "On *The Color Purple*, Stereotypes, and Silence." *Black American Literature Forum* 18 (1984): 155–61.

Hawkes, Terence. *Structuralism and Semiotics*. Berkeley: University of California Press, 1977.

Hawthorne, Nathaniel. "Young Goodman Brown." 1835. In Hawthorne, *Tales and Sketches*. New York: Library of America. 276–89.

Hegeman, Susan. "Native American 'Texts' and the Problem of Authenticity," *American Quarterly* 41, no. 2 (June 1989): 265–83.

Hemesath, James B. Review of *Medicine River*, by Thomas King. *Library Journal* 115, no. 13 (August 1990): 143.

Hemingway, Ernest. *The Short Stories of Ernest Hemingway*. New York: Scribner's, 1938.

——. *The Sun Also Rises*. New York: Scribner's, 1926.

Hilbert, Vi (Taqʷsəblu). *Coyote and Rock and Other Lushootseed Stories*. In Lushootseed and English. Caedmon, 1992.

——, trans. and ed. *Haboo: Native American Stories from Puget Sound.* Seattle: University of Washington Press, 1985.

Hobson, Geary. "The Rise of the White Shaman as a New Version of Cultural Imperialism." In *The Remembered Earth: An Anthology of Contemporary Native American Literature,* ed. Hobson. Albuquerque: Red Earth, 1979. 100–108.

Hoefel, Roseanne. "Gendered Cartography: Mapping the Mind of Female Characters in D'Arcy McNickle's *The Surrounded.*" *Studies in American Indian Literature* 10, no. 1 (spring 1998): 45–64.

Hogan, Linda. *Mean Spirit.* New York: Atheneum, 1990.

Hollander, John. *Rhyme's Reason: A Guide to English Verse.* New Haven: Yale University Press, 1981.

——. *Types of Shape.* 2d ed. New Haven: Yale University Press, 1991.

Homans, Margaret. "'Women of Color' Writers and Feminist Theory." *New Literary History* 25 (winter 1994): 73–94.

hooks, bell. *Talking Back: Thinking Feminist, Thinking Black.* Boston: South End, 1989.

——. *Teaching to Transgress: Education as the Practice of Freedom.* New York: Routledge, 1994.

Hughes, Langston. *Good Morning Revolution: Uncollected Social Protest Writings.* Edited by Faith Berry. Westport, Conn.: Lawrence Hill, 1973.

Hugo, Richard. "Introduction: Young American Indian Poets." *American Poetry Review* 2, no. 6 (November–December 1973): 22.

Huhndorf, Shari M. *Going Native: Indians in the American Cultural Imagination.* Ithaca: Cornell University Press, 2001.

Hum-ishu-ma (Mourning Dove). *Cogewea, The Half-Blood.* 1927. Reprint, with an introduction by Dexter Fisher, Lincoln: University of Nebraska Press, 1981.

Hunter, Carol. "The Historical Context in John Joseph Mathews' *Sundown.*" *MELUS* 9, no. 1 (spring 1982): 61–72.

——. "The Protagonist as a Mixed-Blood in John Joseph Mathews' Novel: *Sundown.*" *American Indian Quarterly* 6 (1982): 319–37.

Hymes, Dell. "Anthologies and Narrators." In Swann and Krupat, eds., *Recovering the Word,* 41–84.

——. *"In Vain I Tried to Tell You": Essays in Native American Ethnopoetics.* Philadelphia: University of Pennsylvania Press, 1981.

——. "Poetry and Anthropology." *Dialectical Anthropology* 11 (1986): 407–11.

Iisaw: Hopi Coyote Stories. With Helen Sekaquaptewa. Prod. Larry Evers. University of Arizona, 1978. Available from Norman Ross Publishing, (800) 648–8850. Videocassette.

"Indians at Work on Soil-Saving Dam, Osage Agency." *Indians at Work,* 15 January 1935, 17.

"Indians Tell Graphic Story of Holland Prairie Tragedy." *Daily Missoulian,* 20 November 1908, 5.

In the Trail of the Wind: American Indian Poems and Ritual Orations. Edited by John Bierhorst. New York: Farrar, 1971.

Irigaray, Luce. *This Sex Which Is Not One.* Translated by Catherine Porter. Ithaca: Cornell University Press, 1985.

Jacobson, Cardell K. "Internal Colonialism and Native Americans: Indian Labor in the United States from 1871 to World War II." *Social Science Quarterly* 65, no. 1 (1984): 158–71.

Jaimes Guerrero, M. Annette. "Academic Apartheid: American Indian Studies and 'Multiculturalism.'" In *Mapping Multiculturalism*, ed. Avery F. Gordon and Christopher Newfield. Minneapolis: University of Minnesota Press, 1996. 49–63.

Jakobson, Roman. "Concluding Statement: Linguistics and Poetics." In *Style in Language*, ed. Thomas A. Sebeok. Cambridge: MIT Press, 1960. 350–77.

Jaskoski, Helen, ed. *Early Native American Writing: New Critical Essays*. Cambridge: Cambridge University Press, 1996.

"J. J. Mathews, Osage Writer, Named Fellow." *Daily Oklahoman* (Oklahoma City), 27 March 1939.

Joffe, Natalie F. "The Fox of Iowa." In *Acculturation in Seven American Indian Tribes*, ed. Ralph Linton. New York: D. Appleton-Century, 1940. 259–331.

Johnson, James Weldon, ed. *The Book of American Negro Spirituals*. New York: Viking, 1925.

Jones, William. *Ethnography of the Fox Indians*. Edited by Margaret Welpley Fisher. Bureau of American Ethnology, Bulletin 125, 1939.

——. "Notes on the Fox Indians." *Journal of American Folk-lore* 24 (1911): 209–37.

K. "Sundown—The Indian Struggle." Review of *Sundown*, by John Joseph Mathews. *Daily Oklahoman* (Oklahoma City), 11 November 1934, C9.

Kallet, Marilyn. "The Arrow's Own Language." *American Book Review*, April 1991, 10.

Kaufman, Kenneth C. "The Indian's Burden." Review of *Sundown*, by John Joseph Mathews. *Christian Science Monitor*, 18 November 1934, 18.

Kelly, Ernece B., ed. *Searching for America*. Urbana, Ill.: NCTE, 1972.

Kelly, M. T. "The Subtle Trickster." Review of *Medicine River*, by Thomas King. *Globe and Mail* (Toronto), 3 February 1990, C19.

Kickingbird, Kirke, and Karen Ducheneaux. *One Hundred Million Acres*. New York: Macmillan, 1973.

King, Thomas. "Border Trickery and Dog Bones: A Conversation with Thomas King." Interview by Jennifer Andrews. *Studies in Canadian Literature* 24, no. 2 (1999): 161–85.

——. "Godzilla vs. Post-colonial." *World Literature Written in English* 30, no. 2 (1990): 10–16.

——. *Green Grass, Running Water*. New York: Houghton, 1993.

——. Interview by Hartmut Lutz. In Lutz, *Contemporary Challenges: Conversations with Canadian Native Authors*. Saskatoon, Sask.: Fifth House, 1991. 107–16.

——. "Interview with Thomas King." Interview by Jeffrey Canton. *Paragraph* 16, no. 1 (1994): 2–6.

——. "Interview with Tom King." Interview by Constance Rooke. *World Literature Written in English* 30, no. 2 (1990): 62–76.

——. "Inventing the Indian: White Images, Native Oral Literature, and Contemporary Native Writers." Ph.D. diss., University of Utah, 1986.

——. *Medicine River*. Toronto: Penguin, 1989.

Works Cited 225

——. *One Good Story, That One.* Toronto: Harper, 1993.

——. *Truth & Bright Water.* New York: Grove, 1999.

——, ed. *All My Relations: An Anthology of Contemporary Canadian Native Fiction.* Toronto: McClelland and Stewart, 1990.

Kinkade, M. Dale. "Bluejay and His Sister." In Swann and Krupat, eds., *Recovering the Word,* 255–96.

Kirchhoff, H. J. "Indian Tales, This Time from the Pen of a Native." *Globe and Mail* (Toronto), 3 January 1990, A17.

Knack, Martha C., and Alice Littlefield. "Native American Labor: Retrieving History, Rethinking Theory." In Littlefield and Knack, eds., *Native Americans and Wage Labor,* 3–44.

Koch, John. "A Deserving First Novel." Review of *Medicine River,* by Thomas King. *Boston Sunday Globe,* 9 September 1990, B90, B92.

Kroeber, Karl. "Deconstructionist Criticism and American Indian Literature." *Boundary 2* 7 (1979): 73–89.

——. "The Wolf Comes: Indian Poetry and Linguistic Criticism." In *Smoothing the Ground: Essays on Native American Oral Literature,* ed. Brian Swann. Berkeley: University of California Press, 1983. 98–111.

Krupat, Arnold. *Ethnocriticism: Ethnography, History, Literature.* Berkeley: University of California Press, 1992.

——. *For Those Who Come After: A Study of American Indian Autobiography.* Berkeley: University of California Press, 1985.

——. "On the Translation of Native American Song and Story: A Theorized History." In Swann, ed., *On the Translation of Native American Literature,* 3–32.

——. *The Turn to the Native: Studies in Criticism and Culture.* Lincoln: University of Nebraska Press, 1996.

——. *The Voice in the Margin: Native American Literature and the Canon.* Berkeley: University of California Press, 1989.

La Bossiere, Camille R. "Coyote Agape: Thomas King's Wording for Love." *River Review/La Revue Rivière: A Multidisciplinary Journal of Arts and Ideas/Revue Multidisciplinaire d'Arts et d'Idées* 1 (1995): 47–57.

La Farge, Oliver. "The Realistic Story of an Indian Youth." Review of *Sundown,* by John Joseph Mathews. *Saturday Review of Literature,* 24 November 1934, 309.

Larson, Charles R. *American Indian Fiction.* Albuquerque: University of New Mexico Press, 1978.

Larson, Sidner. *Captured in the Middle: Tradition and Experience in Contemporary Native American Writing.* Seattle: University of Washington Press, 2000.

Lauter, Paul. *Canons and Contexts.* New York: Oxford University Press, 1991.

——. "Introduction." *Reconstructing American Literature: Courses, Syllabi, Issues,* ed. Lauter. Old Westbury, N.Y.: Feminist Press, 1983. xi–xxv.

——. "Race and Gender in the Shaping of the American Literary Canon: A Case Study from the Twenties." *Feminist Studies* 9 (1983): 435–63.

The Law School of Harvard University Announcement, 1933–34. Cambridge: Harvard University, 1933.

Leap, William L. *American Indian English.* Salt Lake City: University of Utah Press, 1993.

Lee, Don L. "Toward a Definition: Black Poetry of the Sixties (After LeRoi Jones)." In Gayle, ed., *The Black Aesthetic,* 235–47.

Lemon, Lee T., and Marion J. Reis, eds. and trans. *Russian Formalist Criticism: Four Essays.* Lincoln: University of Nebraska Press, 1965.

Lévi-Strauss, Claude. *Tristes Tropiques.* Translated by John and Doreen Weightman. New York: Atheneum, 1974.

Lincoln, Kenneth. *Native American Renaissance.* Berkeley: University of California Press, 1983.

Littlefield, Alice, and Martha C. Knack, eds. *Native Americans and Wage Labor.* Norman: University of Oklahoma Press, 1996.

Logsdon, Guy. "John Joseph Mathews—A Conversation." *Nimrod* 16, no. 2 (1972): 70–75.

Longhurst, Derek. "'Not for All Time, but for an Age': An Approach to Shakespeare Studies." In *Re-reading English,* ed. Peter Widdowson. London: Methuen, 1982. 150–63.

Lord, Albert. *The Singer of Tales.* Cambridge: Harvard University Press, 1960.

Lurie, Nancy Oestreich. "Money, Semantics, and Indian Leadership." *American Indian Quarterly* 10, no. 1 (winter 1986): 47–63.

Mackie, Mary M. "Status, Mixedbloods, and Community in Thomas King's *Medicine River.*" *Journal of American Studies of Turkey* 8 (1998): 65–71.

Malin, Wm. G. "Report Concerning Indians in Iowa. Report of Agent for Sac and Fox Agency." *Annual Reports to the Department of the Interior for the Fiscal Year Ended June 30, 1902.* Indian Affairs. Part 1. Washington, D.C.: GPO, 1903. 212–17.

Mathews, John Joseph. Letters to W. S. Campbell, tss. 5 March 1929; 4 March, 24 March, and 3 December 1930. W. S. Campbell Collection, box 32, folder 27. Western History Collections, University Libraries, University of Oklahoma, Norman.

——. *The Osages: Children of the Middle Waters.* Norman: University of Oklahoma Press, 1961.

——. *Sundown.* 1934. Reprint, Norman: University of Oklahoma Press, 1988.

——. *Talking to the Moon.* 1945. Reprint, Norman: University of Oklahoma Press, 1981.

——. *Wah'Kon-Tah: The Osage and the White Man's Road.* Norman: University of Oklahoma Press, 1932.

Matthews, Washington, collector and trans. *Navaho Legends.* Boston: Houghton, 1897.

——. *The Night Chant, a Navaho Ceremony.* Memoirs of the American Museum of Natural History 6 (Whole Series 6; Anthropology 5). New York: Knickerbocker Press, 1902.

Mattina, Anthony. "North American Indian Mythography: Editing Texts for the Printed Page." In Swann and Krupat, eds., *Recovering the Word,* 129–48.

Mayfield, Julian. "You Touch My Black Aesthetic and I'll Touch Yours." In Gayle, ed., *The Black Aesthetic,* 24–31.

McNickle, D'Arcy. *The Hungry Generations.* Edmund E. Ayer Collection, Newberry Library, Chicago.

——. *The Indian Tribes of the United States.* London: Oxford University Press, 1962.

——. Letter to William Gates, ts. 25 March 1934. Edmund E. Ayer Collection, Newberry Library, Chicago.

——. Letter to Ruth Rae, ts. 28 November 1935. Edmund E. Ayer Collection, Newberry Library, Chicago.

——. "Meat for God." *Esquire,* September 1936, 86, 120, 122. Reprinted in McNickle, *The Hawk Is Hungry,* ed. Birgit Hans. Tucson: University of Arizona Press, 1992. 25–34.

——. Papers and manuscripts, courtesy of the Edward E. Ayer Collection, Newberry Library, Chicago.

——. *The Surrounded.* 1936. Albuquerque: University of New Mexico Press, 1978.

——. *They Came Here First: The Epic of the American Indian.* Rev. ed. New York: Harper, 1975.

——. "Train Time." *Indians at Work,* 15 March 1936, 45–48. Reprinted in McNickle, *The Hawk Is Hungry,* ed. Birgit Hans. Tucson: University of Arizona Press, 1992. 47–52.

——. *Wind from an Enemy Sky.* 1978. Reprint, with afterword by Louis Owens, Albuquerque: University of New Mexico Press, 1988.

McTaggart, Fred. *Wolf That I Am: In Search of the Red Earth People.* 1976. Reprint, Norman: University of Oklahoma Press, 1984.

Review of *Medicine River,* by Thomas King. *Books in Canada* 19, no. 4 (May 1990): 49.

[Merriam, Harold G.] Review of *The Surrounded,* by D'Arcy McNickle. *Frontier and Midland: A Magazine of the West* 16, no. 3 (spring 1936): 238–39.

Mihesuah, Devon A. *American Indians: Stereotypes and Realities.* Atlanta: Clarity Press, 1997.

——, ed. *Natives and Academics: Researching and Writing about American Indians.* Lincoln: University of Nebraska Press, 1998.

Miles, L. J. [Report of Agent for Osage Agency.] *Annual Report of the Commissioner of Indian Affairs to the Secretary of the Interior for the Year 1885.* Washington, D.C.: GPO, 1885. 89–91.

Miller, Walter B. "Authority and Collective Action in Fox Society." In Gearing, Netting, and Peattie, *Documentary History,* 126–66.

——. "Two Concepts of Authority." *American Anthropologist* 57 (1955): 271–89.

Mitscher, O. A. "Report of Agent for Osage Agency." *Annual Reports to the Department of the Interior for the Fiscal Year Ended June 30, 1902.* Indian Affairs. Part 1, *Report of the Commissioner and Appendixes.* Washington, D.C.: GPO, 1903. 292–96.

Momaday, Natachee Scott. *Owl in the Cedar Tree.* Boston: Ginn, 1965.

Momaday, N. Scott. *House Made of Dawn.* New York: Harper, 1968.

Moore, David L. "Myth, History, and Identity in Silko and Young Bear." In *New Voices in Native American Literary Criticism,* ed. Arnold Krupat. Washington, D.C.: Smithsonian, 1993. 370–95.

——. "Ray A. Young Bear." *Native Writers of the United States,* ed. Kenneth M. Roemer. Vol. 175 of *Dictionary of Literary Biography,* 5th ser. Detroit: Gale, 1997. 322–30.

Moses, Johnny. *American Indian Voices Presents Johnny Moses, Storyteller from the*

Northwest Pacific Coast. Video and audio cassettes. Johnny Moses, P. O. Box 1210, LaConner, Wash. 98257.

Mourning Dove (Hum-ishu-ma). *Cogewea, The Half-Blood: A Depiction of the Great Montana Cattle Range.* 1927. Reprint, Lincoln: University of Nebraska Press, 1981.

Mulvey, Laura. "Visual Pleasure and Narrative Cinema." 1975. In Mulvey, *Visual and Other Pleasures.* Bloomington: Indiana University Press, 1988. 14–26.

Murray, David. *Forked Tongues: Speech, Writing, and Representation in North American Indian Texts.* London: Pinter, 1991.

Neal, Larry. "The Black Arts Movement." 1968. Rpt. in Gayle, ed., *The Black Aesthetic,* 272–90.

Neale, Steve. *Cinema and Technology: Image, Sound, Colour.* Bloomington: Indiana University Press, 1985.

Neihardt, John G. *Black Elk Speaks: Being the Life Story of a Holy Man of the Oglala Sioux.* 1932. Reprint, Lincoln: University of Nebraska Press, 1979.

Nelson, Cary. *Repression and Recovery: Modern American Poetry and the Politics of Cultural Memory, 1910–1945.* Madison: University of Wisconsin Press, 1989.

Niatum, Duane. "On Stereotypes." 1978. In Swann and Krupat, eds., *Recovering the Word,* 552–62.

Niranjana, Tejaswini. *Siting Translation: History, Post-structuralism, and the Colonial Context.* Berkeley: University of California Press, 1992.

Oaks, Priscilla. "Introduction." In Mathews, *Sundown.* Boston: Gregg, 1979. v–xi.

"Oil Royalties for Osages Are Beginning to Decline." *New York Times,* 8 January 1928, sec. 3, 1.

Okpewho, Isadore. *African Oral Literature: Backgrounds, Character, and Continuity.* Bloomington: Indiana University Press, 1992.

Olivier, Sydney. *White Capital and Coloured Labour.* London: Independent Labour Party, 1906.

Ong, Walter J. *Orality and Literacy: The Technologizing of the Word.* London: Routledge, 1982.

Ortiz, Simon. "Towards a National Indian Literature: Cultural Authenticity in Nationalism." *MELUS* 8, no. 2 (summer 1981): 7–12.

"Osage Indians Face Loss of Oil Wealth." *New York Times,* 27 August 1929, 40.

Oskison, John M. *Black Jack Davy.* New York: Appleton, 1926.

——. *Wild Harvest: A Novel of Transition Days in Oklahoma.* New York: Appleton, 1925.

Owens, Louis. *Other Destinies: Understanding the American Indian Novel.* Norman: University of Oklahoma Press, 1992.

——. "The Red Road to Nowhere: D'Arcy McNickle's *The Surrounded* and 'The Hungry Generations.'" *American Indian Quarterly* 13, no. 3 (1989): 239–48.

——. Review of *Word Ways: The Novels of D'Arcy McNickle,* by John Lloyd Purdy. *American Indian Quarterly* 15, no. 4 (1991): 557–59.

Palumbo-Liu, David. "Introduction." In *The Ethnic Canon: Histories, Institutions, and Interventions,* ed. Palumbo-Liu. Minneapolis: University of Minnesota Press, 1995. 1–27.

Parins, James W. *John Rollin Ridge: His Life & Works.* Lincoln: University of Nebraska Press, 1991.

Parker, Dorothy R. "D'Arcy McNickle: An Annotated Bibliography of His Published Articles and Book Reviews in a Biographical Context." In Purdy, ed., *Legacy,* 3–29.

———. *Singing an Indian Song: A Biography of D'Arcy McNickle.* Lincoln: University of Nebraska Press, 1992.

Parker, Robert Dale. "Texts, Lines, and Videotape: The Ideology of Genre and the Transcription of Traditional Native American Narrative as Poetry." *Arizona Quarterly: A Journal of American Literature, Culture, and Theory* 53, no. 3 (1997): 141–69.

———. "'Where You Want to Go Now': Recharting the Scene Shifts in the First Section of *The Sound and the Fury.*" *Faulkner Journal* 14, no. 2 (spring 1999): 3–20.

———. "Who Shot the Sheriff: Storytelling, Indian Identity, and the Marketplace of Masculinity in D'Arcy McNickle's *The Surrounded.*" *Modern Fiction Studies* 43, no. 4 (winter 1997): 898–932.

Parman, Donald L. "The Indian and the Civilian Conservation Corps." *Pacific Historical Review* 40 (February 1971): 39–56.

Parry, Benita. "Problems in Current Theories of Colonial Discourse." *Oxford Literary Review* 9, nos. 1–2 (1987): 27–58.

The Path on the Rainbow: An Anthology of Songs and Chants from the Indians of North America. Edited by George W. Cronyn. New York: Boni, 1918.

Peattie, Lisa. "Being a Mesquakie Indian." In Gearing, Netting, and Peattie, eds., *Documentary History,* 39–62.

Peters, Robert. *Hunting the Snark: A Compendium of New Poetic Terminology.* New York: Paragon, 1989.

"Peyton's Body Brought to Missoula by Warden Scott." *Daily Missoulian,* 22 October 1908, 1.

Phillips, Robert. *The Confessional Poets.* Carbondale: Southern Illinois University Press, 1973.

Poetry: A Magazine of Verse 9, no. 5 (February 1917).

Poetry: A Magazine of Verse 15, no. 4 (January 1920).

Pokagon, Simon. *O-gî-mäw-kwî Mit-i-gwä-kî (Queen of the Woods).* Hartford, Mich.: C. H. Engle, 1899.

Polgar, Steven. "Biculturalism of Mesquakie Teenage Boys." *American Anthropologist* 62 (1960): 217–35.

Posey, Alexander. *The Fus Fixico Letters.* Edited by Daniel F. Littlefield Jr. and Carol A. Petty Hunter. Lincoln: University of Nebraska Press, 1993.

Pound, Ezra, trans. *Cathay.* London: E. Mathews, 1915.

Powell, Timothy B. *Ruthless Democracy: A Multicultural Interpretation of the American Renaissance.* Princeton: Princeton University Press, 2000.

"Proceedings of the Osage Tribal Council." Minutes, ts. 17 October 1934. National Archives and Records Administration, Southwest Region, Fort Worth, Texas, Record Group 75.

———. Minutes, ts. 18 December 1935. National Archives and Records Administration, Southwest Region, Fort Worth, Texas, Record Group 75.

Propp, V. *Morphology of the Folktale.* 1928. Translated by Laurence Scott and Louis A. Wagner. Austin: University of Texas Press, 1968.

Purdy, John Lloyd. *Word Ways: The Novels of D'Arcy McNickle.* Tucson: University of Arizona Press, 1990.

——, ed. *The Legacy of D'Arcy McNickle: Writer, Historian, Activist.* Norman: University of Oklahoma Press, 1996.

Rainwater, Catherine. *Dreams of Fiery Stars: The Transformations of Native American Fiction.* Philadelphia: University of Pennsylvania Press, 1999.

Ramsey, Jarold. *Reading the Fire: The Traditional Indian Literatures of America.* Rev. ed. Lincoln: University of Nebraska Press, 1999.

——. "The Wife Who Goes Out Like a Man Comes Back as a Hero: The Art of Two Oregon Indian Narratives." *PMLA* 92 (1977): 9–18.

A reader from Canada. "One Big Seinfeld Episode (Sort Of)." Review of *Medicine River,* by Thomas King. Amazon.com, 28 September 1997.

Reising, Russell. *The Unusable Past: Theory and the Study of American Literature.* New York: Methuen, 1986.

Revard, Carter. *Family Matters, Tribal Matters.* Tucson: University of Arizona Press, 1998.

Rice, Julian. *Deer Women and Elk Men: The Lakota Narratives of Ella Deloria.* Albuquerque: University of New Mexico Press, 1992.

Ridge, John R. *Poems.* San Francisco: Henry Payot, 1868.

——. *A Trumpet of Our Own: Yellow Bird's Essays on the North American Indian.* Edited by David Farmer and Rennard Strickland. San Francisco: Book Club of California, 1981.

Rimmon-Kenan, Shlomith. *Narrative Fiction: Contemporary Poetics.* London: Methuen, 1983.

Roediger, David R. *The Wages of Whiteness: Race and the Making of the American Working Class.* Rev. ed. London: Verso, 1999.

Roemer, Kenneth. "The Nightway Questions American Literature." *American Literature* 66 (1994): 817–29.

Roof, Judith, and Robyn Wiegman, eds. *Who Can Speak? Authority and Critical Identity.* Urbana: University of Illinois Press, 1995.

Rose, Wendy. *Bone Dance: New and Selected Poems, 1965–1993.* Tucson: University of Arizona Press, 1994.

——. "Just What's All This Fuss about White Shamanism Anyway?" In *Coyote Was Here: Essays on Contemporary Native American Literary and Political Mobilization,* ed. Bo Schöler. Spec. issue of *Dolphin* 9 (1984): 13–24.

Ross, Gayle. *How Rabbit Tricked Otter and Other Cherokee Animal Stories.* Caedmon, 1991. Audio recording.

——. *To This Day: Native American Stories.* Fredericksburg, Tex.: Gayle Ross, 1986. Audio recording.

Ross, Scott. "Natives Make Up 20 Per Cent of Calgary's Battered Wives." *Kainai News* (Stand Off, Alberta), 3 May 1989, 7.

Rothenberg, Jerome. *Shaking the Pumpkin: Traditional Poetry of the Indian North Americas.* Garden City, N.Y.: Doubleday, 1972.

——. "'We Explain Nothing, We Believe Nothing': American Indian Poetry and the Problematics of Translation." In Swann, ed., *On the Translation of Native American Literature,* 64–79.

"Rudolph Arrives in Missoula." *Daily Missoulian,* 23 October 1908, 1.

Ruoff, A. LaVonne Brown. *American Indian Literatures: An Introduction, Bibliographic Review, and Selected Bibliography.* New York: Modern Language Association, 1990.

——. "John Joseph Mathews's *Talking to the Moon*: Literary and Osage Contexts." In *Multicultural Autobiography: American Lives,* ed. James Robert Payne. Knoxville: University of Tennessee Press, 1992. 1–31.

Ruppert, James. *D'Arcy McNickle.* Western Writers Series. Boise: Boise State University, 1988.

——. "Discovering America: Mary Austin and Imagism." In Allen, ed., *Studies in American Indian Literature: Critical Essays and Course Designs,* 243–58.

——. *Mediation in Contemporary Native American Fiction.* Norman: University of Oklahoma Press, 1995.

——. "Outside the Arc of the Poem: A Review of Ray Young Bear's *Winter of the Salamander.*" *Studies in American Indian Literature,* o.s., 6, no. 3 (1982): 6–10.

——. "The Poetic Languages of Ray Young Bear." In *Coyote Was Here: Essays on Contemporary Native American Literary and Political Mobilization,* ed. Bo Schöler. Spec. issue of *Dolphin* 9 (1984): 124–33.

——. "The Reader's Lessons in *Ceremony.*" *Arizona Quarterly* 44, no. 1 (spring 1988): 78–85.

——. "Textual Perspectives and the Reader in *The Surrounded.*" In *Narrative Chance: Postmodern Discourse on Native American Indian Literatures,* ed. Gerald Vizenor. Norman: University of Oklahoma Press, 1989. 91–100.

——. "The Uses of Oral Tradition in Six Contemporary American Indian Poets." *American Indian Culture and Research Journal* 4 (1980): 87–110.

Russ, Joanna. *How to Suppress Women's Writing.* Austin: University of Texas Press, 1983.

Sarris, Greg. *Keeping Slug Woman Alive: A Holistic Approach to American Indian Texts.* Berkeley: University of California Press, 1993.

Schoolcraft's Indian Legends. Edited by Mentor L. Williams. East Lansing: Michigan State University Press, 1965.

Scott, Nathan A., Jr. "The Dark and Haunted Tower of Richard Wright." In *Five Black Writers,* ed. Donald B. Gibson. New York: New York University Press, 1970, 12–25. Reprinted in *Richard Wright: A Collection of Critical Essays,* ed. Richard Macksey and Frank E. Moorer. Englewood Cliffs, N.J.: Prentice-Hall, 1984, 149–62.

"Secretary Ickes Signs the Flathead Constitution and By-Laws." *Indians at Work,* 15 November 1935, 23–24.

Sedgwick, Eve Kosofsky. *Between Men: English Literature and Male Homosocial Desire.* New York: Columbia University Press, 1985.

——. *Epistemology of the Closet.* Berkeley: University of California Press, 1990.

Senier, Siobhan. *Voices of American Indian Assimilation and Resistance: Helen Hunt*

Jackson, Sarah Winnemucca, and Victoria Howard. Norman: University of Oklahoma Press, 2001.

———. "A Zuni Raconteur Dons the Junco Shirt: Gender and Narrative Style in the Story of Coyote and Junco." *American Literature* 66, no. 2 (June 1994): 223–38.

Sequoyah, Jana. "How (!) Is an Indian?: A Contest of Stories." In *New Voices in Native American Literary Criticism,* ed. Arnold Krupat. Washington, D.C.: Smithsonian, 1993. 453–73.

Seyewailo: The Flower World: Yaqui Deer Songs. Prod. Larry Evers. University of Arizona, 1978. Available from Norman Ross Publishing, (800) 648–8850. Videocassette.

Seymour, Peter J. *The Golden Woman: The Colville Narrative of Peter J. Seymour.* Edited by Anthony Mattina. Translated by Anthony Mattina and Madeline deSautel. Tucson: University of Arizona Press, 1985.

Sheridan, Michael. "Secret Places." Review of *Winter of the Salamander,* by Ray Young Bear. *Southwest Review* 66 (1981): 427–29.

Sherzer, Joel. "Modes of Representation and Translation of Native American Discourse: Examples from the San Blas Kuna." In Swann, ed., *On the Translation of Native American Literature,* 426–40.

———. *Verbal Art in San Blas: Kuna Culture through Its Discourse.* Cambridge: Cambridge University Press, 1990.

Sherzer, Joel, and Anthony C. Woodbury, eds. *Native American Discourse: Poetics and Rhetoric.* Cambridge: Cambridge University Press, 1987.

Shklovsky, Victor. "Sterne's *Tristram Shandy:* Stylistic Commentary." In Lemon and Reis, eds., *Russian Formalist Criticism,* 25–57.

Shotwell, L. W. "End of an Era—Beginning of a New?" *Indians at Work,* n.d. [c. August 1936], 29–30.

Silko, Leslie Marmon. "The Border Patrol State." In Silko, *Yellow Woman and a Beauty of the Spirit.* New York: Simon & Schuster, 1996. 115–23.

———. *Ceremony.* 1977. New York: Penguin, 1986.

———. "Fences against Freedom." In Silko, *Yellow Woman and a Beauty of the Spirit.* New York: Simon & Schuster, 1996. 100–114.

———. "Listening to the Spirits: An Interview with Leslie Marmon Silko." Interview by Ellen L. Arnold. In *Conversations with Leslie Marmon Silko,* ed. Arnold. Jackson: University Press of Mississippi, 2000. 162–95.

———. "An Old-Time Indian Attack Conducted in Two Parts." *Yardbird Reader* 5 (1976): 77–84.

Simard, Rodney. Review of *Medicine River,* by Thomas King. *Studies in American Indian Literature,* 2d ser. 3, no. 3 (fall 1991): 72–75.

Sinfield, Alan. "Give an account of Shakespeare and Education, showing why you think they are effective and what you have appreciated about them. Support your comments with precise references." In *Political Shakespeare: New Essays in Cultural Materialism,* ed. Jonathan Dollimore and Alan Sinfield. Ithaca: Cornell University Press, 1985. 134–57.

Skinner, Constance Lindsay. "Conflicts of an Osage Boy: A Relentlessly True

Novel of a Puzzled Modern Indian with an Ancient Heritage." Review of *Sundown*, by John Joseph Mathews. *New York Herald Tribune Books*, 2 December 1934, 4.

The Sky Clears: Poetry of the American Indians. Edited by A. Grove Day. New York: Macmillan, 1951.

Slowik, Mary. "Henry James, Meet Spider Woman: A Study of Narrative Form in Leslie Silko's *Ceremony.*" *North Dakota Quarterly* 57, no. 2 (1989): 104–20.

Smith, Barbara Herrnstein. *Contingencies of Value: Alternative Perspectives for Critical Theory.* Cambridge: Harvard University Press, 1988.

——. "Value/Evaluation." In *Critical Terms for Literary Study*, ed. Frank Lentricchia and Thomas McLaughlin. Chicago: University of Chicago Press, 1988. 177–85.

Smith, Candace. Review of *Medicine River*, by Thomas King. *Booklist*, 1 October 1990, 255.

Smith, Steven. "Modern Native Images That Counter Cliches." Review of *Medicine River*, by Thomas King. *Toronto Star*, 24 March 1990, M10.

Snodgrass, W. D. *After Experience: Poems and Translations.* New York: Harper, 1968.

——. "Powwow (Tama Reservation, Iowa, 1949)." *New Yorker*, 2 June 1962, 28. Reprinted in *The New Yorker Book of Poems.* New York: Viking, 1969. 566–67.

"Some Osages Broke. Oil Depression Finds Many without Adequate Income." *New York Times*, 16 August 1931, sec. 3, 6.

Spivak, Gayatri Chakravorty. "Can the Subaltern Speak?" In *Marxism and the Interpretation of Culture*, ed. Laurence Grossberg and Cary Nelson. Urbana: University of Illinois Press, 1985. 271–313.

——. "Can the Subaltern Speak? Speculations on Widow-Sacrifice." *Wedge* [7E] (winter/spring 1985): 120–30.

——. *A Critique of Postcolonial Reason: Toward a History of the Vanishing Present.* Cambridge: Harvard University Press, 1999.

——. *In Other Worlds: Essays in Cultural Politics.* New York: Routledge, 1987.

——. *Outside in the Teaching Machine.* New York: Routledge, 1993.

——. "Three Women's Texts and a Critique of Imperialism." *Critical Inquiry* 12 (autumn 1985): 243–61.

"Squaws Return to Headquarters." *Daily Missoulian*, 27 October 1908, 4.

"Story of Peyton's Murder Told by Returning Hunters." *Daily Missoulian*, 21 October 1908, 1, 10.

Review of *Sundown*, by John Joseph Mathews. *Sooner Magazine*, December 1934.

Review of *Sundown*, by John Joseph Mathews. *Tulsa World*, 8 November 1934.

Review of *The Surrounded. Buffalo* [N.Y.] *Times Post*, 10 February 1936.

Review of *The Surrounded. Camden* [N.J.] *Post*, 22 February 1936.

Review of *The Surrounded. Miami Herald*, 19 April 1936.

Review of *The Surrounded. Oakland Tribune*, 1 March 1936.

Review of *The Surrounded. Washington Star*, 22 February 1936.

Review of *The Surrounded. Waterville* [N.Y.] *Times*, 25 August 1936.

Swan, Edith. "Healing via the Sunwise Cycle in Silko's *Ceremony.*" *American Indian Quarterly* 12, no. 4 (1988): 313–28.

———. "Laguna Prototypes of Manhood in *Ceremony.*" *MELUS* 17, no. 1 (spring 1991–92): 39–61.

———. "Laguna Symbolic Geography and Silko's *Ceremony.*" *American Indian Quarterly* 12, no. 3 (1988): 229–49.

Swann, Brian, ed. *On the Translation of Native American Literatures.* Washington, D.C.: Smithsonian, 1992.

Swann, Brian, and Arnold Krupat, eds. *Recovering the Word: Essays on Native American Literature.* Berkeley: University of California Press, 1987.

Taylor, Charles. "The Politics of Recognition." In *Multiculturalism: Examining the Politics of Recognition,* ed. Amy Gutmann. Princeton: Princeton University Press, 1994. 25–73.

Tedlock, Dennis. *Breath on the Mirror: Mythic Voices & Visions of the Living Maya.* San Francisco: Harper, 1993.

———. "Learning to Listen: Oral Narrative as Poetry." In Ronald J. Grele with Studs Terkel et al., *Envelopes of Sound: The Art of Oral History.* 2d ed. New York: Praeger, 1991. 106–25.

———. "On the Translation of Style in Oral Narrative." In Tedlock, *The Spoken Word and the Work of Interpretation,* 31–61.

———. "Questions Concerning Dialogical Anthropology." *Journal of Anthropological Research* 43 (1987): 325–37.

———. *The Spoken Word and the Work of Interpretation.* Philadelphia: University of Pennsylvania Press, 1983.

———, trans. *Finding the Center: The Art of the Zuni Storyteller.* Translated from live performances in Zuni by Andrew Peynetsa and Walter Sanchez. 2d ed. Lincoln: University of Nebraska Press, 1999.

———, trans. *Finding the Center: Narrative Poetry of the Zuni Indians.* Translated from performances in the Zuni by Andrew Peynetsa and Walter Sanchez. 1972. Reprint, Lincoln: University of Nebraska Press, 1978.

———, trans. *Popol Vuh: The Definitive Edition of the Mayan Book of the Dawn of Life and the Glories of the Gods and Kings.* New York: Simon & Schuster, 1985.

Thomas, Keith. "Work and Leisure in Pre-industrial Society." *Past and Present* 29 (December 1964): 50–66.

Thompson, E. P. "Time, Work-Discipline and Industrial Capitalism." *Past and Present* 38 (December 1967): 57–96.

Thoreau, Henry D. *Walden.* 1854. Edited by J. Lyndon Shanley. Princeton: Princeton University Press, 1971.

Thorson, Connie Capers. "Bibliography." In *Leslie Marmon Silko: A Collection of Critical Essays,* ed. Louise K. Barnett and James L. Thorson. Albuquerque: University of New Mexico Press, 1999. 285–300.

Tinker, Sylvester. "What the IECW Means to the Osages." *Indians at Work,* 15 September 1935: 18.

Toelken, Barre. "Life and Death in the Navajo Coyote Tales." In Swann and Krupat, eds., *Recovering the Word,* 388–401.

Toelken, Barre, and Tacheeni Scott. "Poetic Retranslation and the 'Pretty Languages' of Yellowman." In *Traditional Literatures of the American Indian: Texts and Interpretation,* ed. Karl Kroeber. Lincoln: University of Nebraska Press. 65–116.

Tolstoy, Leo. *Anna Karenina.* 1873–77. Translated by Constance Garnett. New York, Modern Library, n.d.

Tomashevsky, Boris. "Thematics." In Lemon and Reis, eds., *Russian Formanist Criticism,* 61–95.

Tompkins, Jane. *Sensational Designs: The Cultural Work of American Fiction.* New York: Oxford University Press, 1985.

Trosper, Ronald Lloyd. "The Economic Impact of the Allotment Policy on the Flathead Indian Reservation." Ph.D. diss., Harvard University, 1974.

Trumpener, Katie. *Bardic Nationalism: The Romantic Novel and the British Empire.* Princeton: Princeton University Press, 1997.

United States. *Race Relations in Tama County: A Report Prepared by the Iowa Advisory Committee to the U.S. Commission on Civil Rights.* Washington, D.C.: GPO, 1981.

Utter, Jack. *American Indians: Answers to Today's Questions.* Lake Ann, Mich.: National Woodlands, 1993.

Vestal, Stanley. *Mountain Men.* Boston: Houghton, 1937.

Vizenor, Gerald. *Bearheart: The Heirship Chronicles.* Rev. ed. Minneapolis: University of Minnesota Press, 1990.

——. *Manifest Manners: Postindian Warriors of Survivance.* Hanover, N.H.: Wesleyan University Press, 1994.

Vorse, Mary Heaton. "End of the Trail." Review of *The Surrounded,* by D'Arcy McNickle. *New Republic,* 15 April 1936, 295–96.

——. "From Flathead to Blackfeet." *Indians at Work,* 15 September 1935, 31–36.

Walker, Cheryl. *Indian Nation: Native American Literature and Nineteenth-Century Nationalisms.* Durham: Duke University Press, 1998.

Walker, Willard B. "Native Writing Systems." In *Languages,* ed. Ives Goddard. Vol. 17 of *Handbook of North American Indians,* ed. William C. Sturtevant. Washington, D.C.: Smithsonian, 1996. 158–84.

Walton, Eda Lou, and T. T. Waterman. "American Indian Poetry." *American Anthropology,* n.s., 27 (1925): 25–52.

Walton, Percy. "'Tell Our Own Stories': Politics and the Fiction of Thomas King." *World Literature Written in English* 30, no. 2 (1990): 77–84.

Wanatee, Donald. "The Lion, Fleur-de-lis, the Eagle, or the Fox: A Study of Government." In *The Worlds between Two Rivers: Perspectives on American Indians in Iowa,* ed. Gretchen M. Bataille, David M. Gradwohl, and Charles P. Silet. Ames: Iowa State University Press, 1978. 74–83.

Warrior, Robert Allen. *Tribal Secrets: Recovering American Indian Intellectual Traditions.* Minneapolis: University of Minnesota Press, 1995.

Waseskuk, Bertha. "Mesquakie History—As We Know It." In *The Worlds between Two Rivers: Perspectives on American Indians in Iowa,* ed. Gretchen M. Bataille, David M. Gradwohl, and Charles P. Silet. Ames: Iowa State University Press, 1978. 54–61.

Weaver, Jace. *That the People Might Live: Native American Literatures and Native American Community.* New York: Oxford University Press, 1997.

——. "Thomas King." *Publisher's Weekly,* 8 March 1993, 56–57.

White, Richard. *The Middle Ground: Indians, Empires, and Republics in the Great Lakes Region, 1650–1815.* Cambridge: Cambridge University Press, 1991.

Wiebe, Rudy. *The Temptations of Big Bear.* Toronto: McClelland and Stewart, 1973.

Wiget, Andrew. *Native American Literature.* Boston: Twayne, 1985.

———. "Telling the Tale: A Performance Analysis of a Hopi Coyote Story." In Swann and Krupat, eds., *Recovering the Word,* 297–336.

Wilson, Terry P. "John Joseph Mathews." *Native Writers of the United States,* ed. Kenneth M. Roemer. Vol. 175 of *Dictionary of Literary Biography,* 5th ser. Detroit: Gale, 1997. 154–62.

———. "Osage Oxonian: The Heritage of John Joseph Mathews." *Chronicles of Oklahoma* 59 (fall 1981): 264–93.

———. *The Underground Reservation: Osage Oil.* Lincoln: University of Nebraska Press, 1985.

The Winged Serpent: An Anthology of American Indian Prose and Poetry. Edited by Margot Astrov. New York: John Day, 1946.

Womack, Craig S. *Red on Red: Native American Literary Separatism.* Minneapolis: University of Minnesota Press, 1999.

Wong, Hertha Dawn. *Sending My Heart Back across the Years: Tradition and Innovation in Native American Autobiography.* New York: Oxford University Press, 1992.

The Woodland Singers. *Traditional Mesquakie Songs.* Canyon Records, CR-6194, 1987.

Wright, James. *Above the River: The Complete Poems.* New York: Farrar, 1990.

Wright, Richard. *Black Boy: A Record of Childhood and Youth.* 1945. Reprint, New York: Harper, 1966.

Yamamoto, Traise. "Different Silence(s): The Poetics and Politics of Location." In *Reviewing Asian America: Locating Diversity,* ed. Wendy L. Ng, Soo-Young Chin, James S. Moy, and Gary Y. Okihiro. Pullman: Washington State University Press, 1995. 137–45.

Yellow Bird (John Rollin Ridge). *The Life and Adventures of Joaquín Murieta, the Celebrated California Bandit.* 1854. Reprint, Western Frontier Library, Norman: University of Oklahoma Press, 1955.

Young Bear, Ray A. *Black Eagle Child: The Facepaint Narratives.* Iowa City: University of Iowa Press, 1992.

———. "Connected to the Past: An Interview with Ray Young Bear." In *Survival This Way: Interviews with American Indian Poets,* ed. Joseph Bruchac. Tucson: University of Arizona Press, 1987. 337–48.

———. "For the Rain in March: The Blackened Hearts of Herons." *American Poetry Review* 7, no. 2 (March/April 1978): 41–44.

———. "From the Land of the Red Earths: Gaming gains and losses add up to . . ." *Des Moines Sunday Register,* 26 April 1998, 4AA.

———. "in disgust and in response to indian-type poetry written by whites published in a mag which has rejected me too many times." *Poetry Northwest* 17, no. 2 (summer 1976): 18–20.

———. "An Interview with Ray A. Young Bear." Interview by Elias Ellefson. In *Speaking of the Short Story: Interviews with Contemporary Writers,* ed. Farhat

Iftekharuddin, Mary Rohrberger, and Maurice Lee. Jackson: University Press of Mississippi, 1997. 35–44.

———. "In the First Place of My Life." In *Townships,* ed. Michael Martone. Iowa City: University of Iowa Press, 1992. 198–206.

———. *The Invisible Musician.* Duluth, Minn.: Holy Cow! 1990.

———. "Journal of a Mesquakie Poet: Notes Leading to 500 Years After." *Des Moines Sunday Register,* 4 October 1992, 1C–2C.

———. "A journey to Onion Creek: Swimming away (temporarily) from the Central Camp of Relatives." *Des Moines Sunday Register,* 17 November 1991, 1C.

———. Poetry reading. Champaign, Ill., 15 October 1991.

———. Poetry reading. Urbana, Ill., 31 October 1992.

———. "Reaching Out, Keeping Away." Interview. *Tamaqua* 2, no. 2 (1991): 19–29.

———. *Remnants of the First Earth.* New York: Grove Press, 1996.

———. *The Rock Island Hiking Club.* Iowa City: University of Iowa Press, 2001.

———. "Staying Afloat in a Chaotic World: A Conversation with Ray Young Bear." Interview by David Moore and Michael Wilson. *Callaloo* 17, no. 1 (winter 1994): 205–13.

———. "The Sun's Glint on an Eagle's Wing." *Ornament* 18, no. 2 (winter 1994): 50–53.

———. *Winter of the Salamander: The Keeper of Importance.* San Francisco: Harper, 1980.

Zolbrod, Paul G. *Reading the Voice: Native American Poetry on the Page.* Salt Lake City: University of Utah Press, 1995.

Index